Practicing New Worlds
Abolition and Emergent Strategies

ANDREA J. RITCHIE

Foreword by Alexis Pauline Gumbs
Introduction by adrienne maree brown

AK
PRESS

Praise for *Practicing New Worlds*:

"In *Practicing New Worlds*, Ritchie brings her wisdom—drawn from decades of researching, theorizing, organizing, and convening movement spaces—into an altogether new kind of dream work. In a feat of originality, Ritchie stretches the conceptual paradigms of emergent strategy into entirely new places, grounding it deeply in struggle: specifically, Black feminist, abolitionist movement work. In doing so, she accomplishes a rare feat, gifting us a text that is expansively visionary and pragmatic."—**Robyn Maynard, author of** *Policing Black Lives*

"*Practicing New Worlds* is essential reading for all who don't merely dream of a better world but who have embraced the daunting task of bringing one into being. Ritchie draws insights from organizing victories, setbacks, and especially the tireless groundwork—behind the scenes and out of the spotlight— required for all advances in social justice. She emboldens us to address the burning questions Grace Lee Boggs posed to movement builders, 'How can we make the ideal more real? How can we make the real more ideal?'" —**Scott Kurashige, coauthor of Grace Lee Boggs's** *The Next American Revolution*

"*Practicing New Worlds* is right on time. As organizers look for different ways to navigate multiple crises, Andrea Ritchie offers generative ideas at the intersection of emergent strategy and PIC abolition. She suggests this is the time for creativity, experimentation, and imagination, and calls on us to be braver. Let this book be a life raft for you as you swim a little farther from shore. By the end of the book, I promise that you'll be inspired to try the deep end of the organizing ocean. Andrea's invitation is to come on in, the water will hold you."
—**Mariame Kaba, author of** *We Do This 'Til We Free Us*

"Andrea Ritchie demonstrates her brilliance and generosity through her broad and deep respect for a vast expanse of teachers and comrades, woven intricately and intimately throughout this book." —**Mimi E. Kim, founder of Creative Interventions and cofounder of INCITE!**

"I thought I understood emergent strategies, and then I read *Practicing New Worlds*. With equal parts rigor and vulnerability, Andrea shares a breathtaking theoretical exploration of the principles of emergent strategies alongside examples grounded in the everyday practice of creating abolition. *Practicing New Worlds* left me hopeful, curious, and eager. I will turn to it, again and again, in the years to come." —**Angélica Cházaro, Seattle Solidarity Budget and Mijente**

"While words and phrases related to abolition and emergent strategy circulate widely these days, their meanings have become elusive. Andrea firmly grounds *Practicing New Worlds* in the collaborative practices that people are engaging in right now to dismantle state violence, showing us why making our work local, decentralized, interdependent, nimble, responsive, relational, and adaptive is the way forward for survival and liberation." —**Dean Spade, author of *Mutual Aid: Building Solidarity During This Crisis (And The Next)***

"This is a necessary book, and I can't think of a better person to take us on this journey than Andrea. For decades, her organizing and scholarship have been foundational in creating the conditions for liberation and abolition to feel possible and tangible. I'm honored to have my ideas in conversation with Andrea's abolitionist brilliance. In this book, Andrea puts hands in dirt to collectively grow more liberation for us all." —**Walidah Imarisha, author of *Angels with Dirty Faces* and coeditor of *Octavia's Brood***

Practicing New Worlds: Abolition and Emergent Strategies
Emergent Strategy Series No. 9
© 2023 Andrea J. Ritchie
Foreword © 2023 Alexis Pauline Gumbs
Introduction © 2023 adrienne maree brown
This edition © 2023 AK Press (Chico / Edinburgh)

ISBN: 978-1-84935-511-7
E-ISBN: 978-1-84935-512-4
Library of Congress Control Number: 2022948752

AK Press   AK Press
370 Ryan Avenue #100   33 Tower St.
Chico, CA 95973   Edinburgh EH6 7BN
USA   Scotland
www.akpress.org   www.akuk.com
akpress@akpress.org   akuk@akpress.org

Please contact us to request the latest AK Press distribution catalog, which features books, pamphlets, zines, and stylish apparel published and/or distributed by AK Press. Alternatively, visit our websites for the complete catalog, latest news, and secure ordering.

Cover design by Herb Thornby
Cover illustration by Amir Khadar
Printed in the United States of America on acid-free paper

"To Build a Future Without Police and Prisons, We Have to Imagine It First," by Walidah Imarisha was first published in *OneZero* on October 20, 2020, onezero.medium.com.

"Tending the Acre" by Shawn Taylor and "Albina Zone" by Lisa Bates were originally published in Wakanda Dream Lab's *Black Freedom Beyond Borders: Memories of Abolition Day* (New York: Policy Link, 2020).

Molly Costello's *Keep Practicing the Future* and *Tending My Mycelium Network* used by permission.

for all who practice(d) abolitionist futures and
for the future generations who will live them

Another world is necessary, another world is possible, another world has already started.

—GRACE LEE BOGGS

Systems and structures dominate.
But as human beings we have choices.
As individuals those choices are limited.
But collectively our choices add up to a force.

—FAHD AHMED, DESIS RISING UP AND MOVING (DRUM)

Contents

Foreword

by Alexis Pauline Gumbs

Nanny of the Maroons was an emergent strategist. Yes. The Jamaican spiritual revolutionary who outsmarted the colonizing British army, who led and fed a community of Africans who escaped the plantation and refused to return, was in deep partnership with the plants, animals, and elements of the mountains, she had a life-saving knowledge of root vegetables, and she knew how to listen to her ancestors and her collaborators *at the same time.* This is why to this day the Jamaican Maroons call Queen Nanny *the great scientist.*

Maroon science is an earlier name for what Octavia Butler called Earthseed theology, our intentional relationship to divine change in apocalyptic circumstances, a life-giving precedent for what our beloved series editor adrienne maree brown calls "emergent strategy." Nanny and all Maroons by all names in the Americas were abolishing slavery by practicing freedom. Because yes, Maroon community members often went on missions to bring other Africans off the plantation, but what ultimately brought the plantation system down, according to the colonizers themselves, was how the idea that there were formerly enslaved people somewhere practicing freedom made captive plantation workers ungovernable. The very fact that— here in this new world, cut off from the communities enslavers stole them from—there was another form of life beyond plantation domination? It activated a million acts of resistance of many different sizes that eventually made the plantation system unprofitable for the Europeans. Which, as every materialist knows, is the only reason they stopped.

And what did the Maroon scientists do? They created a composite language through which they could listen to and pray to all of their ancestors who spoke hundreds of different tongues and came from various sites on the continent of Africa. They created a bridge of listening across everything we supposedly lost.

And isn't this why the founders of Critical Resistance made the poetic and political choice to call this movement to bring home our folks, and to live in sustainable peace, prison industrial complex *abolition*? Because in its very language, it connects this work to our ancestor's knowing. Because the prison industrial complex (PIC) enforces legalized kidnapping and forced labor, an adaptation of slavery for our time. It is out of this knowing, this long experiment of Black liberation, that our strategy must emerge.

As Ruthie Gilmore teaches, "abolition is presence." And our love is a presence as old as the universe, so I could have started this preface anywhere. But I started in Jamaica because our brave, persistent, rebellious, committed Jamaican author, our always-showing-up movement lawyer for liberation, our weaver of testimony, fiction and theory, our cherished Andrea Ritchie has offered us what the Jamaican Maroons call the *abeng*: the conch shell that becomes a freedom trumpet when you put it to your lips and breathe your truth.

Beloved reader, may you be as curious as you are committed. May our wonder outmatch our wounds. May our listening reach back so far it generates a future we will only recognize when we return to it.

Let this book be your Maroon map. Let it guide you in creating and supporting what Black Organizing for Leadership and Dignity (BOLD) calls Maroon practice space. Let it remind you of what every great scientist knows:

the seeds are in the compost
the ancestors are in the soil
our love is older than any wall
the roots break through

Love always,
Alexis Pauline Gumbs

Introduction
by adrienne maree brown

Andrea J. Ritchie is an unlikely Emergent Strategy Series contributor. She is a Capricorn movement lawyer, generally most comfortable with a linear plan of action to execute. I've known and admired Andrea's legal and organizing work for almost two decades. I always felt we were in parallel efforts—her attending to the legal and policy struggles of the present while I do the imaginative space-holding work of collaborative dreaming of the future. I have often felt indulged by organizers like Andrea, "Ok, dream on, but in the meantime we gonna get people free right now."

This is why I was astounded to find myself at a conference in Hawai'i, on a panel dedicated to a wide breadth of responses to emergent strategy, holding back tears as Andrea gave a talk on how emergent strategy had changed her worldview, life, and work toward abolition.

Andrea and I are both abolitionists, meaning we are working to abolish the system of US policing and prisons and, more broadly, shift our species from punitive approaches to justice to transformative ones. This means we both seek to transform the conditions of our society from the root up, such that the conditions that create what is then criminalized—poverty, inequality, and discrimination—are fundamentally eradicated. We both feel the pressure of urgency inside of intersecting crises for our peoples and our planet. It is challenging to be experimental in the face of such pressure, because it means acknowledging that the strategies we are more familiar with, even skilled in, are not enough to get us where we need to be: free, able to practice authentic accountability, in communities of care.

I think one of the ways we ended up at that talk, and with this book, is that we both developed a relationship to Detroit. I became a student of Detroit in 2006 and moved there in 2009 for what became a twelve year education in adaptation in the face of crises. Every summer, Andrea would come to town for the Allied Media Conference (AMC), a gathering of media-making change agents envisioning new worlds and sharing practical tools for the communication of survival technologies. For me, the AMC has been the cauldron in which I have experimented with my new recipes for justice and liberation.

I held an Octavia E. Butler summit there and early Emergent Strategy workshops, as well as Pleasure Activism sessions and Visionary Fiction writing workshops. Andrea also used this as a space to build her networks for policy-shifting legal work, and at times we overlapped. I got to facilitate gatherings of organizers and lawyers she was building with. We found each other on the dance floor in a shared community of activists, artists, journalists, and visionaries.

Beyond being the physical location of these gatherings, Detroit was a point of inspiration and education, showing us a people who had figured out paths of survival in the seemingly impossible conditions of racial capitalism. In these Detroit summers, I noticed that, alongside her pragmatism, Andrea was interested in magic. I learned that she was a secret sailor and thus had a relationship of respect and awe with the more-than-human natural world.

When Andrea began showing interest in emergent strategy, I felt excited and nervous—emergent strategy is both emerging modern theory and wisdom based in ancient understandings and visible patterns of the world around us. I could feel the depth of my faith in emergent strategy up against the anticipation of a cross examination. But then that made me more excited—I want people to keep unveiling more of emergent strategy, and to help keep it rooted in its radical soil, which can be very difficult in the reductionist landscape of social media and viral trends. This requires a critical look at where emergent strategy comes from, how it has landed and been received, how it works with and beyond existing political frameworks, and where there are gaps in applying it to organizing.

With *Practicing New Worlds*, Andrea offers us a deepening of emergent strategy. In addition to her own reflections and scholarship of how emergent strategy and abolitionist movements intertwine, Andrea lets us in on a conversation among all kinds of people doing this work, about how the small, relational, and visionary moves we make can accumulate, converge, and ultimately shift culture at the largest scale. This is how change *has* happened, both in abolition work and throughout human history.

Andrea uncovers histories of emergent strategy that even I was unfamiliar with, histories that make me even more excited to be in the river of these ideas. She pulls in comrades and collaborators like Walidah Imarisha, ill weaver, Sage Crump, Mia Herndon, Ejeris Dixon, Mariame Kaba, Paula Rojas, Shira Hassan, Woods Ervin, Amanda Alexander, kai lumumba barrow, Mia Mingus, Damon Williams, the Spirit House crew, and so many more to weave this story, explore these lessons.

By looking at abolition through the lens of emergent strategy, element by element, Andrea uplifts the organizing strategies that are already creating more possibilities for our collective liberation, and points to the experiments and practices we can be in to advance toward the world we are co-creating. She even includes a radical bit of original mermaid fiction, so we can see how her own imagination has been unleashed in this journey. I am so grateful to Andrea for taking the risk to ask these questions, to let the answers in, and to deeply consider the possibilities offered through emergent strategy. I am so excited for you all to read this equally pragmatic and visionary and vulnerable work.

Introduction
by Andrea J. Ritchie

I am an unlikely emergent strategist.

I am a linear thinker in search of certainty and concrete solutions. I see a problem and try to solve it with a ten-point plan. I respond to conditions, rather than seeking to shape them. I am more inclined to react to the present than to dream of the future.

For much of my life, I have turned to tools many of us take for granted—laws, policies, institutions—to attempt to make the change I want to see in the world. For the astrologically inclined, I am a quintessential Capricorn—give me a clear structure, a job to do, rules, and a series of steps to follow, a checklist, a mountain to climb, and I will crush it. Ask me to step outside of existing structures and into fluidity and uncertainty to imagine and practice something different . . . well, it's a struggle, especially under pressure.

I was raised in, and for most of my life have practiced, approaches to making change rooted in traditional organizing strategies and understandings of how change happens: you assess material conditions; develop a political analysis of root causes; ascertain where the power to shift them lies; build a base among people directly impacted by the conditions you want to change; develop an agenda (usually focused on changing laws or policies) that advances your overall vision and a strategy to win it; analyze strengths, weaknesses, opportunities, and threats;

1

build power (through relationships with people in power and/or mass mobilization) to pressure your target to make the change you want; celebrate wins; and then move to the next step that will bring you closer to your vision in a linear fashion. For a significant part of my life, the end goal was to seize state power to serve the people.

Over the past four decades that I have been researching, organizing, advocating, litigating, and agitating toward more liberatory futures, I have learned that building power, making a case, and pressing demands on people in power to change laws, policies, and institutions is not the entirety of how we get to the future I long for—a world in which everyone's material, emotional, and spiritual needs are met, and we all have what we need to reach our highest human potential, in sustainable and reciprocal relationships with each other and the rest of the natural world, free of policing, punishment, deprivation, and exile. In other words, an abolitionist future.

Much of my work has focused on documenting the violence of policing and criminalization, most often through the lens of the experiences of Black women, queer and trans folks, and of women and LGBTQ people of color—as a Black woman, a lesbian, a migrant, daughter of a migrant, descendant of many migrants, and as a survivor of police and interpersonal violence.[1] Although it is certainly not my only (or even my primary) identity or work, I became a lawyer in my early thirties after more than a decade of organizing and advocacy in anti-apartheid, Black liberation, racial, gender, reproductive, migrant, and environmental justice, labor, and anti-violence movements. I have never believed that justice could be found in courts, or that the law could bring about the future I seek—a conviction that was only affirmed by what I learned in law school. But, like many policymakers, politicians, advocates, organizers, and everyday people, I have turned to laws, policies, and rules to address the harm of current systems.

I have participated in many legislative and policy campaigns—to ensure the right to abortion, to stop construction of new nuclear power plants and the burial of nuclear waste on

Indigenous lands, to forestall cuts to social programs. Most of my legal and policy work has focused on policing, particularly as it impacts women, queer, and trans people—including reshaping the Toronto Police Service search of persons policy in the late 1990s and NYPD policies with respect to interactions with LGBT people in the early 2010s, and participating in litigation and legislative campaigns to eliminate sex offender registration requirements for people accused of prostitution-related offenses in Louisiana under the leadership of Women With a Vision.[2] I've led challenges to the use of possession or presence of condoms as evidence of intent to engage in prostitution, developed model policies and practices to address police sexual violence, and played a leadership role in a campaign to pass the most comprehensive anti-profiling legislation in the United States in New York City.[3] I have also represented people in criminal and family courts, and successfully litigated against the NYPD in a dozen cases involving police violence against women, girls, and trans people.

Some of these victories chipped away at the state's power to do harm, kept people out of jail, freed people from prison or carceral surveillance, or provided compensation to individuals who were harmed by policing and punishment. Yet in most cases, these victories offered only temporary relief. Often, they produced changes on paper but not in practice. They did not transform systems, communities, or conditions enough to prevent the harm from continuing in the same or new forms. In some cases, the campaigns to win them replicated existing relations of power in their methodology.

Through these experiences and more, I have come to understand that there is no single ten-point plan, no legislative agenda, no legal strategy that can get us out of the conditions we find ourselves in amid the death throes of racial capitalism. There is no top-down approach that will yield the world we want. We can't legislate, policy-make, or litigate our way out of economic, climate, or political collapse—or out of the violence of policing.

These lessons feel even more poignant and pressing as we once again collectively grapple with how to respond to the brutal killing of Tyre Nichols by the Memphis Police Department—and of least two dozen more Black people in the first quarter of 2023.[4] Once again, people and politicians are looking to law and policy for answers: prosecute individual cops, launch a federal investigation of the department, document traffic stops, change police policies, increase police training, end qualified immunity in civil lawsuits.[5] As I and others have argued extensively elsewhere, none of these approaches would have prevented Tyre's gruesome death, or the next one, at the hands of police. All of them pour more power, money, and legitimacy into an institution doing exactly what it was set up to do.[6]

We can't continue to organize in ways that replicate and legitimize the systems we are seeking to dismantle. We can't afford to waste time and energy trying to use the same old frameworks and tools to make radical change. Black feminist and critical race theory teach us that laws and policies perpetuate existing structures of power; consequently, they carry in their DNA the systems we are trying to shift. They are of the world we are trying to undo and make anew. This is why, in the oft-cited words of Audre Lorde, the master's tools cannot dismantle the master's house.

That doesn't mean there is no role whatsoever for law and policy in our movements. Certainly, we need to resist with all our might laws and policies that would deny and seek to eliminate the existence of trans, queer, and disabled people; exert control over our bodies and access to healthcare; destroy public institutions; and deny us access to resources and decision-making about our lives. And, as veteran abolitionist organizer Rachel Herzing argues in her essay "Big Dreams and Bold Steps Toward a Police-Free Future," some laws and policies—often referred to as "non-reformist reforms," defined by André Gorz as "changes designed to make a practical difference in the short run, while also building toward larger transformations,"—bring us closer to the worlds we want by removing barriers or by creating conditions that make it easier for us to fight.[7] Transformative demands for laws or policies that defund the police, curtail the power of systems of policing and punishment, end criminalization, ensure that everyone's material needs are met without conditions, and that increase the legitimacy and resources available to abolitionist community-based safety strategies build our movement.

Interrupting Criminalization's *So Is This Actually an Abolitionist Proposal or Strategy?* gathers tools offering guidance around legislative or policy approaches that might fall into this category.[8] But they are a means to ends, not the ends themselves. At best, they create more favorable terrain to build toward a world that does not rely on the violence of policing and make it possible for more people to join in those efforts. In terms of the kind of change we need to make, they are just the tip of the iceberg.

Over the past four decades, I have learned that the majority of the work to build the worlds we want happens outside of the structures that manufacture and preserve existing relations of power. I've developed a deeper awareness and understanding that we must step beyond what we know to experiment with, build, and practice new ways of being in relationship with each other and the planet.

Yet, as conditions worsen and urgency increases, as millions are increasingly mired in economic and climate crises while billionaires bank on our suffering, as the Right rises around the globe and comes for our throats with a clear intention to obliterate communities I am part of and care deeply about, the destruction of so much of the planet we call home looms large, and as police, state, and white-supremacist violence and repression intensify and multiply, it feels harder and harder to try on different strategies to resist and persist. It feels riskier to experiment; to reach for different ways of thinking, being, and relating; to imagine and create conditions for something new to emerge. The more pressure we are under, the more urgency, uncertainty, and fear we face, the stronger our instincts are to cling to the familiar. Under pressure, we are more likely to double down on strategies that have largely failed in the past, and turn to the institutions and structures that manufacture, produce, and sustain the current order in the hopes of changing them—or of at least staving off the worst of what's to come. We fight harder but continue to fight in the ways we know.

This is precisely the time when we most need to critically examine the ways we are seeking to make change, and to explore where and how we need to shift our approach.

This moment calls on us to practice new ways of relating, new forms of governance, and new modes of being that enable the worlds we want to emerge instead of relying on top-down, law and policy-based strategies that are mired in the illusion that we can change systems and institutions doing exactly what they were created to do: produce and maintain societies that promote extractive accumulation by the few at the expense of the many and of the planet, structured by laws, policies, and institutions that distribute life chances through surveillance, policing, punishment, and exclusion.

Philosopher, organizer, and beloved movement elder Grace Lee Boggs would often begin conversations by asking, "What time is it on the clock of the world?" According to Grace, one answer is that "in the midst of this epochal shift, we all need to practice visionary organizing." For her, that meant moving beyond protest organizing: "Instead of viewing the US people as masses to be mobilized . . . we must have the courage to challenge ourselves to engage in activities that build a new and better world by improving the physical, psychological, political, and spiritual health of ourselves, our families, our communities, our cities, our world, and our planet."[9] In her view, visionary organizing "begins by creating images and stories of the future that help us imagine and create alternatives to the existing system."[10]

In *The Next American Revolution: Sustainable Activism for the Twenty-First Century*, Grace writes with Scott Kurashige: "The tremendous changes we now need and yearn for in our daily lives . . . cannot come from those in power or from putting pressure on those in power. We ourselves have to foreshadow or prefigure them from the ground up."[11] In other words, we need to stop looking exclusively to the same places we always have looked, doing the same things we have always done, being the same people we have always been. Instead, we must seek out new ways of thinking, doing, and being in everyday actions, with the intention of shifting large and complex systems and relations of power. We need to seek out as many portals as we can find into futures we cannot currently imagine and practice them every day.

I have come to believe that emergent strategies offer important clues to help us to find new paths forward, to step outside of what we know and into the futures we want to create, to survive, and to resist the futures racial capitalism and Right-wing forces seek to make inevitable.

Emergent Strategy and emergent strategies

adrienne maree brown's book, *Emergent Strategy: Shaping Change, Changing Worlds*, has served as an introduction to emergent strategies for hundreds of thousands of people, including me.* It summarizes a broader set of ideas about how to create, shift, and change complex systems—including human society— through relatively simple interactions. Emergent strategies, as adrienne describes them, focus on starting small and making space for and learning from uncertainty, multiplicity, experimentation, adaptation, iteration, and decentralization.

These ideas are not new—*Emergent Strategy* draws on a much deeper body of work rooted in the workings of the natural world, Indigenous lifeways, complexity science, change theory, Grace Lee Boggs's later writings, the work of the Complex Movements Collective, and the observations of scholars and organizers across generations. In many ways, *Emergent Strategy* distills and invites us to hone key principles already at play in effective organizing efforts and movements.

Emergent strategies, by definition, require attention to emergence—what becomes possible under certain conditions when we:

---

* I use *Emergent Strategy* to refer to adrienne maree brown's book of that name, and emergent strategies to refer to the broader body of work the book draws on.

- start small and focus on critical connections,
- build decentralized networks,
- iterate and adapt with intention, and
- cooperate toward collective sustainability,

rather than trying to control or impose change through law, policy, and other top-down strategies.

While this approach may feel counterintuitive given the scale of the problems we face and the growing political power of authoritarian forces, change scholars Margaret Wheatley and Deborah Frieze argue that emergence has made large-scale resistance and societal shifts possible. According to them, these shifts happened through "many local actions and decisions, most of which were invisible and unknown to each other, and none of which was powerful enough by itself to create change. But when these local changes coalesced, new power emerged. What could not be accomplished by diplomacy, politics, protests, or strategy suddenly happened."[12] Under this theory, the 2020 Uprisings, the Occupy movement, the Arab Spring, the Zapatista Uprising, and other widescale and sustained resistance movements in the Global South that led to historical moments of systemic change were in fact the products of a multitude of networked actions, guided by a shared politic and intention over extended periods of time. shea howell, a member of the Council of the Boggs Center in Detroit, pointed out in a conversation with me that while on the surface these appeared to be spontaneous mass mobilizations—much like the anti-globalization protests at the 1999 meeting of the World Trade Organization in Seattle (a.k.a. the Battle of Seattle)—they were actually made possible through critical connections and small networks.[13] "If you think of the most successful mass demonstrations, they were connections of affinity groups. . . . We can think about larger power formations as instances when lots of small spaces come together for a particular moment in a particular direction."** In other

---

** Unless otherwise noted, quotes are from individual and collective conversations that took place between 2019 and 2023.

words, making systems change at the scale we want and need to in this moment requires attention to the process of emergence.

shea emphasizes that emergent strategies offer counter-narratives to the conventional wisdom that arose in the context of industrialization: mobilization for change must match the scale of the systems we seek to affect. In other words, emergent strategies call into question the notion that just like we need mass production, we need mass uprisings to shift conditions, mass safety (which comes in the form of police and prisons), and mass "solutions" to social problems that can be replicated everywhere. Emergent strategies prompt us to ask critical questions about this approach offered by kai lumumba barrow, a longtime Black feminist abolitionist organizer and sistercomrade who served as National Organizing Director for Critical Resistance, a national organization that has shaped thinking and organizing toward abolition of the prison industrial complex (PIC) for the past twenty-five years. kai asks: "Do we need a mass movement, or do we need networks of active cells that are able to intervene, prevent, and transform the everyday violences that we're experiencing? Do we need a mass movement to tell us all what we should be doing, or do we need small groups raising our awareness?" For kai, emergent strategies point us toward alternate answers to these questions, toward networks of "small, decentralized groups sharing information and resources, that employ collective processes for decision-making around shared things that everyone can access, and that are guided by a set of shared principles."

That said, practicing emergent strategies doesn't mean that we no longer try to affect large systems. It "doesn't mean eschewing the systemic for the interpersonal or vice versa. Emergence is an invitation to hold a dual focus."[14] As someone living in a time of climate collapse, mounting fascism, and rising rates of white-supremacist, gender-based, homophobic, transphobic, colonial, and anti-Black violence, I am painfully aware that large systems are increasingly constraining possibility at every scale. As a Black feminist, I am committed to what the Combahee River Collective Statement describes as "the development of integrated analysis and practice based upon the fact that the major systems of oppression are interlocking," and on the premise that "if Black women were free that would mean everyone else would have to be free because our freedom would necessitate the destruction of all systems of oppression."[15] None of the changes I want to see in the world are possible without eliminating a global economic system built on racial capitalism and the structural violence it requires and produces along the axes of race, gender, sexuality, disability, class, and nation, operating in the lives of Black women, trans and gender nonconforming people, and our communities everywhere. By definition, this requires large-scale, systemic change.

The knowledge that what happens at the small-scale replicates, coalesces into, and shapes larger social structures and systems simply shifts the primary focus of transformation to our relationships, interactions, networks, and communities instead of strategies that rely exclusively on mass mobilization and top-down legislative and policy initiatives. Emergent strategies invite us to act based on shared values and principles at a smaller scale, and to connect our actions across time and space into networks with the power to shape complex systems. They remind us that we are constantly learning and adapting to changing conditions at the individual and collective levels. They point to critical guidance offered by the natural world on building resilience under pressure through decentralization, cooperation, and interdependence. They urge us to ask generative questions; move beyond binaries; value uncertainty; practice while learning from our mistakes; and to create more possibilities. They invite us to engage our radical imaginations and to center joy and pleasure in our efforts.

As shea puts it, "We cannot stop fascism with small steps alone. On the other hand, without those small steps, we are not going to get to the larger action and the larger society. I think this is the piece that is missing. The only way [is] through slow, patient organizing—there's just no quick way. I wish there was." Grace Lee Boggs points out that this approach "lacks the drama and visibility of angry masses making demands on the power structure" and thus "doesn't seem practical to those who think of change only in terms of quick fixes, huge masses, and charismatic leaders."[16] Both studied the work of Charles Payne, who said, writing about the civil rights movement in *I've Got the Light of Freedom*, "Overemphasizing the movement's more dramatic features, we undervalue the patient and sustained effort, the slow, respectful work, that made the dramatic moments possible."[17] Drawing on Payne and Wheatley's work, Grace concludes that "the real engine of change is never 'critical mass;' dramatic and systemic change always begins with 'critical connections.'"[18] That is where shaping the future begins.

Why Emergent Strategies Matter in a Time of Fascism

Even if you are not convinced that emergent strategies can play an important role building toward the worlds we want, there are still important reasons to learn about them. In fact, I have come to believe that we can't afford to not to be emergent strategists in this time—because emergent strategies are part of how we got to where we are.

Over the past six decades, the religious Right has leveraged the power of relatively small interactions—in church basements and prayer circles, over harvest and coffee—to shape the systems and conditions we are now living. While the use of law, policy, political parties, think tanks, and judicial appointments to advance Right-wing agendas is more visible, these strategies represent the tip of the iceberg in terms of how the Right built the power they are now exercising in an attempt to dominate what they describe as the seven mountains or pillars of society: economy, education, family life, religion, media, culture, and government.[19] While our collective focus has rightly been on authoritarian, top-down Christian evangelical efforts, led by charismatic leaders, to pass legislation to ban abortion and gender-affirming care, attempt to eradicate the public existence of trans and queer people, to take over and overturn systems of government, and to impose a white-supremacist, patriarchal Christian theocracy, there is much more at play.

The Christian Right has adopted the strategy of calling on its followers to "go and make disciples" and to "invade" each of these seven arenas with the intention of shifting larger systems further toward white supremacy and cisheteropatriarchy. Supporters are encouraged to advance theocratic values through critical connections: in their workplaces, faith communities, social media posts, and conversations with families and friends.[20] Neo-Nazis are similarly deploying decentralized strategies reliant on small groups of people to form "a web, instead of a chain of command."[21] ¡No Pasarán!: Antifascist Dispatches from a World in Crisis contributors Emmi Bevensee and Frank Miroslav write, "One of the most concerning developments is the shift by various strands of fascism into becoming more horizontal and to using distributed organizing mechanisms . . . There are a number of reasons this kind of distributed white terror is becoming more popular; the most obvious of which is that it works."[22] In a particularly alarming turn, the Patriot movement is bastardizing "dual power" approaches that originate in revolutionary struggles of the Global South and focus on both challenging state power and building prefigurative community institutions.[23] In the Patriots' case, they do so by creating militias and common law courts that prefigure the dictatorship they seek to impose on broader society.[24] Alt-Right groups are likewise seeking to dismantle centralized states while upholding patriarchal non-state "tribal" systems rooted in male dominance.[25] In other words, Right-wing movements are also manifesting decentralized, adaptive, and iterative approaches to shaping the world that build on critical connections and networks to shift larger systems.

As a result, as organizer and strategist Suzanne Pharr, longtime student of Right-wing, white-supremacist movements, puts it, "They are so pervasive as to be obscured and normalized to the extent that they are simultaneously everywhere all the time and difficult to detect."[26] Like a virus, they infect communities, replicate themselves, and spread.[27] To resist, Pharr calls us to engage in local work aimed at transforming individuals and communities, to recognize that "the bridges we build one by one between individuals are the strongest," to understand our struggle as one of fundamental values, and to move with the knowledge that "every step toward liberation must have liberation in it."[28] As organizer Shane Burley writes in *¡No Pasarán!*, "The antidote to fascism in all its manifestations is community-building."[29] Emmi Bevensee and Frank Miroslav argue that, "Whereas fascists use complexity to promote their violent and overly simplistic worldview, antifascists can use complexity to cultivate richly diverse and evolving networks of resistance." In other words, to fight a competing world vision that is rapidly spreading in part through what could be characterized as emergent strategies, we need to at least understand and practice them ourselves.

Detroit Roots of *Emergent Strategy*

The book *Emergent Strategy*—as well as the Emergent Strategy Podcast and Emergent Strategy Ideation Institute that emerged from it—grew out of study groups and conversations among Detroit-based organizers beginning in the late 2000s.[30] These explorations were rooted in Detroit's unique conditions at the time: the city was experiencing the height of organized abandonment and the failure of state institutions, and organizers were heeding the call of Detroit organizer Charity Hicks to "wage love" in response.[31] Importantly, ideation around application of emergent strategies to social movements took place in a majority-Black city that Detroit-native, filmmaker, and organizer dream hampton has described as "one long, beautiful experiment." Others—including adrienne maree brown—have described Detroit as an "emergent strategy city" built on "making a way out of no way" in ways that prefigure abolitionist futures.

The organizers shaping *Emergent Strategy* were also informed by a long legacy of resistance to the violence of policing, from the Great Migration, to the 1963 police shooting of a Black woman named Cynthia Scott, to the 1967 Detroit rebellion, to intensive organizing against dozens of policing killings since then. By 1996, the city led the country in police violence, leading organizers to establish the Detroit Coalition Against Police Brutality, and one of its founders, Ron Scott, to dub Detroit "ground zero for police brutality."[32] Under Ron's leadership, communities organized into Peace Zones 4 Life, training people in de-escalation, mediation, and violence interruption in an effort to keep cops out of neighborhoods. Speaking at the 2010 Allied Media Conference, Ron articulated his vision: "It's about rebuilding family, rebuilding connections, resolving disputes before we invite police, about de-escalating violence among us so we don't have to have somebody come in and police us."[33] More recently, the resistance continues through Detroit Will Breathe and 313 Liberation Zone's demands to cut police funding and increase investments in community-based safety programs, as well as campaigns to stop Project Green Light and ShotSpotter, both of which would install police surveillance cameras and recording equipment throughout the city. Black youth in Detroit surveyed community members about their visions for safety through the Greenlight Black Futures campaign, while community members launched a "green chairs not green lights" initiative, inviting people to watch out for each other instead of allowing the state to sell them an illusion of safety through surveillance.[34]

Organizers evolving a framework for applying emergent strategies to social movements were also deeply informed by engagement with Indigenous organizers on Turtle Island and in Palestine; with movements across the Global South; by conversations coalescing through the World Social Forums (gatherings of global left movements under the theme "Another World is Possible" that began in 2001 as an effort to build counterpower to the forces of racial capitalism gathering at the World Economic Forum); and by the US Social Forum, first held in Atlanta in 2007, adding "Another US Is Necessary" to the title. I, too, was profoundly shaped by these conversations as one of the thousands who traveled first to Atlanta and then to Detroit to attend the second US Social Forum in 2010—which adrienne co-organized—under the additional tag line, "Another Detroit Is Happening."

Detroit organizers exploring emergent strategies were also central to the Allied Media Conference (AMC), which I have been attending since it first relocated to Detroit in 2007. I still vividly remember finding my way to my first AMC by happenstance, at the suggestion of a friend, unsure of what I would find or offer at a media conference. In my previous life, I was the communications director for a national women's organization in Canada, and all I could imagine was a room full of movement flacks talking about how to get more column inches. I couldn't have been further from the truth. I have returned to the AMC every year since then, bringing dozens of people and organizations with me, describing myself in my conference bio as an AMC evangelist.

The conference is a space where emergent strategies are beautifully embodied and practiced—even as the conference has grown from several hundred participants to thousands of people from around the globe, first gathering in person, then virtually at the height of the pandemic, and now in hybrid form—around the time of the summer solstice. AMC consciously seeks to spark visionary organizing by focusing on critical connections between people and communities, like those between resistance mural creators in Northern Ireland and Southwest Detroit; between Indigenous youth on Turtle Island and in Palestine; between Black communities in Detroit and New Orleans; between South African shack dwellers and Detroit housing and water warriors. The AMC is structured to nurture interaction between conference participants beyond programming, through collective meals and collaborative open spaces, making the AMC a place where relationships are built and connective tissue between organizing communities is strengthened. Many of the people I consider my closest comrades, beloved movement family, and my most influential teachers are people I met and built with at the conference. The first year I attended, I had the honor of sitting at Grace's feet (literally, in a packed room, as she spoke on a closing plenary), the universe magically placed me in a dorm suite with Alexis Pauline Gumbs, and I attended a workshop on participatory research hosted by Jenny Lee, ill weaver, and Detroit Summer youth.[35] Since then, the conference has connected me with dozens of people I have loved and struggled alongside in multiple formations over the years.

AMC content is co-created in a decentralized fashion by participants and takes the shape of network gatherings, practice spaces, and workshops. Over the years I have participated in the selection and facilitation of programming; served on the conference's advisory committee; and hosted tracks and network gatherings, including INCITE!/SpeakOut Women of Color tracks highlighting organizing and cultural production by radical feminists of color. The 2016 Say Her Name/Black Trans Lives Matter network gathering I co-hosted grew into the In Our Names Network, a constellation of over twenty organizations and individuals across the United States working to end police violence against Black women, girls, queer, and trans people.[36] I have reveled in the conference's seamless integration of art, technology, music, play, and dance. The AMC is where I made my first zines, learned about pirate radio, light actions, mud stenciling, and 3D printing; where I was taught how to make a robot by a twelve-year-old Black girl and played intergenerational games of revolutionary red rover. I have regularly experienced transcendence during opening and closing ceremonies carefully designed to explode our hearts and imaginations with joy and possibility, as well as on the dance floor of the conference's legendary musical showcases and parties.

Mine is just one of many stories within the broad ecosystem of the AMC. As Jenny Lee, former conference coordinator and Allied Media Projects (AMP) director points out on the *Critical Connections: Stories from Twenty Years of the Allied Media Conference* podcast, "The AMC is not a single organism. It is a forest, it is an underground network of mushrooms, it is a galaxy—we have no end of metaphors. But the best one is probably that it is fertile ground."[37] According to Jenny, the AMC plays the role of earthworms in creating conditions for building and growing critical connections: "We're cultivating the soil. We're decomposing the shit that's not working and turning it into valuable nutrients. We're aerating, making space for roots to grow. We're cultivating this really rich soil that then a seed can fall in, and all of a sudden it's going to blossom." This is what distinguishes AMC from traditional conference spaces where parameters and agendas are already set, the goal and outcomes pre-determined—and what makes it such a rich soil for the practice of emergent strategies.

For me, AMC has served as fertile ground for growing my understanding that we won't get to the world I long for by just documenting the problems, engaging in issue- and policy-based advocacy, or focusing on what Grace described as top-down mobilization of "the faceless masses." It is where I first grappled with the truth that personal transformation is essential to being in right relationship with political change and that it happens in community and practice with others. Since then, personal transformation has happened for me again and again through the experiences of being held in the AMC community. AMC is where I first experienced processes of creation, communication, and envisioning the world we are creating (even as we can't yet fully imagine it) as transformative. The AMC also taught me that our movements must be so joyful, attractive, and compelling that, like the AMC, they become spaces that people are more often drawn to than recruited to, where they are able to find countless points of entry and engagement. I have returned year after year to be restored, refreshed, reminded, reinspired, and regrounded in what it means to build the world we long for in every interaction, in an expansive understanding of change and transformation, and in how we shape the containers we learn, grow, and play in to make it possible. Whenever I would get pulled into legal strategies and policy campaigns, the AMC reminded me that the relationships we nurture, the communities we create, and the principles we live by and practice every day are what bring us closer to liberation. I often describe the AMC as a gathering that shines a flashlight into the future we are trying to build—and I return every year to catch glimpses of what the flashlight illuminates. It is not an exaggeration to say the AMC has completely transformed me and the way I do my work. Importantly, the AMC is where I was first introduced to emergent strategies through workshops hosted by adrienne and Complex Movements. In other words, it is the soil in which this book germinated.

Over the years, the AMC has intentionally adapted and iterated to respond to internal challenges and changing conditions in Detroit, the US, and the world. Organizers traced its impacts by mapping connections and ripples emanating from the fractal relationships nurtured at the conference. Participants evolved a set of principles (reproduced at the end of this chapter) and practices around disability, transformative, gender, and healing justice that guide many of us as we practice visionary organizing beyond the conference. After twenty years, Allied Media Projects, the organization that hosts the AMC and dozens of projects that emerged from it, engaged in a year-long period of intentional reflection, guided by the metaphor of a caterpillar entering a chrysalis to emerge fully transformed.[38] As shea put it, the AMC is "a space where you're free, where you feel for that brief minute, 'This is what the future could be.' But you're actually in it. It's about how we can practice freedom now so that we can get the muscles for it, a taste for it, a feel for the space we should be heading toward." And, as Nandi Comer, who has played multiple roles in coordinating the conference and now serves as the director of the AMP Seeds program created to spread the AMC experience beyond the now-biennial conference, points out, "It's also still a space where we have to navigate harm and talk about restorative practices, even in a place where most people feel like they have this space of freedom." In other words, it is a place where participants have practiced abolitionist futures through conflict, failures, lessons, and triumphs, building community safety teams and healing justice practice spaces as part of the process.

The Detroit Safety Team (DST) emerged from this collective practice of creating safer spaces without policing at the

Allied Media Conference. As John Sloan, DST's co-director put it on the *One Million Experiments* podcast:

> Detroit Safety Team believes that this current system of policing and justice, as it's built, is doing exactly what it was designed to do, which is not to keep a large group of people safe, it's to maintain a social order and status quo.
>
> Detroit Safety Team exists to be able to say, "What's going to exist in its place? What systems can we build that center the needs of the community, that put more agency into the community members to define what safety looks like for them, for their block, for their neighborhood, for their city?"
>
> . . . Safety is a process. It's an understanding of how we're working through this process, in collaboration with those people in our environment.[39]

DST facilitates a process of moving toward greater community safety and well-being by building and strengthening communities, individual skills and capacities, and holding restorative processes when harm occurs.[40] Like the AMC, DST engages in constant evaluation to assess whether what community members believed would create greater safety still represents the path they want to take. Recognizing that community safety practitioners are up against well-resourced systems invested in the status quo, DST co-director Curtis Renee nevertheless asserts, "We can match that in creativity, in how we're having the conversation house to house, neighbor to neighbor, at our kitchen table." DST's guiding question is "How are we providing more opportunity across the city of Detroit to be able to have these conversations?"[41]

The AMC is not only a practice space unto itself; it is also part of, shaped by, and an amplifier of Detroit's response to organized abandonment and of its commitment to rebuild the world anew. When I first visited Detroit in the 1990s, and again during tours of the city led by community organizers during the AMC, I learned about how the city was shaped by white capital and white flight.[42] I also learned that migrant workers were taking over abandoned factories to make tamales to feed their communities. I learned that students at shuttered schools were taking back the abandoned buildings, inviting adults in the community to teach them what they wanted to know and the skills they needed, while others were using music and spoken word to gather and amplify their experiences in the remaining heavily policed schools. I learned that people combating food apartheid were taking over abandoned lots and creating community gardens—which have multiplied from a few hundred to over a thousand across the city, many of which allow community members to harvest what they need.[43] I learned about the possibilities of community resilience and transformation.

PG Watkins, a nonbinary organizer, facilitator, trainer, and coach from Detroit who is a member of the Boggs Center Council and a facilitator with the Emergent Strategy Ideation Institute (ESII) says, "Some of that possibility has come because of all of the ways that this city has been disinvested in, and all the ways that it's been discounted by folks." They add, "The people who have been here for their whole lives or for a very long time have had to figure out shit on their own, have had to practice interdependence, have had to practice resiliency in creating these possibilities out of their own money, out of their own homes, on their own blocks because the city wasn't looking out for us."[44]

Erin Butler, an abolitionist organizer who was also born and raised in Detroit, similarly talks about how growing up in the city shaped her politics and understandings of what is possible. "Divestment created the structure where we have to share resources and be in multiple movements because we've experienced multiple forms of disinvestment at the same time." It also led to a lived experience of abolitionist practices. Erin describes their family jumping in to de-escalate fights in front of the house, walking out and saying, 'Hey, what the fuck are you doing?!' when someone was breaking into their garage, staying up one night to push cars that were stuck in the snow during storms, mowing the lawn on abandoned lots. "It wasn't an active political choice," she explains. "We weren't trying to enact abolition as a family, we were just trying to get by. There was no one you could call, no back-up plan, no infrastructure. We were it, so you had to act like it." Erin says these realities created the conditions to become an abolitionist organizer. "It gave me frameworks for when people said, 'We have to find ways to do that without the cops.' I thought, 'Oh, I already know how to do that.' It was harder for people who lived in places where the cops were more present to imagine and figure out."

Halima Cassells, an interdisciplinary artist with deep roots in Detroit whose work intersects social, land, food, and community justice, points to how the Great Migration, which brought so much of Detroit's population to the city and led so many of Detroit's youth to be sent back to the South for the summer, also shaped possibilities. "A lot of these practices are rooted in Black people's survival of the South, and their ancestral expertise in thriving community traditions," she says. The organizing she does these days focuses on gathering people in her home and at art venues for critical conversations, practicing mutual aid by hosting Free Market of Detroit swap events, supporting people in telling Detroit stories by advising the Detroit Narrative Agency, and encouraging young people to speak out about what they are most passionate about.[45] Halima has also been involved in creating conditions to support this work through policy-based initiatives such as with the People's Platform and community benefits agreements, Arts in a Changing America, and participatory budgeting, but strategies focused on community connections and resilience are at the heart of her work.[46]

In other words, place matters in the evolution of conversations about emergent strategies. Reflecting on Detroit, shea highlights the instability produced when an economy driven by the auto industry, and the capitalist institutions that upheld it, foundered. The fallout was compounded by the state's organized abandonment, making way—for the most part outside of the watchful gaze of authorities—for practice and experimentation with building community organizations and institutions to fill the gaps that could prefigure a world beyond them. "It's because those capitalist institutions are so shaky that the values that enabled humans to survive but were buried by capital—values of care, cooperation, joy, love, pleasure, dreaming—are now emerging as people try to survive where capitalism left us," shea says. "That's why Detroit matters. Abolitionist practices emerged when the state failed. It is failing in other places in different ways, but it seriously failed here . . . paying attention to what's emerging in the most dispossessed places is our best chance."

While it's true that visionary organizing shaped by emergent strategies is more likely to flourish and bear fruit in places like Detroit, we need to meet those conditions by practicing emergent strategies with a clear connection to the values we believe must shape it. shea cautions that the collapse of late-stage racial capitalism doesn't automatically lead to opportunities to practice and build the world we want; the same conditions can fan the flames of white supremacy and fascism. "The values of cruelty, of greed, of self-protection are also on the rise," shea warns. "Unless we place emergent strategies within a certain value orientation, we're not going to win what's actually a contest for the future." For me, Black feminism, abolition, and internationalism serve as the values that shape my understanding and practice of emergent strategies.

Emergent Strategies, Black Feminism, and Global Struggle

There are several reasons the ideas and practices in evidence in the AMC, US Social Forums, and Detroit-based organizing resonated with me so deeply. I come to organizing informed by family, community, time spent growing up in the Global South, and by study of global liberation struggles. As an adult, I organized with and learned from Black feminist abolitionists, including Beverly Bain, Angela Y. Davis, Beth Richie, Ruth Wilson Gilmore, Barbara Smith, Barbara Ransby, kai lumumba barrow, Tourmaline, Che Gossett, Kenyon Farrow, Alisa Bierria, Shana M. griffin, Cara Page, Alexis Pauline Gumbs, Robyn Maynard, and of course, my beloved friend, comrade,

Interrupting Criminalization cofounder, and coauthor of *No More Police: A Case for Abolition*, Mariame Kaba, along with many more Black women, queer, and trans organizers I have had the privilege of struggling alongside. Both Black feminism and exposure to movements outside the United States attuned me to what emergent strategies have to offer.

Black feminism theorizes from the lived experiences of Black women, girls, and trans people and frames political struggle through a commitment to their inherent value. Black feminist author and organizer Barbara Smith describes Black feminism as "a political stance and a political choice."[47] It prioritizes the critical consciousness and connections that shape historic and present-day practices of collective care that have made our survival possible. It names the controlling narratives operating in service of interlocking systems of oppression that constrain our perceptions of ourselves, of each other, and of possibilities for living otherwise. Black feminism requires dismantling what Beth Richie describes as a matrix of state, community, and interpersonal violence that entraps Black women, girls, and trans people—and that we do so everywhere.[48] As Mariame and I wrote in *No More Police*, "Black feminism invites us to liberate our imaginations so that we can conceive of new ways of understanding and creating collective safety and well-being, and to believe that it is possible to make them real through everyday actions."[49] Black feminist scholar Hortense Spillers submits that, "What Black feminisms might teach the current social order begins with concernful care for other human beings,"[50] while Toni Cade Bambara asserts that it starts with a practice of liberation in the present in order make it possible in the future.[51] Many of these principles and practices of Black feminism align with those of emergent strategies.

Organizing in solidarity with revolutionary movements in South Africa, Nicaragua, and El Salvador in the late 1980s, and studying resistance to neoliberalism in Central and South America in the late 1990s and 2000s with comrades in INCITE! Feminists of Color Against Violence and the Another Politics is Possible (APP) study group in New York City, similarly contributed to my openness to emergent strategies.[52] Former fellow INCITE! national collective member Paula X. Rojas in particular profoundly shaped my thinking around the framework of "making power" and "taking power," which draws on dual power strategies deployed by movements in Chile, Mexico, Brazil, and Argentina described in her influential article "Are the Cops in Our Heads and in Our Hearts?" first published in the INCITE! anthology *The Revolution Will Not Be Funded: Beyond the Non-Profit Industrial Complex.*[53] INCITE! affiliate Sista II Sista, which Paula co-founded, put this framework into action by turning away from the state as a target, and toward each other as a community to transform conditions that produce gender-based violence.[54] Learning about and witnessing this work opened me up to more relationship- and community-based approaches to organizing.

At the same time, the APP study group was reading and writing about decentralized, non-hierarchical movements that were practicing new social relations as they fought for systemic change. Writing in the mid-2000s about the Zapatistas in Mexico, the landless people's movement in Brazil, the shack-dweller movement in South Africa, and resistance to neoliberal economic policies in Ecuador, Bolivia, and Argentina, Marina Sitrin, author of *Horizontalism*, describes

> an upsurge in prefigurative revolutionary movements: movements that create the future in the present. These new movements are not creating party platforms or programs. They do not look to one leader but make space for all to be leaders. They place more importance on asking the right questions than on providing the right answers. They do not adhere to dogma and hierarchy, instead they build direct democracy and consensus. They are movements based in trust and love.[55]

Rather than focusing on building "power over" by seizing the state, the movements Sitrin was writing about were building "power with" through direct democracy in communities. "Unlike past movements," she wrote, "social change isn't deferred to a later date by demanding reforms from the state, or by taking state power and eventually instituting these reforms."[56] Instead, communities were creating new worlds in the present. Communities focused on making change through relationships and on sharing information, resources, and decision-making through networks of local neighborhood assemblies and occupied workplaces. And they had significant systemic impacts. For instance, in December 2001, millions in Argentina "spontaneously took to the streets, and without leaders or hierarchies, forced the government to resign, and then through continuous mobilizations, proceeded to expel four more governments in less than two weeks" in response to neoliberal economic policies.[57] While a combination of repression and cooptation eventually eroded movement gains, participants believed they would nevertheless have lasting, systemic effects based on their methods: "Something changed in them as people, as well as in how they relate to each other. These changes could not be undone, even if the structures of the organizations changed."[58] What I learned in study and conversation about these movements aligned with elements of what I now understand as emergent strategies.

Later, as a board member of another INCITE! affiliate, the Young Women's Empowerment Project (YWEP), I was introduced to what former co-director Shira Hassan calls "liberatory harm reduction."[59] She defines this as "a philosophy and set of empowerment-based practices that teach us how to accompany each other as we transform the root causes of harm in our lives" through relationship and community building, rather than reliance on laws and policies.[60] Shira taught me, as we were struggling to find ways to reduce the violence of policing as experienced by YWEP's constituency, that we needed fewer laws and policies, not more, to do so.

Based on these experiences, though I continued to engage in work focused on law, policy, and litigation, I became increasingly disillusioned with both process and outcome, at times finding myself deeply out of alignment with my politics and values.

When *Emergent Strategy* was published in 2017, much of what had been "won" through campaigns and policy advocacy efforts I was involved in had evaporated under profound shifts in political conditions. While some of the policies and laws I was part of writing and winning remain on the books, the practices they sought to change persist and in some cases have even expanded. I was in a place where the ideas about emergent strategies gathered in the book struck a chord, shifting and expanding my theory of change within a Black feminist abolitionist and internationalist politic.

What *Emergent Strategy* Is NOT

Before going any further, it is important to note at the outset that *Emergent Strategy* does not, despite the name, outline a political or organizing strategy per se, nor does the book identify or adhere to any particular political theory or ideology. This can lead readers who, like me, emerge from leftist material traditions to experience it as somewhat ungrounded. As Ejeris Dixon, movement strategist and founder of consulting firm Vision, Change, Win points out, *Emergent Strategy* does not describe a singular *strategy* to build and contend for power in the sense of the goal, strategic objective, target, tactics organizing methods and vocabulary we were both raised on.

Instead, *Emergent Strategy* is a collection of ideas about *how* change happens—or, more specifically, how the change we need could happen. adrienne acknowledges this in the book's introduction, characterizing her offering as "a cluster of thoughts in development, observations of existing patterns, and questions about how we apply the brilliance of the world around us . . . to transform the crises of our time."[61] In other words, *Emergent Strategy* points us toward a set of practices rooted in a particular understanding of the process of change.

It is helpful to remember that the principles offered in *Emergent Strategy* grow out of a practice of facilitation, of creating and holding generative containers in which political ideologies and organizing strategies can be developed, assessed, tweaked, implemented.[62] This becomes even clearer in the second book in the Emergent Strategy Series, *Holding Change: The Way of Emergent Strategy Facilitation and Mediation*, in which adrienne delves more deeply into how the principles explored in *Emergent Strategy* can shape facilitation goals and practices. Both books focus on the *process* of change, the methods we use as we work together toward liberation.

The importance of these offerings should not be underestimated. I, along with many other abolitionist organizers I spoke with about this book, point to *Emergent Strategy*, *Holding Change*, and ESII trainings as invaluable contributions to our facilitation practice. Many of us named this as the most transformative aspect of emergent strategies—their emphasis on the importance of moving away from rigid, packed, and unsustainable agendas and spaces that leave people exhausted and uninspired. Emergent strategies point us toward the necessity of creating luscious, generative spaces and practices that make room for visioning the world we want and inviting people into creating it with us, iteration and adaptation to meet the needs of participants and of the moment, opportunities to learn from our mistakes and for fostering transformation and building resilience. In short: of practicing the world we want in the spaces we hold as we build it. Because, as dream hampton observes, as existing systems collapse, "facilitation becomes governance."[63]

That said, emergent strategies are not a substitute for rigorous assessment of material conditions or for taking concrete action. shea reminds us: "One thing about emergent strategy is you have to place it in the moment. You still have to ask, 'What are the opportunities capital has created? Where are the contradictions we can exploit?' We don't think of strategy out of nowhere; we think of it in relation to the main contradiction, the opportunities for action. We can't give up on political analysis." Emergent strategies simply point to how we might apply a political analysis in action.

Woods Ervin, a beloved former co-conspirator at Interrupting Criminalization and longtime member (and now co-director) of Critical Resistance, the longest-standing national abolitionist organization in the US, describes emergent strategies as "a set of organizing tools that can help bring people into formations that can do the work of building a world without surveillance, prisons, and policing." Or, as kai lumumba barrow, former national organizer at Critical Resistance, put it, emergent strategy principles are "core practices for how an abolitionist ideology is materialized." Like shea, Woods emphasizes that emergent strategies are an "additive not a substitution" for an analysis, a politic, a set of values, an intention, a set of material changes we want to achieve. According to Woods, emergent strategies serve as a reminder to remain flexible, fluid, creative, curious, and to be rigorous (disciplined in our attention and actions) without being rigid (unable to adapt to changing conditions) as we organize to build power to bring the future we want into being. Or, as Sendolo Diaminah described on the *Emergent Strategy Podcast*, to practice "more devotion, less discipline."[64] Practicing emergent strategies doesn't mean we don't clearly envision and articulate our overall strategic objectives as we organize through critical connections, networks, and communities of practice to dismantle structures and systems of power. It also doesn't mean discipline and structure aren't required as we do so. Emergent strategies simply invite us to practice devotion to learning about how to achieve the change we seek from the complex systems we are part of. In other words, to move fractally, with flexibility, making room for adaptation and iteration, in service of an abolitionist politic and political strategy.

Emergent Strategy also does not lay out a brand-new approach to organizing. It points us to the best of organizing that is already happening, to what we are already doing that we need to do more of. It also helps us recognize when we are operating at cross purposes with the changes we want to create and when our efforts are likely to keep leading to dead ends. Attempting to read *Emergent Strategy* as a "new," fully formed organizing strategy rather than as a set of methodological guideposts for collective action within an existing politic, strategy, and set of values can lead to potentially dangerous places.

For instance, some of the ways in which *Emergent Strategy* and the ideas it touches upon have been further simplified, decontextualized, and abstracted beyond the organizing contexts from which they emerged as the book's reach has grown have contributed to confusion as to what application of emergent strategies to organizing means in practice. Internet memes abound with messages drawn from the book like "what is easy is sustainable—birds coast when they can" or "be like mushrooms." Practicing emergent strategies toward abolitionist futures is neither comfortable nor easy—although kai muses that the notion that it is both comfortable and easy may be part of *Emergent Strategy*'s broad appeal: people don't want to be uncomfortable and are drawn to the fallacy that emergent strategies don't require them to be. In fact, the opposite is true. While looking for ways to ride the winds of change is important, increasing collective sustainability under current conditions is no small feat and will no doubt require a significant amount of discomfort. Practicing emergent strategies toward building sustainable and effective abolitionist movements does not mean checking out of the hard work of organizing altogether in search of ease and comfort.

Practicing emergent strategies also does not mean simply making one-to-one analogies between human societies and non-human organisms. While mushrooms do amazing things, they often take hundreds or even thousands of years to do them and function quite differently than humans. Becoming emergent strategists means asking ourselves what we might learn from nature to enhance the efficacy of existing organizing efforts—how do we build the kinds of expansive and resilient networks mushrooms create underground? How do we attend to detoxification in the material, movement, and societal realms? It does not mean acting as though the change we seek we need will suddenly spring up, seemingly out of nowhere, like mushrooms do after a rain.

In other words, some of the ways that *Emergent Strategy* has been taken up outside of the larger politic and organizing contexts it came out of does a disservice to the ideas it articulates. In some cases, the principles articulated in *Emergent Strategy* have been divorced from emergent strategies' invitation to collective action to the point of being read mainly as a "social justice self-help book." At worst, these principles have been mobilized in ways that can be downright *dis*organizing. For example, exploring emergent strategies does not mean just showing up to see what emerges, expecting something magical to take the place of the hard work of assessing and organizing to change conditions. Or, as shea put it, saying, "Oh, I'll take a vacation, and everything will be alright." In her book *As We Have Always Done*, Michi Saagig Nishnaabeg scholar and organizer Leanne Betasamosake Simpson reminds us that as we celebrate the complexity and mystery of natural systems, we need to see ourselves as agents of change within them.[65] We need to move as though "living is a creative act."[66] In other words, action is required. It is how knowledge, and a different future, is generated. When it comes to building critical connections, as Ejeris points out, "It is not enough to recognize the importance of talking to strangers, you have to actually talk to strangers, you have to actually dream and put dreams into practice. You have to say, 'Here are the actions that build, here are the actions that change.'"

As the principles articulated in *Emergent Strategy* have become increasingly unmoored from their theoretical and organizing roots, some have questioned what, if anything, they might have to offer abolitionist struggles in this moment. Maurice Mitchell, the national director of the Working Families Party and one of the architects of the Movement for Black Lives, shares an important corrective in a 2022 article offering an assessment of the state of left movements in the United States. He points out that disconnection of principles from the contexts in which they emerged is a manifestation of a broader tendency to superficially reference but not engage in the rigorous study and practice of frameworks like emergent strategies. Invocation of phrases such as *Emergent Strategy*'s "small is all," or Audre Lorde's assertion that "caring for myself is not self-indulgence, it is self-preservation, and that is an act of political warfare," without internalizing the Black feminist organizing contexts and political commitments that they emerged from undermines our ability to develop and enact collective liberatory strategies.[67] The same is true of vague gestures to the "non-profit industrial complex" that do not take into account the theoretical framework and structural analysis behind the phrase and the global Black, Indigenous, and women of color feminist (largely unpaid) organizing contexts it emerged from.[68] Doing emergent strategies—and Black feminist thought—justice requires that we situate these principles within an analysis and political commitment to action aimed at dismantling interlocking systems of oppression at every scale.

Even in their fullest expression, there are serious gaps in the emergent strategies framework. For instance, what happens when countervailing forces also deploy emergent strategies, as Right-wing forces are increasingly demonstrating their ability and inclination to do? What happens when the state recognizes our capacity to generate large-scale systemic shifts through emergent strategies and directly targets our connections, networks, and communities of practice?

kai offers a series of cautions and concerns along these lines. "While emergent strategies may not appear threatening on the surface, once we start to deploy them to create self-sustaining communities that are connected in ways that challenge white-supremacist patriarchal capitalist institutions, that not only shift our identities but how we relate to institutions, then we become a threat." Under those circumstances, she points out, "we haven't come up with a viable, sustainable response to the direct violence of the state." In light of this, kai sees emergent strategies as practices and methodologies that can be successful in prefiguring abolitionist futures in small communities of activists, who in turn can have an impact in larger geographic communities through networking. In other words, "Emergent strategies reflect how I roll in my personal relationships, with people I am in alignment with, with people I am hoping to build with," she says. Indeed, Meg Wheatley and other emergent strategy theorists focus on finding and building networks and communities of practice with other people with shared values. "I think these are the ways that we are structuring ourselves to be envisioning and practicing this world, creating what we hope to leave behind for every generation following us until we get there," kai concludes. But once we become a threat, what's the plan? How do we "defend ourselves from the violence of the state in a way that is aligned with our values?" How do we ensure that organizing shaped by emergent strategies is not "eradicated before we are able to materialize our vision?" INCITE! cofounder Mimi Kim shares these concerns, pointing to the fragility of the complex systems emergent strategies look to as metaphors for organizing:

> On the other side of the beauty of starfish, spores, and viruses, biological forms evoked in current treatises on social movement innovation, lies precarity. . . . Constant also is the precarity of anti-state, anti-institutional countermovements that have persisted and prevailed but face the ever-present threat of disappearance.[69]

To be sure, there is still value in moving in the face of violence in ways that are interconnected, decentralized, adaptive, and resilient. But kai wonders if emergent strategies can move us from being on the defense to being on the offense. "What's missing to me," she says, "is the struggle. There's a lot of violence around us at all times. We're surrounded by violence, but we're not talking about violence. How are we directly intervening in and dismantling, declawing, shifting the violence that is coming into our communities, to our planet? Emergent strategies can be one of our stockpile of strategies, but I do think there's a missing piece about how we contest for power in this situation."

A clue to this piece of the puzzle lies in geographies in which emergent strategies have found footholds. For instance, it is notable that when conversations about emergent strategies were at their height in Detroit, the city was experiencing a particular form of governmental collapse and organized abandonment. The state and oppositional forces had largely withdrawn from the field, leaving a vacuum into which emergent strategies could be practiced with less risk of being targeted by a police state. There is still much to learn about how emergent strategies can build resistance and shape change under acutely adverse and repressive conditions.

Despite these limitations, I believe that the framework of emergent strategies that *Emergent Strategy* draws from, applied within a broader abolitionist organizing politic and practice, can open up new possibilities and create more fertile ground for more liberatory futures to blossom.

The 2020 Uprisings: Emergence in Action?

Many longtime abolitionists will tell you that we never—in our wildest dreams—believed that abolitionist ideas and demands would enter the mainstream the way they did following the police killings of George Floyd, Breonna Taylor, and hundreds more in the days, months, and years since May 25, 2020. The presence of over twenty-six million people in the streets of cities, suburbs, and small towns across Turtle Island—many united around an abolitionist demand to defund the police—was not the product of a planned, top-down approach. I, along with many of the people I spoke with while writing this book, was one of a group of more than sixty abolitionist organizers who gathered in Miami in January 2020 to assess, plan, and discuss how to strengthen movements to divest from and abolish police. At the end of two days together, we concluded that there was a long way to go to build a mass movement to that end—only to find ourselves in the midst of a massive uprising taking up those very demands less than six months later. That said, it's important to note that the 2020 Uprisings did not spontaneously pop up out of nowhere. Decades of abolitionist theorizing and organizing, the networks of abolitionist formations that took shape over that time, and the relationships among abolitionist organizers and groups we mapped during the gathering were all critical to its emergence.

Arguably, the 2020 Uprisings reflected key principles of emergent strategies at work. They were not coordinated by a central organizing body, nor were they focused on a single policy or piece of legislation. They were the product of highly decentralized organizing efforts, guided by a simple set of principles: the violence of policing cannot be reformed; to end it, we must divest from institutions that fail to prevent and instead perpetuate violence against our communities, and we must invest in the things individuals and communities need to survive and thrive.

Organizers adapted those demands to their local contexts, iterating as conditions shifted and as they learned from their efforts and those of others. They are building critical connections by engaging community members in conversations about what safety looks like, feels like, and requires. They are engaged in visionary organizing, prefiguring the world they wanted through mutual aid and by building responses to crisis beyond policing and punishment. They are practicing new forms of governance through participatory budgeting and people's movement assemblies. They are shifting conversations and conditions, continuing to build and share lessons and strategies through national networks, and opening portals into new possibilities in ways that could not have been predicted.[70] While the backlash is fierce and furious—a testament to the power of the demand and the crisis of legitimacy it produced for police—these efforts are producing seismic shifts in possibilities for abolitionist struggles.

In *#DefundPolice #FundthePeople #DefendBlackLives: The Struggle Continues*, Interrupting Criminalization gathers important insights from abolitionist organizers about lessons learned in the process, some of which point to emergent strategies. The first is that mass mobilization represented a critical flashpoint, but ongoing, deep place- and relationship-based organizing is necessary to sustain and grow the flame. The second is that as conditions change, strategies and tactics must adapt. The third is that, throughout the Uprisings and beyond, abolitionist networks and communities of practice remain essential to continuing to build our collective capacity to shift systems—whether it's the

Community Resource Hub Invest/Divest Learning Communities, which met weekly throughout 2020 and 2021 and continue to gather monthly to collectively strategize, share skills, create resources, brainstorm around challenges and celebrate successes; or the Building Coordinated Crisis Response practice space and the Creating Ecosystems of Collective Care Cohort hosted by Interrupting Criminalization.[71]

Exploring how emergent strategies might guide us in bringing about the changes we want to see at this particular moment—under political, social, and economic conditions in which white supremacy and fascism are flourishing, multiple pandemics rage out of control, racial capitalism is collapsing on itself, and climate catastrophe is upon us—feels simultaneously essential and risky. When adrienne and AK Press invited me to write this book in 2019, based on a talk I gave at the American Studies Association conference that year, I went back and forth about whether I should. Then 2020 happened, and many, many, many more people became engaged in conversation and action around abolition, including policymakers, organizers, philanthropists, the mainstream media, and everyday community members. Many reached for the tools they have always used—legislation, policies, top-down, mass mobilization—to advance a politic they had not studied or practiced in any great detail before that point. As a result, many have fallen prey to the inevitable pitfalls of attempting to enact a revolutionary politic through the policymaking machine of a carceral state. And many seem to be grappling with issues I and many other abolitionists have struggled with over the past two decades: How do we get to abolition? How do we completely reshape society to eliminate policing and punishment—along with the systems they manufacture and uphold—and to create safer, thriving communities? How do we avoid chasing red herrings and simplified policy "solutions" that lead us to dead ends, or worse yet, to making demands that expand rather than shrink the footprint of surveillance, policing, and punishment?

Emergent strategies, and the organizing practices they invite, helped me to better understand: there is no ten-step program to abolition. There is no single policy agenda and no simple set of solutions to the multitude of issues for which society has been offered a single response: police. In a video she released in 2021 offering guidance to new abolitionists, Critical Resistance cofounder and former director Rachel Herzing emphasized that any tool can be used toward abolitionist ends provided we are guided by an abolitionist politic.[72] As time went on, it felt more and more like this book might be a useful contribution to explore in greater depth how emergent strategies are and can be tools for abolitionist organizing.

As the current conjuncture deepens, it is becoming increasingly evident that we are in a battle among vastly different visions of the future—a future in which access to diminishing resources and livable spaces is increasingly violently policed or one in which we meet the current and coming collapse of existing systems and climates with collective care, recognizing a deep interdependence that extends beyond borders. Grace Lee Boggs teaches that "every crisis, actual or impending, needs to be viewed as an opportunity to bring about profound changes in our society."[73] Indeed, Kelly Hayes, organizer, coauthor of *Let This Radicalize You*, and host of Truthout's *Movement Memos* podcast, describes us as "builders in a time of collapse." The question is how we can advance our abolitionist visions of the future, how we can pivot from *what is* to *what can be*, how we can, as Lorraine Hansberry invites us to do, "impose beauty on our future," and what strategies will enable us to most effectively do so.[74]

Who Is This Book For?

This book is an invitation to people who have been drawn to the book *Emergent Strategy* over the past five years to gain greater clarity and to enter into deeper engagement with the abolitionist politics and organizing that informed it. As part of the Emergent Strategy Series, it engages the ideas contained in that book, along with others in the series, but also goes beyond them.

It is also an invitation to people newly organized to abolitionist politics to think beyond mass mobilizations and solutions that center law and policy. Importantly, it is *not* a primer on abolition—many more expansive books on the subject have already been written, including *Abolition Geographies*: *Abolition. Feminism. Now.*; *No More Police: A Case for Abolition*; and *Abolition Feminisms* volumes 1 and 2, to name just a few published in 2022 alone.[75] It *is* an effort to engage people who catapulted into an embrace of abolitionist politics in the context of the 2020 Uprisings through policy and budget-based demands to #DefundPolice in an exploration of how emergent strategies might move us under current conditions toward abolitionist futures. And it offers an opportunity for those of us who are already committed to abolitionist politics and practice to explore how emergent strategies are already at play in abolitionist organizing and to reflect on how we might deploy them most effectively to bring us closer to the abolitionist horizon.

Regardless of where you fall on this spectrum, this is a book about organizing: the process of bringing new people into organizations and movements for change, with the goal of shifting collective consciousness and building power to make the change we want to see. As Black feminist icon Barbara Smith emphasized in her 2023 lecture "What I Believe," organizing requires us "to make material change, that means change on Earth, in *this* galaxy."[76] Organizing is an ongoing process that extends beyond protests and mass mobilization, that is rooted in building relationships, sharing knowledge, analysis, and skills, and strengthening communities. It requires us to build organizations that can serve as spaces for political education, skills building, mutual aid, as well as what emergent strategists refer to as communities of practice and network nodes. I firmly believe that organizing is necessary to build the world we want.

That said, shifting the process of *how* we organize within an existing political framework and set of values can open new possibilities for achieving different results. As Leanne Betasamosake Simpson teaches, "It became clear to me that *how* we live, *how* we organize, *how* we engage the world—the process—not only frames the outcome, it is the transformation. *How* molds and then gives birth to the present. The *how* changes us. *How* is the theoretical intervention."[77]

I have come to understand over the past three decades, in part through learning more about emergent strategies, that the *how* of struggling for the futures we want through top-down organizing strategies that rely on and replicate existing structures is impeding rather than furthering our ability to enact those futures. Emergent strategies, their lineage, and the practices they point to, invite us to exercise rigor, curiosity, and commitment to shared values in everyday actions and relationships. Emergent strategies teach that a proliferation of connections, networks, and communities of practice can create conditions that will allow us to dream and shift systems toward the worlds we want. In other words, emergent strategies articulate ways of being that can help us engage in the prefigurative organizing Grace called for by practicing "forms of social relations, decision-making, culture, and human experience that are the ultimate goal."[78]

Emergent strategies have helped me extend beyond my own limits of linear thinking and training in traditional approaches to change toward understanding how we might collectively meet this moment to bring liberatory futures into being. They have expanded my vision beyond top-down strategies and tactics focused on a distant set of end goals, to the exclusion of the everyday practices that help us get there. Rather than narrowing options to one "perfect" path forward and a single-minded pursuit of that goal, emergent strategies create an abundance of possibilities.[79] Emergent strategies have also helped me better understand that the work I now spend most of my time doing—nourishing connections, cross-pollinating between organizations and movements, building networks, supporting communities of practice—is an important part of how we impact larger systems. In many ways, this book could be called "A Capricorn's guide to better understanding how emergent strategies can help us move toward abolitionist futures."[80]

More than anything, this book is an offering to those who are struggling to let go of the old to play a part in making way for the new in the cauldron of the present.

Allied Media Projects Network Principles

Allied Media Projects (AMP) is a network of people and projects rooted in Detroit and connected to hundreds of other places across the globe. Together, we grow and exchange ways of using media to create the world we need.[1]

We begin by listening.

Every year we face new challenges and opportunities. Our work changes constantly, and there is no perfect formula for how we do this work. Embedded throughout our organizing is a set of principles which we have distilled from listening to our network.

- We are making an honest attempt to solve the most significant problems of our day.
- We are building a network of people and organizations that are developing long-term solutions based on the immediate confrontation of our most pressing problems.
- Wherever there is a problem, there are already people acting on the problem in some fashion. Understanding those actions is the starting point for developing effective strategies to resolve the problem, so we focus on the solutions, not the problems.

- We emphasize our own power and legitimacy.
- We presume our power, not our powerlessness.
- We spend more time building than attacking.
- We focus on strategies rather than issues.
- The strongest solutions happen through the process, not in a moment at the end of the process.
- The most effective strategies for us are the ones that work in situations of scarce resources and intersecting systems of oppression because those solutions tend to be the most holistic and sustainable.
- Place is important. For the AMC [Allied Media Conference], Detroit is important as a source of innovative, collaborative, low-resource solutions. Detroit gives the conference a sense of place, just as each of the conference participants bring their own sense of place with them to the conference.
- We encourage people to engage with their whole selves, not just with one part of their identity.

We begin by listening.

Glimpses of Emergent Strategies

One of the many transformative moments I experienced at the Allied Media Conference (AMC) was the Sailing for Social Justice workshop in 2018.

Earlier that day, I had co-moderated a plenary highlighting INCITE's legacy of organizing to support survivors of gender-based violence at the hands of the state, family, and communities with Allied Media Projects board member and fellow former INCITE! national collective member Emi Kane. After the panel, I co-led a workshop with beloved Black feminist comrade Robyn Maynard on resisting police violence against Black women, girls, and trans people across Turtle Island.

In other words, I had come from spaces firmly rooted in my public, political, and organizing life, and conversations that would more traditionally be understood to be about organizing toward abolition.

That day, the space I was most curious and excited about was one that spoke to my lifelong but deeply personal and private love of sailing. The Sailing for Social Justice workshop blew open my heart, mind, and spirit by highlighting histories of sailing as a practice deeply rooted in Indigenous and Black cultures and communities across the globe, in sharp contrast to the privileged, white, "Yacht Rock" culture it is generally associated with.[1] We talked about the ways that people around the world have reclaimed sailing to tell decolonized histories and organize in decentralized ways across geographies.

But what struck me most were the lessons sailing offers our movements that were shared by Tala Khanmalek, the workshop organizer and founder of Sailing for Social Justice. For instance, sailing requires you to keep an eye on the boats around you and to constantly adapt and shift your weight, your course, and the trim of your sails to make the most of the wind and conditions, to move at the pace of the elements. I immediately saw the applications to organizing: we need to be aware of, care for, and tend to each other and our surroundings, and continuously adapt our containers, positions, and directions based on conditions while staying a course shaped by a politic toward liberation. The wisdom Tala shared is clearly connected to emergent strategies' call to focus on critical connections, adaptation, and building capacity to simultaneously move within and shape larger systems.

Years later, Maura Bairley, a brilliant facilitator and movement builder who also attended the Sailing for Social Justice workshop, invited me to join her on a scuba diving trip. In casual conversations over lunch we listened for similar lessons for organizing from our underwater adventures. Always move with a buddy. Always be aware of how much air is in your tank—and theirs. Your breath can serve as ballast, buoyancy, or balance. Again, we found lessons for organizing rooted in emergent strategies—tend to and stay connected to yourself and those around you, move in a way that is informed by your individual and collective capacity, adapt your strategies based on the direction you need to move as your objectives and the environment around you shift.

Fast forward five years. In the early morning hours of former AMC director Jenny Lee's fortieth birthday, a group of us went hot air ballooning. Later that night, as we were all reeling from the Supreme Court's decision in *Dobbs*, some of us took comfort, on a text thread, in riffing on how resistance movements might learn from hot air ballooning by adapting to changing conditions with intention.[2] "Relinquish control, follow the wind but move to different elevations to catch new wind directions," one of us texted. "Move when the air is calm and cool," another responded. "Be prepared to shift your plans regularly to adapt to conditions and to not know where you will land." "Be prepared to drop into a field that is in hostile territory." "Notice what you can see and hear from a different vantage point that is imperceptible from where you usually are." All of these guides to floating across the sky on the wind felt like important lessons to bring to bear as the political winds shifted in the wake of the ruling. We need to shift greater focus and resources to different "elevations" rather than simply relying on court-based strategies, get better at operating in increasingly hostile territory, and, above all, remain flexible and adaptable to harness the winds of outrage toward ensuring access to abortion care for as many people as possible.

The practice of seeking and finding insights in our interactions with the world around us that bring us closer to the world we want is one we carry with us from the AMC. This is what emergent strategies teach us: look for signposts and clues to the path to liberation in joy, in connection, in relationship, in experimentation and learning, and in communities of practice and care. Once you start to see them, you will find them everywhere.

What Is Abolition?

Abolition is presence.

—RUTH WILSON GILMORE

Prison Industrial Complex (PIC) abolition is a political commitment to and a practice of a world without surveillance, police, prisons, jails, or cages of any kind, including immigration detention centers, forced medical interventions, or locked hospital wards. It is a world without policing or punishment in any form—including the policing each of us perpetuate in our daily lives, the kinds of punishments we wish for when we experience or witness harm or injustice, or pre-conditions on meeting our basic needs. It is also a world where these things are no longer possible, where the material conditions, carceral logics, social and economic arrangements, and values that produce and justify their existence no longer exist. As abolitionist scholar Eric Stanley writes: "Abolition is not simply a reaction to the prison industrial complex but a political commitment that makes the PIC impossible."[1] Abolition therefore requires profound transformation within each of us, in how we see, experience, and relate to the world around us, and of the societies we create and perpetuate.

In *No More Police: A Case for Abolition*, Mariame Kaba and I outline abolitionist principles reflecting this political commitment:

- We oppose surveillance, policing, or incarceration in any form—including in response to state and white-supremacist violence.
- Policing is beyond reform. The changes we work toward must divest resources, power, weaponry, and legitimacy from police and reinvest those funds and resources into community-accountable institutions and practices that provide real safety.
- Real change comes from material redistribution of resources and access to healing, not simply shifting or renaming systems of policing while maintaining inequalities and relations of power. For example, real change comes from meeting mental health needs through universal, accessible, quality, and voluntary preventive and supportive care for everyone, not renaming violent police and coercive responses to unmet mental health needs as "crisis intervention teams" or diverting people into carceral and punitive mental health systems.
- We need experimentation and innovation toward building safety specific to each community— there is no single "evidence-based," one-size fits all solution.
- We are committed to disability justice and to dismantling interlocking systems of oppression rooted in ableism, patriarchy, transphobia, homophobia, racial capitalism, and imperialism.
- We are committed to collective governance and Black feminist practices of collective care that center the safety, needs, visions, and well-being of Black women, queer, and trans communities.
- We practice hope and radical imagination as a discipline.[2]

As many abolitionists emphasize, abolition is not just a process of dismantling, "an erasure, an absence, a lack, a nothing," as Ruth Wilson Gilmore put it.[3] It is a luscious process of imagining and filling the world with what we want instead of policing and punishment—or, as she describes it, "presence."[4] In other words, abolition is a set of prefigurative practices that reflect these principles—which require us to imagine, experiment with, and grow new ways to prevent, interrupt, transform, and heal from harm beyond policing. As Critical Resistance articulates,

> An abolitionist vision means that we must build models today that can represent how we want to live in the future. It means developing practical strategies for taking small steps that move us toward making our dreams real and that lead us all to believe that things really could be different. It means living this vision in our daily lives.[5]

Abolition is building the skills, relationships, and institutions we need to meet our individual and collective material needs.[6] It is a process of exploring how to be in right relationship with each other and the world around us. It therefore requires us to unlearn and unmake colonialism, racial capitalism, ableism, cisheteropatriarchy, and imperialism in order to make way for a world where policing and punishment are no longer possible—nor required to manufacture and uphold existing systems of economic, political, and social domination.

Sage Crump, formerly chief culture strategist at the Emergent Strategy Ideation Institute (ESII)—a hub for experimentation, facilitation, learning, and sharing emergent strategies—emphasizes that abolition requires shifting culture, which boils down to "how we be together." As Sage lays out in their "Cultural Strategy Toolkit," culture shift toward abolition requires attention to, reimagination of, and experimentation with economic structures, social relations, history, and imagination. Sage describes emergent strategies as a cultural intervention that invites us to think about shifting these complex systems through simple interactions.[7] Understanding abolition as a culture shift helps us to see that abolition isn't a singular destination but "an ever-evolving set of practices that are embedded in how we care for each other and how we value each other." Abolitionist healer and organizer Susan Raffo, author of *Liberated to the Bone: Histories. Bodies. Futures*, describes the cultural work of abolition as "creating spaces for people to listen to each other, build relationships, deepen into both an understanding of conditions and of future possibility."[8] In other words, abolition is a shifting horizon in the future.[9] And, as Ruth Wilson Gilmore teaches, it is a place we choose to create and in the now.[10]

I remember the exact day and time I became an abolitionist—March 21, 1999—because it was the day Angela Y. Davis spoke at a Toronto event marking the International Day to End Racism. She powerfully laid out the case for the abolition of the prison industrial complex, and after years of struggling with efforts (including my own) to reform police, the criminal legal system, and responses to violence, I remember thinking: "Wait, we can just get rid of the whole thing and build something different??? SIGN. ME. UP!"[11] My commitment to an anti-capitalist, internationalist, Black feminist politic along with my experience documenting both the violence and denial of protection perpetrated by police against Black women and queer and trans people paved the way for me to quickly embrace an abolitionist politic and praxis. All I needed was someone to help me make that "jailbreak of the imagination."[12]

Part of resistance to abolitionist visions is a resistance to change, a desire to "fix" what exists rather than imagine anew that is rooted in fear of the unknown and illusions about the past and present. So much of US politics is shaped by toxic forms of nostalgia and longings to "go back" to settings or structures that were never safe or sustaining for the vast majority of us. People seek solace in throwbacks to communities where "Officer Friendly" kept the peace (while enforcing borders of sundown towns and segregated neighborhoods); periods of middle-class prosperity (which excluded Black, Indigenous, disabled, queer, trans, and migrant workers); and the "pre-Trump" era (of neoliberalism and a less visible but no less virulent strain of white supremacy). As more and more people are recognizing the violence of policing and that our collective needs, including our need for safety, are not met by current structures of surveillance, policing, and punishment, we nevertheless struggle to discern a path forward. This is both because our imaginations have been so effectively disciplined into conflating policing with safety and because we are overwhelmed by the assignment to imagine and enact something we have never experienced. Our success as abolitionists depends on our meeting this overwhelm and fear of change at psychic and emotional levels, and on catalyzing our imaginations.

"Visionary fiction," exemplified by the *Octavia's Brood: Science Fiction Stories from Social Justice Movements* anthology coedited by adrienne and Walidah Imarisha, is one tool for sparking, reinvigorating, and exercising our imaginations to the fullest extent possible in the face of claims that the abolitionist futures we seek to manifest are impossible.[13] As Walidah pointed out when I spoke with her,

> All real substantive social change has been considered unrealistic at the time people fought for it—until those people changed the world to make it happen. With visionary fiction, we start with the question "What is the world we want?" rather than "What is a win that is possible and realistic?" . . . This is why visionary fiction and other imaginative spaces are key to true liberatory change—because we must be able to imagine something different before we can build it, and we have lived all of our lives within systems that tell us radical change is an impossibility.

One of the most essential tasks of abolitionist organizing is building our collective capacity to create new possibilities in a time where they appear to be increasingly foreclosed. It is to, as Walidah puts it, "make abolition feel tangible, to make people who watch it think, 'Oh, we can do that.'" Each of us must recognize, as Black feminist poet Lucille Clifton wrote: "I cannot create what I cannot imagine." As adrienne says in *Emergent*

Strategy, we are working in "intersecting worlds—the one we've got, the ones we are building, and the ones we are imagining."[14] "The goal of visionary fiction," Walidah emphasized, "is to help us create liberated worlds" in all of these timelines.

Walidah describes being struck by how many organizers are new to visioning: "Your work is visioning!" she exclaimed. Indeed, I am one of the people she is talking about. While I am a fan of sci-fi (particularly when written by Black women and trans people) and *Octavia's Brood* is one of my favorite books of all time, for most of the decades since I became an abolitionist, I left the work of imagining and building a world without police—and all they represent, enforce, and defend—to others. I saw my task as making a case for abolition by documenting the scope, forms, contexts, and harms of policing, criminalization, and punishment as society's predominant approaches to violence, conflict, harm, and need. I dedicated myself to specifically pointing out the ways that policing perpetrates—rather than prevents—racialized, gender-based violence and keeps us from focusing on meeting the needs of survivors in ways that would actually prevent and interrupt violence.[15] I endeavored to help reduce the harms of policing and criminalization by organizing, litigating, and advocating to take tools of violence and criminalization away from cops and by securing compensation and reparations for the people they harm. I worked to expand our collective understanding of why and how abolition of policing, prisons, surveillance, and borders is essential to achieve the goals of each of the movements I have been a part of—and for our collective survival.

In other words, for the most part, I saw my work as beating back the system while snatching people from its sights, all while hoping others would hurry up and build that abolitionist future because the sheer volume of violence and injustice and sheer number of lives destroyed by policing, prisons, and punishment in the present is intolerable. For a significant part of this time, I was one of the people Ruth Wilson Gilmore describes as preoccupied with the "recitation of the problem" and who adrienne maree brown describes in *Emergent Strategy* as "comfortable deferring the work of vision to others."[16] I acknowledged as much in a short video made in 2017 for Critical Resistance's "Breaking Down the Prison Industrial Complex" series, calling on myself and others to recognize that we cannot defer the work of dreaming and practicing new worlds to some imaginary, more visionary people; we need to exercise the discipline of making that work part of our everyday conversations and actions even as we fight the violence of this one.[17] Indeed, what the past three-plus decades have taught me is that I can, we all can, and in fact *we all must* be part of dreaming, envisioning, and practicing worlds beyond surveillance, policing, prisons, and punishment each and every day. It is not only essential for the project to be successful; it is necessary for our own well-being.

This is why *Practicing New Worlds* includes an essay by Walidah that offers a deeper dive into what visionary fiction is and why we need it at the end of this chapter. You will also find works of visionary fiction interspersed throughout the book. They are included as a way of opening our collective imaginations to possibilities for abolitionist futures in ways that facts, figures, and arguments cannot. They also allow us to play out what our ideas might look like in practice so that we can be on the lookout for how policing and punishment creep back into our imaginations as we reach for new approaches to accountability and healing. I included some visionary fiction of my own as a practice of vulnerability and accountability—as a way of extending myself as I believe abolitionist organizing requires all of us to do. They offer a glimpse into my nascent dreaming of otherwise, in the hopes that others will join in.

While I am newer to visioning abolitionist futures, over the past twenty years I have had the opportunity to practice them through projects like the Safe Outside the System collective of the Audre Lorde Project, INCITE! Feminists of Color Against Violence, YWEP, and in individual efforts to support friends, comrades, clients, and neighbors in finding safety and accountability without policing and punishment. I have played a supporting role to co-strugglers and organizations across the country deep in the trenches of imagining practicing abolitionist responses to harm, while steadily making the case for why abolition is the only way for Black women, queer, and trans people to experience authentic and lasting safety. More recently, I have been gradually shifting away from documenting the problems with policing, criminalization, and punishment—although this still makes up a significant part of my work—and moving toward more actively imagining and practicing what a world without police might look like, and building with others around how we get there. The principles of emergent strategies and the work of emergent strategists have been helpful in unlocking new ways of being, orienting myself to the work, and organizing toward liberation.

Importantly, I do this work as a survivor of interpersonal, community, and state violence, as part of a community of survivors. As we emphasize in *No More Police*, abolitionist movements are led by survivors of violence—the majority of whom neither seek nor find safety in policing and punishment, and a significant number of whom find themselves targeted for criminalization rather than protection when they do.[18] For instance, a 2022 study published by the National Domestic Violence Hotline found that more than half of survivors who called the police experienced discrimination; a quarter were threatened with arrest; and almost three-quarters said they would have chosen a different response than police had one been available.[19] There are many reasons for this, including the fact that police intervention in gender-based violence comes with its own risks of violence by police, criminalization, involvement of the family policing system, coerced medical intervention, eviction, detention, or deportation. Interrupting Criminalization's publication *What About the Rapists?*[20] highlights similar trends among sexual assault survivors, while *Shrouded in Silence* documents pervasive patterns of sexual violence *by the police*, including against survivors seeking to report sexual assaults.[21]

In other words, the current system is failing to prevent violence and in many cases perpetrating violence against survivors. Despite increasing and almost exclusive reliance on policing, punishment, and criminalization to address all forms of violence and conflict over the past five decades, neither policing nor top-down laws and policies have proven effective in reducing or eliminating harm.

Contrary to popular assumptions that abolitionists propose to abandon our communities to violence, abolitionists are very much preoccupied with how we prevent, respond to, and transform violence—now and in the future. Indeed, I often quote Erin Miles Cloud, cofounder of Movement for Family Power, who once said, "Everyone cares about somebody's safety somewhere, some of the time. Abolitionists care about everybody's safety, everywhere, all of the time." Our commitment to abolition comes from the recognition that police don't prevent or stop violence. At best, they respond after the fact, often with violence of their own. Survivors want more and better for themselves and each other than what we got for $275 billion spent on policing and punishment in 2021: some of the highest rates of violence—including police violence—in the world.[22] As the Interrupting Criminalization Domestic Violence Awareness Month fact sheet concludes, "Defunding police is a survivor-led anti-violence strategy that stops police from looting resources survivors need to prevent, avoid, escape, and heal from violence—and puts more money into violence prevention and interruption, and meeting survivors' needs."[23]

Abolition invites genuine accountability and prioritizes survivor safety and healing instead of channeling collective resources into systems that fail to offer protection from violence, while often simply relocating and perpetuating it behind and beyond prison walls instead. Far from ignoring violence, abolition requires us to come face to face with violence, to stop delegating responsibility for it to cops acting as violence workers, and to devote our attention and resources to preventing, interrupting, and transforming the conditions that produce violence and the people who enact it. Importantly, there is no singular top-down "alternative" that can take its place. There is no one-size-fits-all solution to the multiple manifestations of violence fueled by racial capitalism. Conversely, successful violence prevention and intervention efforts have evolved at smaller scales, unique to the time, place, and conditions under which they developed. Many of these efforts reflect the principles of emergent strategies, which also point to how they might be woven together into collective ecosystems of community care.

Ultimately, I am hopeful that this exploration of how emergent strategies might help us navigate, survive, and transform harm can be useful to all of us who are committed to abolition but continue to struggle with the "how"—because we have been steeped in linear, singular-solution, policy-based thinking. Mariame often reminds us that the tools of abolition are already in our hands, not in some distant, utopic future. *Practicing New Worlds* posits that emergent strategies are among the many tools we can all use to roll up our sleeves and join in to build toward abolition now.

To Build a Future Without Police and Prisons, We Have to Imagine It First
by Walidah Imarisha

In this essay, Walidah Imarisha emphasizes the critical role of fostering spaces for imagination in abolitionist organizing, as well as the role emergent strategies can play in visioning new futures. She also introduces the Wakanda Dream Lab anthology Black Freedom Beyond Borders: Memories of Abolition Day *from which several pieces of abolitionist visionary fiction reprinted throughout this book are drawn. The essay closes with an invitation to readers practice dreaming worlds without the violence of policing or punishment by responding to a simple writing prompt.*

Grab a piece of paper or open a new document on your computer, and join in.

I have been a prison abolitionist for almost twenty years. I have held firm to the belief that prisons, policing, and all parts of the carceral system have made us less safe, less free, and less human. That we can create community-based institutions to address harm and hold people accountable that focus on healing, transformation, and wholeness, rather than punishment and control. This is also why, for ten years, I have created, nurtured, and taught a practice called visionary fiction—a means of imagining better, more just futures and then doing the work of building them into reality—and why I hope we will embrace it today.

A lifelong nerd, I began to see that not only could science and speculative fiction coexist with social change, but they were

55

intricately connected. I recognized the need for spaces, both real-world and digital, that allow us to imagine beyond the limits of what we are told is possible if we are to build liberated futures. I used the term "visionary fiction" for the first time in a 2010 issue of *Left Turn* magazine where I guest-edited a section called "Other Worlds Are Possible." Visionary fiction is fundamentally concerned with how we reshape this world: it's an all-encompassing term for any fantastical art (speculative fiction, horror, magical realism, fantasy, etc.) that might aid in creating social change and a way to differentiate between more mainstream science fiction that most often reproduces reactionary or society's dominant politics.

Visionary fiction is not utopian. It does not imagine perfect societies, because, while utopias can be useful as thought experiments, we know there are no true utopias, or for that matter dystopias, in reality. As visionary fiction writer Octavia E. Butler once said, "I find utopias ridiculous. We're not going to have a perfect society until we get a few perfect humans, and that seems unlikely." Conversely, as long as even one person can imagine something different, there are no true dystopias because the possibility for change is ever-present. Instead, visionary fiction is any fantastical art that helps us to understand existing power structures and supports us in imagining ways to build more just futures.

To do that, visionary fiction demands us to be unrealistic in our visions of the future because all real, substantive social change has been considered to be unrealistic at the time people fought for it—until those people changed the world to make it happen. With visionary fiction, we start with the question *What is the world we want?* rather than *What is a win that is possible and realistic?*

We can't build what we can't imagine, so it is imperative for us to create spaces that allow us to infinitely stretch our understanding of what's possible. Famed sci-fi/fantasy writer and thinker Ursula K. Le Guin said in her 2014 National Book Award acceptance speech, "We live in capitalism, its power seems inescapable—but then, so did the divine right of kings.

Any human power can be resisted and changed by human beings. Resistance and change often begin in art. Very often in our art, the art of words.": This is why visionary fiction and other imaginative spaces are key to true liberatory change: because we must be able to imagine something different before we can build it, and we have lived all of our lives within systems that tell us radical change is an impossibility.

Visionary fiction pairs perfectly with the abolition movement, as we have all grown up in a society that has told us society would collapse without police and prisons. The idea that a prison- and police-free society might not only be possible but flourish has been mostly absent from mainstream discourse—even as it has been held and nurtured and explored by so many, especially Black women and trans folks of color. It was considered a fantastical idea that belonged in the realm of science fiction, not reality.

And then everything changed.

In 2020, we saw a new wave of Black Lives Matter protests rise up across the nation, this time centered in the framework of "Defund the Police." The question of what that meant, exactly, quickly arose, along with a host of responses that ranged from surface reform to radical transformation of abolition. City councils across the country voted to reduce, in some cases by millions of dollars, police budgets and redirect those resources to communities of color. And yet protests continued in the streets, folks organized online, demanding more. Protesters and organizers challenged the foundations of the institution of policing itself, and said that abolition, and reinvesting those funds into marginalized and oppressed communities, is the real justice we are demanding for those murdered by police.

Minneapolis was the epicenter of this iteration of the Black Lives Matter (BLM) movement. Why Minneapolis? Because of all the police reforms of the past that changed nothing.[2] Folks realized the issue is systemic, not surface. Minneapolis and other cities had done everything possible under reform, and the issue had not fundamentally changed.

So, it was time to do the "impossible."

I watched in amazement as activists successfully called for the defunding and redistribution of the entire Minneapolis Police Department budget, seeing the stuff of futuristic science fiction quickly become our lived reality and part of our political landscape. The fact that it was happening in the midst of a global pandemic blended the horror with the visionary. And while Minneapolis' City Council is now backtracking on their original commitment, it does not take away from the abolitionist organizing and protests that continue unabated till today.[3]

While it may feel like we warped into the future, this moment and this movement did not arise out of nowhere. It came from decades of folks who have been imagining, dreaming, writing, and organizing for something they were told again and again was impossible. Until suddenly it was not only possible—it felt almost inevitable.

This is why we must dream beyond what we are told is possible or realistic. Because we have the power collectively to change what is possible, to lay strong foundations so that when a moment like this arises, we are ready to take advantage of it. Folks like Angela Davis and Ruthie Gilmore and INCITE! and Mariame Kaba and the Black Panther Party and countless others held this work for decades until we as a whole were ready for it.

Police abolition has been held for generations and centuries. From enslaved Black folks being told freedom and an end to chattel slavery was an impossibility, down to the civil rights era and the Black liberation era, the Black freedom struggle has always understood that true liberation for us would always be framed as science fiction by the mainstream.

Even the phrase "Black lives matter" is visionary fiction, and a gift to us from the three Black women/femmes—Alicia Garza, Patrisse Cullors, and Opal Tometi—who coined it, and the countless others who have breathed and continue to breathe life into it. A few years ago, BLM put out a call to answer the prompt, "In a world where Black lives matter, I imagine . . ." an immense gift to make concrete our imaginings, so they are not just vague ether but tangible things we can see and embody and fight for. That prompt made explicit that all of it was visionary fiction in action.

This is the challenge of true liberatory movements—we critique and fight against what exists, but we take on the responsibility of stretching beyond the now, beyond what we have seen and felt and heard, to root in a shared vision of true liberation. And then we do the work of building that into existence.

In 2015, I coedited *Octavia's Brood: Science Fiction Stories from Social Justice Movements* along with adrienne maree brown.[4] It is a collection named in honor of sci-fi writer Octavia E. Butler, and it contains visionary fiction short stories written by organizers, activists, and changemakers. adrienne and I reached out to folks—many of whom had not written fiction, let alone science fiction—who were holding the visions of the future we longed for.

We knew they would create compelling and rich worlds that would help us build better futures because the premise for *Octavia's Brood* is that all organizing is science fiction. Every time we imagine a world without prisons, without police, without borders, without oppressions, that's sci-fi—because we've never seen it in our reality. But we can't build what we can't imagine, so we absolutely need imaginative spaces like sci-fi that allow us to dream.

During the pandemic, we have continued holding visionary events and workshops—virtually, adapting the in-person interactions for our current remote age. One example is a presentation and conversation I called "Better Futures: Visioning in a Time of Crisis," which left space for those attending—around five hundred—to collectively vision a poem about what a liberated world will be like.[5]

This is the time to be *unrealistic* in our demands for change. We are told repeatedly we need to be realistic, but that is just another method of social control. We are told true liberation is an impossible dream by the powers that be, over and over again, because us *believing* that it is an impossible dream is the only thing between here and the new, just futures we want.

The more scared we are, the more in crisis, the more we are told to pull back. But this is the time when anything and everything can change. Let our imaginations grow as large as galaxies.

And then we have to do the work of building those freedom ideations into existence. It is not enough to just dream and envision, we have to roll up our sleeves and dig in. My coeditor adrienne's work on *Emergent Strategy,* for example, is a vision for organizing that focuses on adaptation and creativity and imagination, is connected to the concept of visionary fiction—you could say the ideas grew up together. One of the principles she discusses is being generative, creating more possibilities and entry points.

Every successful movement for social change has used a diversity of tactics and strategies. One of the ways movements are made to fail is that they are pressed into fighting each other over what is the "right" way to struggle and to create change. We cannot allow the very people we are fighting to decide what is a "good" protester or a "bad" protester, what the acceptable avenues for change are, how we reshape the world. When we are rooted in a shared vision and shared principles and values, there is space for all our imaginings. We live in a quantum multiverse where everything that can happen does/has/will, where time is not linear and exists layered upon itself. So how do we engage in quantum organizing that roots in the abundance of futures and presents?

There is an absolute necessity in looking historically, presently, and futuristically for rebellion, for radical struggle, and—most of all—for unity.

If we embrace all of this, we can change the world. We know this because we have already done it. To everyone who has been in the streets, who has struggled on every level, you have already changed the world. Every generation born after this one will see abolition of police and carceral systems as a real, viable option. It may be maligned and degraded, but it will be debated as a real possibility, not as the stuff of fantasy.

That is a huge cultural shift and a win. We must remember that as we continue to struggle for institutional and systemic change because all of those struggles are connected and important.

In the moment, when our focus is explicitly on abolishing the police, we may lose sight of this. Even if we don't win everything we want now, we are still winning. Cultural critic and author Jeff Chang has said we often focus on political change, on events when discussing change, but that cultural shifts are key to real systemic transformational change, and that culture is the purview of artists: "Cultural change always precedes political change."[6]

It is not an either/or. Again, part of visionary fiction and visionary organizing is embracing a quantum framework and recognizing the multiplicities of our movements. There is room for us to celebrate movement forward even as we work harder to create the futures of our dreams.

I was lucky enough to be part of a new Black multimedia abolitionist sci-fi anthology called *Memories of Abolition Day*, put out by Wakanda Dream Lab and PolicyLink.[7] This radical worldbuilding project embodies that notion of Black liberation and quantum organizing both in content and process. In June [2020], a group of Black creators assembled remotely during a global pandemic and collectively imagined an abolitionist world. Then we each wrote a story within that world. We ended up with a timeline that spans five hundred years of abolition, moving from when the last prison closes (Abolition Day) to accountability processes to transformative justice through contact with aliens. The communities in our stories are constantly reimagining abolition because abolition is not just the absence or end of police and prisons, it is the creation of a truly just society. Abolition and liberation are processes, not destinations, and there is room for all of our imaginings and creativity.

The stories in *Memories of Abolition Day* are laid out in a nonlinear order, which allows the reader to see change as fluid and in motion. It also highlights the fallacy of constant linear time. But after six months of lockdown, most of us already know that time can stretch out infinitely, that days can repeat, that the future and the past can exist simultaneously with the present.

We need that understanding when we talk about building better tomorrows because often social change is framed as something that is too far away for us to touch, something we will never experience in our lifetime. But the liberated futures we want don't exist as untouchable distant points out of our reach. When we focus on collective action, mutual aid, self-determination, and centering the leadership of the marginalized, we live the change we want, and we defy linear time. We pull those liberated futures into the present.

That is what this Black-led, Black-dreamed movement is doing right now. Even in the midst of brutal anti-Blackness and continuing Black death, Black people are breathing liberated futures, breathing visionary fiction out with each exhale. This is a hard time, full of grief and pain and anxiety, but oppressed people have always alchemized grief into action, loss into light, trauma into triumph. So, let's keep pulling liberated futures into the present over and over again until we reach the day when that's all there is.

A Visionary Fiction Prompt for 2020:

As part of my work with *Octavia's Brood*, I have worked with many wonderful folks—especially *Octavia's Brood* writer Morrigan Phillips and my coeditor, adrienne—to develop visionary fiction workshops and prompts. A large part of our goal with the anthology is to create spaces where others can engage in collective imagining and dreaming because the future is not the purview of the powerful but belongs to us all. And imagination is a practice, just as Mariame Kaba says that hope is a discipline.

We must practice, joyfully and even playfully, imagining what lies beyond the event horizon society has embedded in our minds.

So, try this: Imagine it's fifty years in the future, and social justice movements have continued winning and advancing liberation. What would your life be like? What would your everyday routine be? You could write out your daily schedule, you could write a journal entry from the year 2070. You could write a letter to a loved one talking about the changes that have occurred over your life.

What Are Emergent Strategies?

Emergent Strategy offers us the opportunity to study and practice the work of shaping change by understanding ourselves as part of the ongoing emergence of nature.

—ALEXIS PAULINE GUMBS, *UNDROWNED*

In essence, emergent strategies are ideas drawn from the natural world, as well as observations of human interactions and societies, about how to shape and shift complex systems through relatively simple, interconnected interactions. shea howell describes emergent strategies "as a summation of the shifting grounds of our knowledge of what it means to be human, how we understand the aliveness of the world around us. They stand in contrast to systems of thought rooted in industrial capital that require us to see the Earth as dead and knowledge as something that is only produced by the material world."

Interestingly, the term "emergent strategy" was used in the early 1970s by Henry Mintzberg, a professor at McGill University. Writing with James A. Waters, a professor at York University, Mintzberg used it to describe patterns he observed in business contexts where

many different actors naturally converge on the same theme, or pattern, so that it becomes pervasive in the organization, without the need for any central direction or control . . . strategy grows out of the mutual adjustment among different actors, as they learn from each other and from their various responses to the environment and thereby find a common, and probably unexpected, pattern that works for them . . . convergence is not driven by any intentions of a central management, nor even by prior intentions widely shared among the other actors. It just evolves through the results of a host of individual actions. Of course, certain actors may actively promote the consensus, perhaps even negotiate with their colleagues to attain it. . . . But the point is that it derives more from collective action than from collective intention.[1]

Mintzberg and Waters contrasted what they described as emergent strategy with planned strategies, built around precise intentions, mechanisms, and guidelines for implementation toward desired outcomes—much like the strategic plans developed by many non-profits, philanthropic organizations, municipalities, and regional governments or what they describe as "ideologically driven strategies" of social movements, "in which a consensus forms around a system of beliefs."[2]

In other words, planned strategies are the linear, ten-point plans, often rooted in mass mobilization toward changes in law and policy, that I and others have been drawn to. According to Mintzberg and Waters, success in realizing planned strategies depends in large part on the accuracy of the planners' predictions; the existence of relatively stable conditions; the power to impose conditions; or some combination of these. In movement terms, this translates to accurately assessing current conditions, correctly predicting the impact of our efforts to change them, and having the power to preserve the changes we make. Because planned strategies often involve detailed blueprints for implementation, adaptation is discouraged—just as deviations from organizational strategic plans or campaign strategies might be, with consequences for our ability to respond to rapidly shifting circumstances. According to Steven Johnson, the author of *Emergence: The Connected Lives of Ants, Brains, Cities, and Software*, corporate America is beginning to recognize the limitations of planned strategies and advantages of the "bottom-up intelligence" emergent strategy makes way for.[3]

Mintzberg and Waters assert that emergent strategy is "especially important when an environment is too unstable or complex to comprehend, or too imposing to defy. Openness to such emergent strategy enables [an individual] . . . to respond to an evolving reality rather than having to focus on a stable fantasy."[4] This points to the potential relevance of emergent strategies in this particular moment of instability precipitated by racial capitalism, ongoing pandemics, climate collapse, wars, and rising fascism.

To be clear, despite Mintzberg's use of the term, emergent strategies as adrienne and I understand them are neither a business proposition nor a product of capital. Far from an invention of the twentieth century, emergent strategies are rooted and embodied in the (often uncredited or vaguely acknowledged) Indigenous ways of knowing and being in relationship, which have been practiced for millennia on Turtle Island and beyond.

In *As We Have Always Done: Indigenous Freedom Through Radical Resistance*, Michi Saagig Nishnaabeg scholar and organizer Leanne Betasamosake Simpson describes Nishnaabewin, the Nishnaabeg system of governance, as "an emergent system reflective of the relationality of the local landscape."[5] Community and nation are characterized by "connectivity based on . . . deep reciprocity, respect, non-interference, self-determination, and freedom."[6] This focus on critical connection is one of the core tenets of what is described here as emergent strategies.

The formation of networks based on these critical connections is an equally essential aspect of emergent strategies. As Simpson describes, "We relied upon process that created networked relationship. . . . Networked because the modes of communication and interaction between beings occur in complex, nonlinear forms, across time and space."[7] Simpson reminds us that the Indigenous communities she is part of are governed by "a series of practices that are adaptable and to some degree fluid . . . a series of complex, interconnected, cycling processes that make up a nonlinear, overlapping emergent and responsive network of relationships of deep reciprocity, intimate and global interconnection and interdependence, that spirals across time and space."[8] These practices include self-determination, consent, honesty, empathy, caring, sharing, self-sufficiency, and internationalism (referring to human, plant, and animal nations, and the natural world). Many Indigenous abolitionist scholars and organizers, including Klee Benally, Morning Star Gali, and Nick Estes offer similarly rich depictions of Indigenous pasts, presents, and futures rooted in similar principles and practices.[9]

These principles and practices—often decontextualized from their roots in Indigenous peoples and communities—are reflected in multiple explorations of emergent strategies, as well as in visions for abolitionist organizing, including those articulated and practiced by Simpson herself.[10] In looking to and honoring the ways that emergent strategies are reflected in Indigenous cultures, we must be careful not to engage in re-colonization or call for a return to an idealized state of being but heed the lessons that can help us to chart bold, new abolitionist futures. As a student of Amilcar Cabral and the revolution of Guinea Bissau, Sage Crump emphasizes that, while we may draw on historical and Indigenous practices as we create abolitionist cultures, "to decolonize is not to go back to an actual culture but to create one that is formed by all the learnings and lived experience to date, including colonization."

Many organizers currently thinking about and practicing emergent strategies—including adrienne maree brown—credit Margaret J. Wheatley's work as a critical spark. A student, researcher, and teacher of organizational and leadership development, Wheatley draws lessons about the operation of complex systems from evolutions in scientific fields such as physics, chemistry, biology, human health, environment, chaos, and organizational theory.[11] Central to her thinking is a move away from scientific understandings that change happens in isolation, mechanically, through force. Instead, Wheatley moves toward holistic understandings of the operation of deeply interconnected and interdependent systems.[12] Writing with her cofounder of the Berkana Institute, Deborah Frieze, Wheatley submits that "in nature, change never happens as a result of top-down, pre-conceived strategic plans, or from the mandate of any single individual or boss. Change begins as local actions spring up simultaneously in many different areas."[13] However, it doesn't stop there. Wheatley and Frieze argue that "when separate, local efforts connect with each other as networks, then strengthen as *communities of practice*, suddenly and surprisingly a new system emerges at a greater level of scale."[14]

Wheatley and Frieze describe the cumulative impact of interconnected networks and communities of practice as a "system of influence" which is not only greater than the sum of its parts, but of a different character altogether. Consequently, this system of influence can create conditions leading to significant shifts within large, complex systems. In their words, a system of influence

> possesses qualities and capacities that were unknown in the individuals. It isn't that they were hidden; they simply don't exist until the system emerges. They are properties of the system, not the individual, but once there, individuals possess them. And the system that emerges always possesses greater power and influence than is possible through planned, incremental change. Emergence is how Life creates radical change and takes things to scale.[15]

According to Wheatley and Frieze, to create systems of influence we need to focus on building and strengthening connections among people with shared values: "Rather than worry about critical mass, our work is to foster critical connections. We don't need to convince large numbers of people to change; instead, we need to connect with kindred spirits. Through these relationships, we will develop the new knowledge, practices, courage, and commitment that lead to broad-based change."[16] Wheatley and Frieze argue that fostering the emergence of networks and communities of practice is necessary for individual

67

actions to connect and coalesce into systems of influence with the power to shift large, complex systems. To this end, they encourage us to explore the following questions:

- Why do networks form? What are the conditions that support their creation?
- What keeps a network alive and growing? What keeps members connected?
- What type of leadership is required? Why do people become leaders?
- What type of leadership interferes with or destroys the network?
- What happens after a healthy network forms? What's next?
- If we understand these dynamics and the life cycle of emergence, what can we do as leaders, activists, and social entrepreneurs to intentionally foster emergence?[17]

Networks can further coalesce into communities of practice, which are self-organized spaces in which people share information, strategies, skills, and support, and come together intentionally to create new knowledge in service of their individual needs and advance the greater good.[18] When systems of influence are generated by networks and communities of practice, "efforts that hovered at the periphery suddenly become the norm . . . practices developed by courageous communities become the accepted standard."[19] In other words, culture shifts, shaping larger structures.

What Wheatley and Frieze describe may explain what appeared to be a "sudden" emergence of abolitionist politics and organizing on the national stage in the context of the 2020 Uprisings. In fact, the entry of abolitionist demands into mainstream discourse was shaped and made possible by abolitionist networks and communities of practice inspired, supported, and nurtured for decades by abolitionist organizations such as Critical Resistance and INCITE! In a moment of opportunity, their influence converged into a force to be reckoned with, shaping discussions and understandings of policing and safety and forcing a response from systems and institutions.

The work of emergence scholars suggests that the most effective way to impact complex systems—societies, economies, ecologies—is at the level of critical connections, networks, and communities of practice, rather than focusing exclusively on top-down interventions that target singular components of the system by force. We effect systems change through relationship and experimentation, not by blueprint.

In the context of abolitionist organizing in the current moment, emergent strategies point to a focus on re-envisioning and practicing how to produce greater safety and well-being beyond police at the individual, relationship, community, and translocal levels. We are building networks of abolitionist organizers and communities of abolitionist practice at regional, national, and international levels to preserve and further the gains of the 2020 Uprisings, resist the forceful backlash that ensued, and continue to strengthen systems of influence that will enable us to effectively resist increasing authoritarianism and fascism and move toward abolitionist futures. In other words, instead of attempting to generate or sustain an unsustainable scale of organizing or recreate mass mobilization, passing more laws or seeking to change policies, it's time to regroup and refocus on healing and deepening our relationships, expanding our networks, and practicing the world we want to build as we till the soil and sow the seeds for the futures we are fighting for.[20]

Diving Deeper: Complexity Science

Emergent strategies are rooted in "complexity science," scientific principles governing the operation of complex systems in nature and society—whether it's bees or human communities, our nervous systems or the Internet.[21] According to #ComplexityExplained, a worldwide collaborative of experts, practitioners, and students, complex systems are made up of individual components that interact with each other and their environment through interdependent networks and systems. Through these interactions, the components generate novel information and structures with the capacity to have impact at greater scale. This process, known as "emergence" is often unpredictable and difficult to understand.[22]

Slime mold is one example of a complex system explored in the popular science book *Emergence: The Connected Lives of Ants, Brains, Cities, and Software* by Steven Johnson. According to Johnson, "Slime mold spends much of its life as thousands of distinct single-celled units, each moving separately from its other comrades. Under the right conditions, those myriad cells will coalesce again into a single, larger organism which then begins its leisurely crawl across the garden floor, consuming rotting leaves and wood as it moves about."[23] The process is mediated by individual actions governed by simple rules: individual cells adjust the amount of a chemical they release based on their individual assessments of their environment, and other cells react accordingly. Interestingly, slime mold coalesces into a single organism under adverse conditions and disperses when food is plentiful—offering additional support to the notion that emergence is a critical tool for collective survival.

Complexity science is the study and exploration of phenomena such as these, examining "how a large collection of components—locally interacting with each other at small scales—can spontaneously self-organize to exhibit non-trivial global structures and behaviors at larger scales, often without external intervention, central authorities, or leaders."[24] Or, as Johnson puts it, how "individual agents in a system pay attention to their immediate neighbors rather than wait for orders from above. They think locally *and* act locally, but their collective action produces global behavior."[25] Johnson describes the process as follows: "In complex adaptive systems . . . agents residing on one scale start producing behavior that lies one scale above them: ants create colonies, urbanites create neighborhoods, simple pattern-recognition software learns how to recommend new books."[26] Importantly, it is impossible to understand the properties of a complex system just by studying its individual components or layers. We also have to understand the process of emergence. Or, as Margaret Wheatley puts it, we have to grasp the "and" in the simple equation "one and one equals two."[27]

Sure, slime mold might be fascinating to someone like me, a researcher who studied science as an undergraduate (another reason I am drawn to emergent strategies). But it's easy to think that studying slime mold is a frivolous distraction in a moment of urgency. What does this have to do with abolitionist organizing? We are not single-celled creatures simply in search of food—we are complex individuals living in complex societies and systems, seeking to dismantle complex systems of power that are doing real harm, right now. Yet students of emergence and complexity science believe that systems like slime mold have important lessons to offer people looking to change human societies. Johnson argues that slime mold offers important lessons on "organizing from below," while the scientists behind #ComplexityExplained believe network science contains keys to disrupting systems of harm, concluding, "If you're trying to do battle against a distributed network like global capitalism, you're better off becoming a distributed network yourself."[28]

Complex Movements, a Detroit-based artist collective that works to support the transformation of communities, has played a pivotal role in popularizing applications of complexity science to organizing. As Sage Crump, a member of both the Complex Movements collective and the Emergent Strategies Ideation Institute, said, "Complex science gives us a new way to think about how change happens in the world."[29] Building on this knowledge, the collective studied and adapted principles of complexity science to reflect, inspire, and focus organizing based on emergent strategies. To help organizers internalize the core concepts of complexity science, they developed a poetic iconographic framework, explored in greater detail in the next section, that uplifts practices of cooperative work and collective sustainability; replication at a small-scale; resistance; resilience; regeneration and decentralization; interconnectedness; valuing

71

both process and outcome; and collective leadership, partnership, and adaptability.[30]

Complex Movements

This section was cowritten with ill weaver, one of the founding members of Complex Movements, and draws from presentations and materials developed by the collective throughout their existence.[31]

Complex Movements emerged in 2010 as a collective made up of graphic designer/fine artist Wesley Taylor, music producer/filmmaker Waajeed, hip-hop lyricist/organizer ill weaver, artist/designer/engineer L05 (Carlos Garcia), and producer/cultural strategist Sage Crump. In some ways, it can be understood as an abolitionist community of practice that is inspired by Grace Lee Boggs's engagement with Margaret Wheatley's *Leadership and the New Science* and evolved in conversation with the ideas reflected in *Emergent Strategy*.[32] In ill's words,

> We were fascinated by the way Grace and Meg Wheatley were framing social justice movements as emerging complex systems. We discovered that specific framework was called complex science . . . the study of emergent system behavior, which seeks to understand how the complex behavior of a whole system arises from its interacting parts. Complex behavior generally cannot be reduced to or derived from the sum of the behavior of the system's components. Exploring these ideas made us ask ourselves, "Can complex science metaphors be useful to local movement building?"[33]

To answer this question, the collective engages in interactive performance juxtaposing complex science and social justice movements to support the transformation of communities.[34]

Complex Movements' evolution was also shaped by multiple organizing heartbreaks, spurred by what ill describes as

"all the top-down, parachuting, national, impositional, patriarchal ways that movement happens." As artists, organizers,
and cultural strategists, Complex Movements sought to offer
a counterpoint to organizing methodologies that are based on
what Mintzberg and Waters might characterize as planned
ideological strategies. These top-down approaches, designed
and implemented by state or national organizations, led by
charismatic leaders bent on "organizing the masses," often
internalize and replicate the systems and relations of power we
are seeking to dismantle.

Complexity science suggests that decentralized networks
are more effective in creating change than models in which
small leadership groups develop campaigns, goals, slogans, and
tactics to be locally implemented in what ill describes as a "franchise model." Complex Movements explored and expressed how
complexity science could inform organizing work that is both
more values-aligned and more effective. The collective took at
their starting point the question, "How can complex systems
and emergent science theories be applied to create new poetic
articulations and metaphors for the work that's already happening, in ways that are compelling, spark radical imagination
toward visionary organizing, and invite more people into new
ways of understanding how change happens and new ways of
acting toward change?"

Through research, informal study groups with organizers, online complexity science courses, and popular science
and urban design literature, collective members engaged in
a wide-ranging study of complexity science, examining how
emergence shaped both the Zapatista Uprisings and religious
fundamentalist movements, and has been used to both build
nuclear bombs and to shape resistance to imperialism.[35] They
were inspired by the decentralized leadership they saw in operation in Tahrir Square during the Arab Spring, in the Occupy
movement, in Chilean Uprisings, and in the movements that
sprang up under the banner of #BlackLivesMatter in response
to the murders of Trayvon Martin and Mike Brown, and
sought to apply decentralized leadership in local organizing

with groups like Detroit Summer, a youth leadership development organization founded by Grace Lee Boggs and Jimmy Boggs.

Based on study and practice, the collective distilled six key metaphoric emblems or signposts to guide visionary organizing to shape and influence complex systems. They are described in a series of posters developed by the collective and reproduced below. As they developed these signposts, Complex Movements asked themselves, "Could these metaphors rooted in complex science be useful to better describe our movements? Can they be a way to invite people into restructuring what they place value on, what to engage in, how they define success, how a movement should feel?" Could they offer methods to move past ideological divides or blockages? Could they enable organizers "to have more qualitative generative conversations about organizing theory and about organizing science because this is how living systems function, this is how brains and cities function"? How might these metaphors "give new language and through new language create new meaning and value to the work of making change?"

The metaphors are not intended to be prescriptive or to become another rigid, top-down framework to be adopted and implemented by rote. Instead, they draw on complexity science to describe what is already occurring in effective movements, and to invite generative questions about what might be possible if we lean more deeply into the principles they represent. After all, as ill points out, "I think people don't understand: we are actually part of natural systems. I don't know why we don't think organizing is part of a natural system. The emblems represent an effort to bring some of that dimension back to our perception."

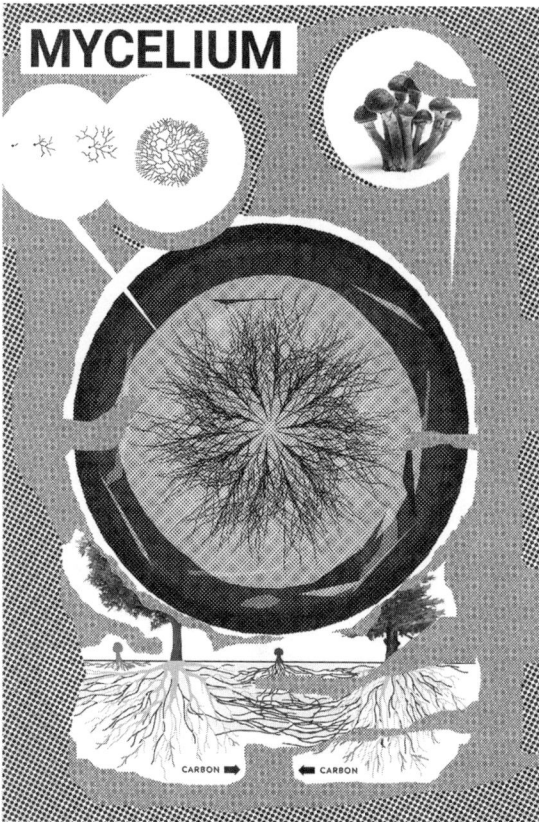

Mycelium: Interconnectedness, detoxification, remediation. Mycelium is the part of the fungus that grows underground in thread-like formations. It connects roots and breaks down plant material to create healthier ecosystems. It is the largest organism on Earth.

We asked ourselves if we could apply lessons from mycelium to detoxify and remediate trauma in our communities and to deepen intersectional solidarity by forming interconnected relationships across silos and sectors.

Within our ecosystems, what do we need to break down in order for life to flourish? What toxins do we need to remediate and heal before we can thrive? What relationships and critical connections (especially unexpected ones) are vital for this to occur?

The Ant: **Cooperative work and collective sustainability**. Ant societies function through individual ants acting collectively in accord with simple local information to carry on all their survival activities: hills are erected and maintained, chambers and tunnels are excavated. Every ant relies on the work of others producing their own, and there is no master or queen ant overseeing the entire colony and broadcasting instructions. The structure applies to other social insects such as bees as well.

What is one of the resource-related obstacles to addressing a challenge in your community? What cooperative economics or collective resourcing practice can be used to address this challenge? What are opportunities for collective work to meet community needs?

The Fern: **Ferns are a form of fractal**. A fractal is an object or quantity that displays self-similarity, which means it looks roughly the same on any scale.

Small-scale embodiment of whole vision at any scale. In a fractal pattern the solution is not to replicate the same solution everywhere (a cookie-cutter/franchise model). A fractal approach uses the same set of principles to build something at all scales even if the particular instance or perspective looks different from place to place.

Fractals force us to think about the patterns that can reverberate out from small-scale solutions to impact the whole system.

Where are examples of highly effective, deeply rooted small-scale practices in your community? What are the dynamics embodied in small-scale solutions that make them work? What would they look like if applied on a different scale?

77

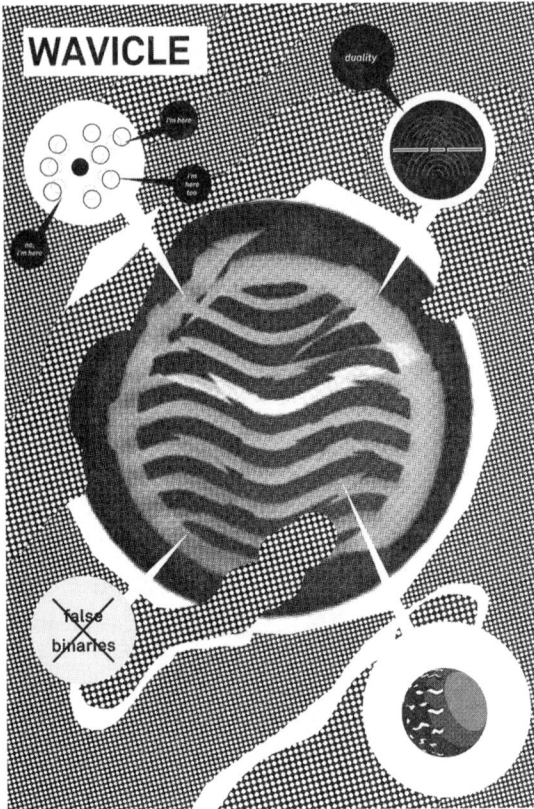

The Wavicle: Uncertainty, doubt, valuing both process and outcome. The wave-particle duality suggests that all objects exhibit both wave and particle properties. Between observations, as the object evolves on its own, it behaves like a wave, distributed across space, exploring different, inter-mixing paths to all possible destinations. However, when its location or speed is measured, it appears definite and concrete like a particle. It is the wave nature that gives measurement a curious property: the more certain we are about either speed or position, the more uncertain we become about the other.

Uncertainty/doubt: According to the scientific method, valuing doubt allows room for unknown possibilities. As soon as you are abso-lutely certain of something, you foreclose the possibility of ever discover-ing anything to the contrary. Being too certain of one thing can make you less certain of something else. This helps us move away from false binaries, valuing doubt and the unknown.

What are the false binaries surrounding dynamics in your community? How can vision and resistance address these dynamics? What are the uncertainties and questions you're still asking in regard to your process and the outcomes you are working toward? How can we embrace uncertainty and avoid the self-righteousness of dogmatic practices? How can we move beyond false binaries that divide and conquer our communities? How can we equally value both process and outcome?

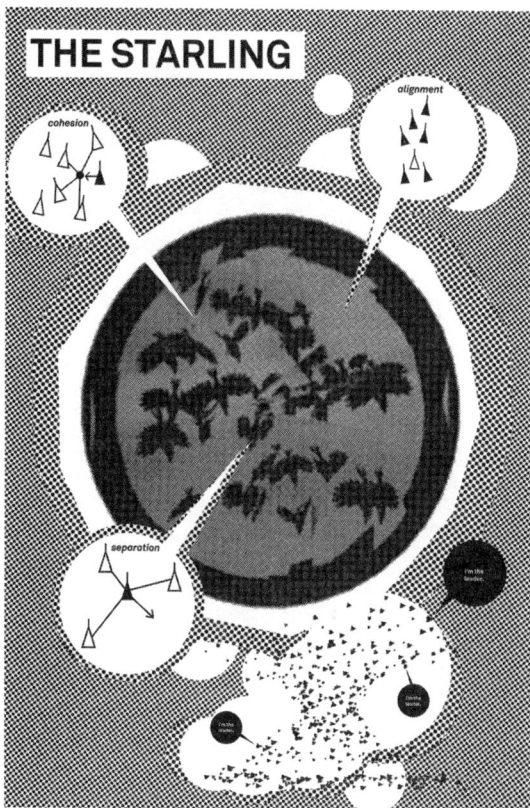

The Starling: Collective leadership and partnership, adaptability. The synchronized movement patterns of a starling flock are also known as a murmuration. Guided by simple rules, starling murmurations can react to their environment as a group without a central leader orchestrating their choices. Instead, each starling influences its neighbors, and these mutual relationships create a network that spans the whole flock. In an instant, any part of the flock can transform the movement of the whole flock.

What would decentralized action to resolve this issue look like? What can we learn from the decentralized, coordinated ways that the murmuration patterns of starlings to apply to the way to take collective action? What would our leadership structures look like, what roles would different people play? What would our collective actions and practices look like (other than a rally or a march)? Can starling murmurations help our communities explore the possibilities of collective leadership and true partnership and decision-making, moving away from charismatic singular leaders?

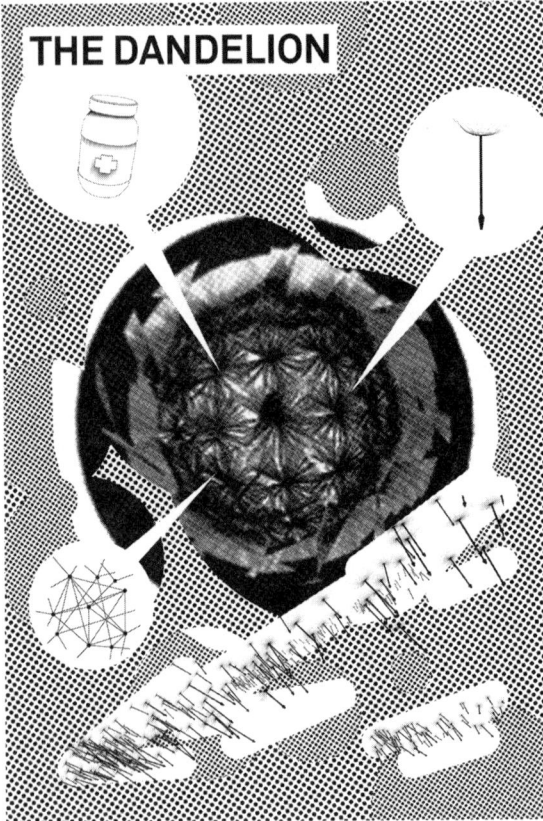

THE DANDELION

The Dandelion: Resilience, resistance, regeneration, decentralization. The dandelion flower head can change into a white globular seed head overnight, each seed a tiny parachute that allows it to spread far and wide in the wind. The entire plant has medicinal properties and is often used in herbal remedies. Dandelions are often mistaken as a weed and aggressively removed but are hard to uproot—the top is pulled but the long tap root stays in the ground, and resprouts.

What are our wind carriers and seeds that carry ideas across communities, into resilient communication systems? How do disruptive ideas and cultures spread that can infect manicured lawns of thought? What are ways to build resilience and stay rooted? How can small-scale and deep-rooted projects form decentralized networks and cross-pollinate lessons? How can Black and Brown economically disenfranchised and criminalized communities in Detroit and other cities stay resilient and resistant and pass on collective models of leadership?

Based on this metaphorical framework, Complex Movements developed *Beware of the Dandelions*, a mobile art installation that functions as a performance, workshop space, and visual arts exhibition, for which the above images were created. Through an immersive audio-visual experience that uses science-fiction narrative, music, interactive performance, video projection, and technology, *Beware of the Dandelions* invites communities to explore how the ideas of complex science are applicable to local social justice issues and connects participants across communities and sectors to cross-pollinate and develop new strategies to create change.[36]

Using visionary fiction, the artists invite participants to think through social change by stepping out of day-to-day realities and conditions to explore and imagine new possibilities. The parable that underlies the performance is intended to incite participants to connect with each other and draw on the story to reimagine current local political struggles. Robin D.G. Kelley describes *Beware of the Dandelions* as

akin to a hip-hop opera, a lyrical play in eleven tracks that moves us through a story of revolt against corporate power, environmental destruction, genetically modified food, industrial farming, land enclosure, "the water hoarders," and prisons. Set in the twenty-fourth century in a small city that bears more than a passing resemblance to Detroit, it is the story of a popular uprising, the Dandelion Revolution, against a ruling class of "Dome Dwellers" who occupy the last unpolluted spaces on the planet. They consume genetically modified "immortality apples" produced by workers who labor in factory farms and live in a state of semi-slavery on a "planetation." The uprising is sparked by an elder who goes on a hunger strike to protest conditions but dies. Songs like "Apple Orchard," "Channel," "Doubt," "Man Made Drought," and "False Solutions" recount how the commodification of resources forced people into "hubs" and a precarious life, and how underground revolutionaries resist the "groundskeepers" who control the land and resources. The story is neither utopian nor dystopian, but like great science fiction it reveals the contradictions we face today. The movement is wracked by internal debates among organizers over whether to fight the system from within or take more radical action. Complex Movements recognizes that movements are, indeed, "complex" and so they resist easy answers or triumphalist narratives.[37]

Beware of the Dandelions can be presented as a single performance or workshop or used to build a cohort in which the collective collaborates with organizers, artists, and activists in a community to curate a series of events designed to "foster and deepen authentic relationships, exchange skills, and build community capacity for visioning."[38] According to ill, the goal of the cohorts is to engage these questions in low-stakes environments as people come together around art that is "energizing, inspiring, beautiful, creative, and generative of both imagination and connection as a way to build relationship." Using the emblems, facilitators would ask questions like: "Think of an issue you're working on within your movement work or within your cultural organizing. What would decentralized collective action to address this issue look like? What different roles would people play? What would our collective actions and practices be that weren't just replicating a rally or march?"

In other words, the goal was not just to point people to phenomena and patterns present in complex systems in the natural world but to engage people in seeing and applying them in the context of organizing they were already doing to effect systems change. Part of this process involved creating "movement memory maps," reflections of cities shaped by stories of how community organizers tried to create change, where they succeeded and where they struggled. ill points out that the memory maps were intended to uncover buried stories, to make them visible rather than iconic, to help people see themselves as part of a larger story, to understand that they hold part of the thread, but they don't have to have all the answers. In other words, to see that "they only need to pay attention to the starlings around them; they don't need to engineer the whole murmuration. That's the piece that's hard—to get people to see the big picture and not feel they have to grab onto the whole picture."

The memory maps traveled between cohorts in Seattle, Dallas, and Detroit, dispersing movement lessons and resilience, nurturing "translocal cross-pollination, learning, and collaboration."[39] Cohorts also formed a network that met annually at the AMC as a way of furthering translocal organizing.[40] In these ways, Complex Movement's work practiced what ill describes as "relationship-based organizing"—organizing through building the critical connections and values-aligned networks Wheatley and Frieze characterize as essential to fostering emergence that can affect large-scale systems.

Over the six years the collective performed and used *Beware of the Dandelions* to share and gather lessons from complexity science for organizers, Complex Movements also served as a fractal, manifesting each of the emblems in its own work: they worked collaboratively, seeking to detoxify the impacts of top-down, patriarchal, mass-mobilization-based movements; endeavored to create the change they wanted to see in the world on the scale of each performance, workshop, or cohort; adapted content to suit each community and set of conditions as well as their own changing capacity over time, recognizing that it would be impossible to accurately measure the full impact of their work; and trusting that the seeds they sowed would spread like dandelions and take deep root in abolitionist organizing.

Emergent Strategy Principles

adrienne maree brown defines emergent strategy as how "humans practice complexity and grow the future through relatively simple interactions."[41] In other words, emergent strategies "leverage relatively simple interactions to affect complex patterns, systems, and transformation using principles of adaptation, interdependence, and decentralization, fractal awareness, resilience, nonlinear and iterative change, creating more possibilities."[42] adrienne builds on this definition in *Holding Change*, stating that *"Emergent Strategy* is fundamentally about how we get in right relationship with change, realigning with an Indigenous worldview that understands the relationality of all things. At the intersection of ancient understanding, science, the sacred, and science fiction sits a set of principles that helps us practice shaping change."[43]

The principles synthesized from this body of work in *Emergent Strategy*—along with strands of thought ranging from Black feminist wisdom ("We are in an imagination battle.") to ancient Buddhist maxims (what you pay attention to grows) to conversations with fellow organizers—offer a set of guideposts that organizers can look for, gravitate toward, and practice within existing political frameworks and organizing work. Over the five years since the book was published in 2017, the principles have influenced thousands of people who read the book, shaped dozens of conversations with organizers on the *Emergent Strategy Podcast*, structured Emergent Strategy "immersions" in Durham, New York City, Detroit, Minneapolis–St. Paul, New Orleans, Washington, DC, Oakland, and Puerto Rico, in which groups came together to explore applications for local organizing. They also informed facilitation trainings hosted by the Emergent Strategy Ideation Institute, which sunset in early 2023.

The principles of emergent strategies—each of which will be explored in greater detail in the chapters that follow—remind us to organize in ways that are:

- Fractal, recognizing that how we are at the small scale is how we are at the large scale. In other words, "Small is good, small is all." Patterns repeat at scale; the large is a reflection of the small. Help people see, celebrate, and build on the small shifts they are making.
- Adaptive, focusing on how we live and grow and stay purposeful in the face of constant change. In other words, change is constant. "Be like water." Help people change with intention.
- Nonlinear and iterative, asking, "How do we learn from this?" recognizing that there are no failures, only lessons, and that what you pay attention to grows. Change comes from cumulative shifts. Reflect how groups are accumulating change, what they are practicing.
- Resilient and transformative, focusing on how we recover and transform, seek understanding, build resilience by building relationships, move at the speed of trust, nurturing critical connections more than critical mass. Keep a systemic view even if it appears in individual behavior.
- Interdependent and decentralized, attending to and supporting authentic relationships, fostering mutual resilience, collaboration, and shared leadership and vision.
- Create more possibilities, focusing on how we move toward life and shape the future toward abundance, and recognizing that there are many pathways and ways to grow the future.[44]

Importantly, as Seattle-based abolitionist organizer Angélica Cházaro observes, the principles outlined in *Emergent Strategy* and *Holding Change* describe things that are *already* happening within effective organizing spaces. For instance, Chicago organizer Damon Williams was not aware of *Emergent Strategy* when he saw the book's principles charted on butcher paper lining the walls of a conference room when he attended a retreat at the Boggs Center in 2017. Yet he recognized them as similar to those he and his fellow organizers adopted during a thirty-day protest encampment the previous year. Similarly, ill weaver describes Complex Movements's iconography as an effort to reflect back to movements the ways that they are already deploying emergent strategies to varying degrees, to help further focus, inform, and structure their work. In other words, the Complex Movement emblems and the principles of *Emergent Strategy* are shaped by existing abolitionist organizing.

And they are also shaping both discourse and practice. Echoes and influences of *Emergent Strategy*—and emergent strategies more broadly—are increasingly reverberating in theoretical and organizing frameworks around how change happens. As INCITE! cofounder and longtime anti-violence organizer Mimi Kim observes, more and more people are exploring emergent strategies as an invitation to reject "the militarized language of organizing campaigns or the corporate discourse of logic models for more nature-inspired models of social change."[45] Mimi theorizes that this is because "nimble organizational forms, porous containers, networks built upon relationships rather than formal structures feel more resonant with the post-modern social, political, economic, and cultural climate."[46] In her book *Viral Justice: How We Grow the World We Want*, scholar Ruha Benjamin explores what she describes as a "microvision of social change."[47] Drawing lessons from nature, she advances a vision for what she dubs "viral justice," which focuses on the role of individual actions, with a recognition of our collective interdependence in shaping change.[48] Like other emergent strategists, Benjamin acknowledges that "we're still taught to only appreciate that which is big and grand, official, and codified," and argues that "a microscopic vision of justice and generosity, love, and solidarity can have exponential effects."[49] A sociologist, Benjamin has largely focused on structural change through policies and institutions and is now reaching beyond these approaches to understand new ways of making change through emergent strategies. She too describes shifting her focus from cataloging crisis to articulating what we want to see emerge from crisis, and invites us to turn attention away from the structures we are struggling to dismantle or transform and toward the power that small things have to change the world. Deepa Iyer of the Building Movement Project also draws on *Emergent Strategy* and natural systems to explore how to cultivate sustainable social change ecosystems in *Social Change Now: A Guide for Reflection and Connection.* Deepa begins with Grace's question about what time it is on the clock of the world, and offers an organizing framework shaped by values that reflect many of the principles of emergence, including interdependence, adaptation, transformation, and complexity.[50]

These are just two of the many schools of thought and action drawing from and building on emergent strategies. The following chapters specifically explore how principles of emergent strategies are reflected and manifesting in abolitionist organizing in the US and beyond.

Emergent Strategies and Abolition

Everything that I've experienced around abolition
falls into this framework.

—ALEXIS PAULINE GUMBS

I think without an emergent strategy, we're
not going to get to abolition.

—SHEA HOWELL

I was surprised to discover that the book *Emergent Strategy*
doesn't actually mention abolition. Yet many of the principles
articulated in the book resonate with abolitionist organizers
and offer critical signposts toward abolitionist horizons. As shea
howell posits, "When emergence, guided by abolitionist politics,
values, and practices, is accompanied by convergence, abolition
becomes possible, maybe even inevitable."

Emergent strategies also resonate with what Mariame and
I refer to in *No More Police* as "Black feminist abolitionist praxis."[1] They teach us that there is no grand master plan to achieve
the profound economic, political, cultural, social, and spiritual
systemic shifts required to dismantle the interlocking systems
of oppression at play in the lives of Black women, girls, and
trans people. So we can stop trying to develop that plan, or in
my case, hoping someone else does, and fast.

Instead, we can focus on building, deepening, and transforming our relationships with each other and the world around us, experimenting, practicing, failing, growing, and learning as we build toward the world we want, guided by Black feminist abolitionist values. As Black feminist abolitionist healer and memory worker Cara Page shared in a discussion of the book she coauthored with Erica Woodland, *Healing Justice Lineages: Dreaming at the Crossroads of Liberation, Collective Care, and Safety,* "As sick, disabled, queer, trans people of color, Indigenous people fighting for our lives . . . reimagining care that's deeply embedded in an abolitionist frame while we're still fighting fascism, while we're still fighting immense poverty and oppression of our people . . . are not separate things. They are all bonded together. . . . To build care is to build safety is to build power at the same time."[2]

Practices aligned with this approach predominated at the inception of US movements to end gender-based, homophobic, and transphobic violence, in the form of localized and decentralized consciousness-raising groups, friend networks, safe houses, and grassroots initiatives aimed at preventing and interrupting violence. Over time, efforts to develop a singular, one-size-fits-all approach to violence, enacted through law and policy and mediated by police and prisons, predominated—despite resistance by women and trans people of color and others who understood the connections between state and interpersonal violence.[3] This "carceral creep," to borrow a phrase from Mimi Kim, left survivors—including survivors of violence *by* police and prisons—out of society's "solutions" to violence, and in many cases, more vulnerable to violence of all forms, including criminalization, while robbing communities of the resources needed to prevent, interrupt, and heal from violence. As we argue in *No More Police*, this is not a failure of a system that can be reformed, it is central to what policing is.[4]

In the summer of 2020, thirty-five coalitions of anti-violence organizers issued a statement entitled "A Moment of Truth," recognizing that increased reliance on policing and punishment over the past four decades has failed to produce safety for survivors of domestic violence and sexual assault. Reflecting on this reality, INCITE! cofounder Nan Stoops, a longtime anti-violence organizer and coauthor of the statement, concludes that ending violence is "not going to happen through a strategic plan and set of policy priorities. We can't do it that way this time. We need to decide what kind of relationships we want, what kinds of communities we want, what kind of world we want and move toward it."[5] As we argue in *No More Police*, we have been sold a top-down carceral vision of safety that does not meet the needs of survivors and communities, but rather of the systems policing was created to uphold, in what amounts to a state-run protection racket. As Mariame and I elaborate in *No More Police*, safety is relative to our relationships with others and with resources. It is something we create together, in community. Or, in the words of Dr. Gabor Maté, safety is "not the absence of threat but the presence of connection."[6]

Ending violence thus requires us to practice elements of emergent strategies at the level of critical connections, networks, and communities of practice that will transform how we think of, experience, and structure society around our individual and collective safety and well-being. As we do so, we need to commit to experimentation, adaption to individual circumstances and local conditions, embracing failure as both an inevitability and a source of critical information and lessons, and iterating toward building community ecosystems of collective care. As longtime anti-violence activist Shannon Perez-Darby puts it, given that the current system is catastrophically failing survivors of violence, all we need to do to start is ask ourselves, "Can we create something better than this?"

The Resonance Network, for which Nan serves as the field liaison, is made up of "over three thousand Black, Indigenous, immigrant, women, femmes, trans, and Two-Spirit people and their co-conspirators who are building a world beyond violence—a world rooted in mutual care, where all people live in dignity, and all beings can thrive." Resonance is embodying emergent strategies by creating spaces for individual and collective transformation, practicing decentralized community-based governance, and engaging in experimentation and innovation toward a world free of gender-based violence in harmony with the Earth.[7] The network is guided by Grace Lee Boggs's assertion that "a revolution that is based on the people exercising their creativity in the midst of devastation is one of the great historical contribution of humankind." They understand their work to be "fractal—that is, existing on a small scale and large scale at the same time." Resonance intentionally organized themselves as a network, noting that "networks are dynamic and flexible, designed to adapt, evolve, and scale in response to changing contexts and current events. This dynamic form not only mirrors the way change happens in the natural world, it makes broad transformation possible." Since its founding, Resonance Network has supported thirty-seven experimental projects through their Innovation Lab and gathered a dozen organizations in a #WeGovern learning community to deepen understanding and practice of collective governance using a set of collaboratively developed principles.[8] While it may take years to see the impacts of these efforts, they represent an important experiment in explicitly deploying emergent strategies toward abolitionist ends.

Despite their appeal, step-by-step linear processes, laws, rules, or a drive to implement a singular "model" program across the country won't bring us genuine and lasting safety beyond policing. The complexity science that undergirds emergent strategies suggests that, guided by and grounded in shared values and visions of abolition, the proliferation of small-scale experiments can, as shea envisions, coalesce into a shape that brings us closer to abolitionist futures than top-down, policy-based approaches. As Mariame often emphasizes, building a world without violence, including the violence of policing, will require "a million different experiments" rather than looking for something that can serve as *the* "alternative" to police.[9] Our goal should be to seed, support, and elaborate localized approaches that are specific to the people, relationships, conditions, and resources unique to each community.

Like many policymakers, politicians, and everyday people, I too would like ready-made, fully formed, tested, proven, and scaled-up solutions to violence, harm, conflict, and need, now. The idea of experimenting with safety is scary to many of us, and relying on small-scale networks to shift the massive systems that produce and perpetuate violence feels counterintuitive. But the truth is, as Mariame often reminds us, we are currently living inside a massive, failed experiment, in which policing has consistently proliferated violence rather than ending it. Heavily resourced, one-size-fits-all, industrial-scale systems are what got us here. Our only hope is to try something new.

And it's important to remember that abolitionist organizers and practitioners of new worlds can't be expected to have built and refined solutions for every possible circumstance overnight, with virtually no time, space, or resources. Nor should we be looking to build structures of safety that are necessarily legible within the current system. As we explore in greater detail in *No More Police*, we need to be wary of replicating policing in new forms and contexts such as forced medical intervention, family policing, carceral "services," or neighborhood watches of the kind that killed Trayvon Martin.

As Woods Ervin puts it, "The people we are can't imagine all of the steps to where we want to go." Emergent strategies can help us find our way to becoming the people we need to be to bring abolitionist futures into being. As shea puts it, "The principles of emergent strategy are essential to creating a different society with different sets of relationships." Emergent strategies articulate a way of being that can enable us to live into an abolitionist politic and to expand our imaginations and practices to end violence in all its forms, in ways that will bring us closer to what can blossom in place of current punitive systems without simply replicating them. While the principles of emergent strategies may appear abstract, they are at work in movements and organizations around the globe (some of which are described in the chapters that follow), shaping how we are building futures without violence, including the violence of policing.

Abolition Is Fractal

"Abolition starts with how you talk to yourself."

The central question I asked myself and the people who generously and graciously agreed to share their vision and wisdom with me was, "How do you see principles of emergent strategies supporting, furthering, and operating in abolitionist organizing?"

The quote that opens this chapter is how Detroit-based organizer PG Watkins answered. Their response literally exploded something deep inside of me. As someone who has, for most of my life, focused my efforts to shift structures of violence externally, the call to begin within was the equivalent of a tectonic shift.

In a similarly heart-opening interaction, my therapist once invited me to reiterate the vision of the world I long for and the kinds relationships it requires and then to contrast it to the way I talk to myself. When I finished responding to his prompts, he bluntly asked, "Why the hell would you want that kind of world inside of you given the world you are trying to build outside yourself?" His question echoed PG's observations on an episode of the *Emergent Strategy Podcast*, "We aren't actually embodying what we want to see in the world. And that's making it harder for us to actually realize that in the world." For PG, the questions to ask as we practice new worlds are, "How do we deeply embody the way we know that we want the world to look after we win? Can we start acting like we've won now, in the way that we work together, in the way that we relate to each other?"[1]

I had internalized the idea that how we interact with each other shapes the larger structures we live in ("the personal is political") but hadn't extended that principle to its logical conclusion: this process begins with the interactions we have with ourselves. So much of my life has been spent driving myself at an unsustainable pace (including while writing this book), constantly pushing myself to do more, think more deeply and work harder, be smarter, sharper, more strategic, more rigorous, a better organizer—without a thought for the world I am building in the ways I am speaking to myself as I do so. I embraced Grace Lee Boggs's axiom that we need to transform ourselves to transform the world, and for many years Mary Hooks's "The Mandate for Black People in This Time"—"To avenge the suffering of our ancestors, to earn the respect of future generations, and to be willing to be transformed in service of the work,"—hung on the wall in front of my desk.[2] But my approach to my own transformation was punishing. I rarely extend myself the grace, kindness, and care I have done my best to offer others in alignment with my values and visions for the future.

PG's words invited me to explore how the way I relate to myself reflects the internalized capitalism Alexis Pauline Gumbs regularly invites us to uproot and what Paula Rojas (quoting "Theater of the Oppressed" practitioner Augusto Boal) calls "the cop in our heads and hearts."[3] Because, despite our best efforts, the way you talk to yourself can bleed into the ways you see and engage the world. As shea put it, we need to "recognize the violence in ourselves and the way that the culture of violence has moved us toward responses that are not life affirming." Failing to attend to the violence within therefore overlooks a critical building block to imagining and practicing a different world.

How you talk to yourself is a reflection of how society is structured and how you are structuring society. As my beloved comrade and friend Robyn Maynard writes to Leanne Betasamosake Simpson in their gorgeous book *Rehearsals for Living*,

"It has been increasingly clear to me that we cannot live in community or move toward political transformation if we are not able to commit, in the most intimate part of our lives, to authenticity within ourselves and to wellness."[4] In the words of Black nonbinary critical theorist and abolitionist Che Gossett, "The revolution—and abolition as both revolutionary and the radicalizing of the terms of revolution itself—are not only external but also internal processes." We need to attend to both.

Emergent strategies teach us that change happens at the smallest levels, that bringing attention to how we talk to ourselves and interact with each other means we can start practicing abolition here, now, and freshly each day, at a scale that is accessible to every one of us. That said, the task of transforming our relationship to ourselves and each other is not an easy one. In her documentary *American Revolutionary: The Evolution of Grace Lee Boggs*, filmmaker Grace Lee challenged her namesake (no relation) about whether she lived her own call to "transform yourself to transform the world," given that she rarely expressed any of the self-doubt or uncertainty that accompanies transformation. Grace Lee Boggs was silent for a few beats, and then responded, "You've given me something to think about. I think our conversation is going to sit with me for a long time."[5] Clearly practicing internal transformation in service of building the world we want is challenging, even for those of us who point to it as essential.

Recognizing that how we relate to each other and the people around us is a central aspect of the world we are practicing doesn't mean writing positive affirmations to ourselves or saying "hi" to our neighbors is the entirety of the work—although it's part of it. We also need to practice the accountability we want to see in the world with ourselves, as Shannon Perez-Darby, founding member of the Accountable Communities Consortium, teaches in her workshops on "self-accountability."[6] We also need to practice it in the simplest interactions with each other, as transformative justice practitioner Mia Mingus emphasizes in her workshops on accountability and the four parts of giving a good apology.[7]

And our charge goes far beyond that. As Sage says, "I think the framework of *Emergent Strategy* sometimes feels like an individual transformation moment, and it is. It is really easy to read this book as 'this is the way *I'm* going to move.' But if we're talking about abolition as the development of a new culture, then *Emergent Strategy* can give us grounding for how we collectively move and what we are moving toward. We have to understand it as more than individual, as collective and systemic, if we are to relate to the complexity of emergent strategies." This is how *Emergent Strategy* transcends the realm of "social justice self-help" into a contribution to conversations about how we shift systems to build abolitionist futures.

One of the core principles of emergent strategies is that complex systems are fractal—a fancy word to describe how small structures are replicated in larger ones—broccoli is made up of tiny broccolis, fern fronds are made up of smaller fronds, snowflakes look like the microscopic crystals of water they're made of, the patterns of our fingerprints are reflected in the shape of galaxies, and so on. In other words, we need to look to the smallest building blocks to understand and shape larger systems. As adrienne puts it in *Emergent Strategy*, "Small is all," because "what we practice at the small scale sets the patterns for the whole system."[8] Or, as I learned through Black Organizing for Leadership and Dignity (BOLD), the way you do one thing is the way you do everything. Therefore, shifting complex systems requires us to act at the individual level to "create patterns that cycle upward."[9]

Erin Butler, a Detroit-based organizer who also happens to be a mathematician, explains that replicating a simple pattern over and over again is how complex systems are generated. The key is to find the pattern that will produce the system you want to create.[10] Translating this mathematical principle to human interactions, Erin says,

It's the idea of replicating patterns in your life at the small scale, at the scale of you, at the scale of you and another person, at the scale of a small group of people, to community gatherings, to larger scale formations. I think about how principles like consent can apply when it's just me, and what consent looks like when it's me and another person, and what consent looks like when it's a group of us, and how to make consent operate at each level of interaction.

The fractal principle points to individuals, critical connections, and networks as sites at which larger systems, like society, are formed, and can—and must—be shaped. In *As We Have Always Done*, Leanne Betasamosake Simpson says that, in the Anishnaabe communities she is part of and descends from, "the ethics and values that individuals use to make decisions in their personal lives are the same ethics and values that families, communities, and nations use to make decisions about how to live collectively."[11]

When it comes to abolitionist organizing, Erin notes, "You have to ask yourself, what was our strategy here? How do we implement that at the next level? It's not something that happens on accident, and you can't stop at just the individual level. You have to recognize the pattern and implement it intentionally at the next stage. Because it's increasing in complexity, it's not going to look the same, so you have to work hard to find the building blocks of the pattern—it takes reflection to find the key." In other words, working through fractals isn't just about finding what will produce a shift at the individual or one-on-one relationship level but the thing that will produce a shift that can magnify to a systems level. It's also about noticing what fractals you are reproducing that are perpetuating the systems that already exist. Policing looks both similar and different at every level that it operates—internally, in relationships, in families, in communities, at the level of the nation-state, on a global scale. We must ask ourselves, what are the building blocks we can replicate at the level of critical connections that can break its hold on our imaginations and actions?

The fact that fractals are simple doesn't mean they are easy to identify or practice, Erin concludes. But, she finds comfort in the idea that what we do as individuals can have an impact on creating and shaping complex systems and that we don't have to wait for something outside ourselves to act—a deity we pray to, a leader we look to, a vision we wait for someone else to have, a movement we wait for someone else to build to get to a world we can't imagine. The simultaneity and inter-relationship between how you talk to yourself, how you are in relationship, and how our societies are structured may be hard to pitch in a ten-minute meeting with a city council member or to break down to a family member or neighbor. But it helps us to understand that it is in our power to shift the world within and around us.

Understanding complex systems as fractal is one of the most important principles of emergent strategies for aboli-tionists, particularly those of us pulled toward ten-point plans. Nikkita Oliver, an organizer, poet, and founding director of Creative Justice in Seattle, told me,

> I used to really be focused on gigantic systems change first. That's still a goal, but especially when we're creating responses to harm, I feel like there is a value in starting small and that the small can add up to something big. This has led to a shift in my own work in how much time I spend on different things. I spend more time on the small experimental incubation of work and building relation-ships within our ecosystem that can endure the impact of the larger ecosystem we're still in. I feel like emergent strategies have led me to think about how we build com-munity infrastructure, even if it's block by block or house by house or friend group by friend group, that could at some point render the systems we're wanting to abolish obsolete. Now that doesn't mean we also don't have ele-ments of large systems change work, but I don't spend 100 percent of my time doing that anymore. I spend a much greater bulk of my time thinking about the fractal elements and how do those add up to a bigger picture.

Understanding abolitionist organizing as fractal also frames the project and practice of abolition on a human scale. The work of tearing down the entire prison, police, military, and surveillance industrial complex—and ensuring they are not replaced by new versions of the same things—while creating conditions to meet everyone's material needs and produce greater safety for communities across the globe can feel daunting, to say the least. But emergent strategies' focus on the fractal brings abolition into the realm of the actionable. As shea puts it, it helps people to "look at the place where they are and ask, 'What are the things we can produce locally that are unique to this place, that sustain life and develop the capacities of our people, while protecting the Earth that's around us?' That's different in every place."

The notion that change takes place on a fractal level makes the task of "turning the world all over," to quote Black lesbian feminist poet and organizer Pat Parker, more tangible and helps to move us from being just "visionary talkers" to visionaries in action.[12] Each of us can begin the work of abolition today and every day by shifting the ways we each respond to harm, conflict, and need—individually and collectively—in our families, communities, and institutions. shea says, "I think the heart of abolition is the belief that if we have relationships of integrity and substance, much of the harm we do each other will not happen. Those aren't just relationships but those are relationships that have established a social, economic, and political base where people feel valued and not threatened. The only place to do that really is in small relations. You can't have a mass approach to safety."

We can examine the ways we engage with ourselves and each other. We can ask ourselves if our behavior is rooted in punishment, exile, and abandonment or if it offers invitations and creates possibilities to transform individual and collective conditions. We can reach toward the world we long for by using every day as a practice-ground in which we generate new possibilities that can proliferate and ultimately reshape our world.

Kat Aaron, beloved member of the AMC community and producer of the *Octavia's Parables* podcast co-hosted by adrienne and musician Toshi Reagon, was one of the early readers and cheerleaders for this book. She enthusiastically agrees, "As a person parenting in the pandemic, I've had so many interactions with my kids that are opportunities to practice these strategies! Trying to sit with their hurt and anger, and my own, and to unpack both where our feelings are coming from and how to repair the harms we cause each other in the day-to-day frustrations."

Mia Herndon, who I first met through INCITE! and the Another Politics Is Possible study group and who was a staff member of the Emergent Strategy Ideation Institute (ESII), similarly described parenting as a practice ground for abolitionist approaches to preventing, interrupting, and healing from harm: "When you are parenting you have to constantly mitigate for unintentional harms over time—like in those times where, in the interests of control, efficiency, order, and meeting multiple needs, children are othered in places where they are supposed to be connected. Those are the times when, as a parent, you need to stop, take a breath, and remember that your intention is to be in relationship, to nurture well-being. It's hard when you don't feel that there is a shared interest or there are competing needs. That's why parenting as an abolitionist practice requires emergent strategies." Mia concludes, "We need to practice accountability and transformation in places of love and community and feel our way to systemic change."

The Storytelling and Organizing Project (STOP) hosted by Creative Interventions gathers examples of people practicing abolitionist responses to harm in their families, neighborhoods, and communities. One of the stories the project collected that has always stuck with me involves a group of friends who are supporting a member of their community who is being financially abused by another. The two people shared a car, which was becoming part of the pattern of abuse. So the friends decided to put a new "club" lock on it to take it out of the equation. They immediately told the person doing the harm that they had changed the lock so that she wouldn't find out by surprise at night and let her know that there were a number of people willing to give her a ride home from work. In other words, they let her know that they cared for her too, even as they were enacting a consequence for her actions. This one simple, creative intervention offered the survivor a sense of relief and possibility for resolution and signaled to the person doing harm that their community knew what was going on and cared enough to act.[13] Each STOP story is different—unique to time, place, people, and circumstance. Each person in need of support or who experienced harm turned to the people closest to the issue—physically or relationally—for solutions, which is often a more effective method than calling on someone far away from the situation, a stranger, or the cops. Creative Interventions's expansive toolkit and workbook gathers tools and lessons from these experiences to increase our individual and collective capacities to practice responses that transform individuals, communities, and conditions and shift us away from policing and punishment.[14]

Often, existing institutions can offer spaces for practice. For instance, shea described learning about a program operating out of a North Philadelphia church that had become something of a "home school" because they couldn't get the kids, mostly young Black men, to go home. Using a program modeled after one the pastor had learned about, when one of them was in crisis, a young person would be asked to identify all the adults in their life to see who could help. The pastor and her team would then meet with each adult to see if they were willing to commit to supporting the young person. Then the young person, the adults who were willing to step up, and the pastor would meet to come up with a plan. For example, if a young person was having trouble waking up after their parent left for work and was in danger of being suspended or expelled as a result, a neighbor would agree to step in and wake them up and help them get ready for school. Statistics show that school suspensions or expulsions can have lifetime impacts. So can avoiding them with the help of a supportive community. Simple, really, but it requires a focus on critical connections and building networks of support. In other words, practicing emergent strategies.

We can also listen and watch for others using simple inter-actions to shift our collective understanding of how we prevent and respond to harm. For instance, I was sitting in the Brooklyn Botanical Garden, in one of my favorite spots, re-reading *Emergent Strategy* as I prepared to turn my 2019 talk into this book when I overheard two people talking. One said, "He was walking me home and asked if I was ever afraid of walking home alone. And I told him, 'Well, statistically speaking you are my biggest threat.'" In a single statement, the speaker acted toward dismantling the mythology of "stranger danger" that currently structures our responses to violence. Recognizing that the primary sources of violence are people we know points all of us to new ways of orienting ourselves toward safety.

Emergent strategies recognize that radical ideas spread through conversations like these, rather than through indoctrination, policing, and punishment.[15] This is what is at the core of organizing—the reality that our ways of understanding and acting in the world shift at the level of relationship and in community, rather than through top-down legal, policy, or "narrative shift" campaigns—although these can help create conditions that are more favorable to organizing and to exploring abolitionist ideas and practices in communities. As discussed in the introduction, despite the higher visibility of their legislative, judicial, and electoral successes, these smaller, less visible inter-actions are also at the core of how the Right has been slowly building toward flexing their power in the current moment: one prayer meeting, post-church coffee hour, online message board post, or truck stop conversation at a time.

Recognizing the power of conversations to better understand and move toward safety, F.A.R. Out (Friends are Reaching Out), a project of the Northwest Network for LGBTQ Survivors, encouraged queer community members in Seattle to create spaces in their lives to speak frankly about relationships and to explore their power dynamics. The program invited everyone to think about how we normalize what might be red flags and how the actions that raise them are inconsistent with the relationships and the world we want. Participants focus on patterns in individual relationships as a strategy to prevent, intervene in, and heal from violence, instead of expending collective energy to pressure the criminal punishment system to address violence in queer relationships, particularly given how, as we point out in *Queer (In)Justice*, it has always policed gender and sexuality and punished LGBTQ+ people instead of protecting us. This, too, is emergent strategy in action.

Shannon, who used to work at the Northwest Network, shared what she describes as a core principle undergirding practices like these:

> I don't know how we're going to make the world out there that we've never experienced. It's not just going to *poof* into existence. The only way I know how to do that is pivot between looking at the small—"How can I get my shit together? How can I be in relationship with one other human?"—and practice that, and then know that can scale to what it needs to be like in our movements, our broader communities, our world. We can't jump to strategies that we can't apply in our everyday. If it doesn't work on that scale, then it won't work on the larger one.

Shannon highlights the importance of building experience and muscle for the world we are constructing through practice:

> What I love about the fractal piece is that I know change is possible because of the transformation I have experienced in relationship with my partner. I have actually experienced all these visions I am trying to create in the world in that relationship. That lets me know it's possible. I don't just have to dream it and then just imagine that someday it's going to come true. What I have to do is figure out how to make this thing I have experienced possible outside of just one relationship. We need to pivot between the small and the large—because when you just focus on the small, it never becomes an organizing strategy.

The Bay Area Transformative Justice Collective's pod-mapping approach and the Fireweed Collective's "Mad Maps" operate at the fractal level as part of an organizing strategy to connect our relationships into networks and communities of abolitionist practice.[16] The pod-mapping worksheet created in 2016 and recently updated invites us to identify and map people, as well as their relationships to us and each other, who we might rely on if we are in crisis; if we experience harm or abuse; if we need support in taking accountability for our own violence, harm, or abuse; if we witness violence; or if someone we care about is being violent or being abused.[17] In other words, "the people in our lives that we would call on to support us with things such as our immediate and ongoing safety, accountability and transformation of behaviors, or individual and collective healing and resiliency."[18] The worksheet reminds us to cast our net wide. Not everyone in our circle needs to be able to meet every single need, respond to every single crisis—each person we are in trusting relationship with can play different roles based on their skills, capacity, and resources.

Organizing projects like the Oakland Power Projects (OPP) operate at the fractal level immediately above pod mapping. Founded in 2015, OPP invites people in Oakland communities to interrogate why they call police and what skills they have or could develop, individually and collectively, to respond to each other's needs instead of relying on the police.[19] Focusing on calls related to mental health, OPP tracked and mapped what currently happens when someone calls 911 for help and then invited community members into dreaming and enacting something different—by learning emotional first aid, drawing on neighbors and community members with relevant skills, and coming up with strategies to prevent mental health crises instead of just responding to them.[20]

Around the same time, longtime abolitionist organizer and former Critical Resistance director Rachel Herzing undertook a similar project under the banner of Build the Block.[21] With the Arab Resource and Organizing Center (AROC), an Arab-led grassroots organizing space, as a key pilot site, Build the Block "was created to pilot strategies aimed at decreasing calls to 911 and contact with law enforcement among residents in Oakland and San Francisco. The project worked with neighborhood groups, formal organizations, and individuals to consider the circumstances under which people may rely on law enforcement intervention and what no-call resources, relationships, knowledge, and practices may be employed to decrease that reliance."[22]

By creating communities of practice focused on moving individuals, organizations and communities away from calling cops and toward offering care, projects like OPP and Build the Block contribute to a shift in how society responds to unmet physical and mental health needs—and how it approaches care altogether. Arguably, the fractal work OPP and Build the Block did in Oakland laid the groundwork for a broader shift toward building individual and community capacity for non-police crisis response, which is evident in organizing projects like Mental Health First in Sacramento and Oakland, in Minneapolis through Relationships Evolving Possibilities (REP), and across the United States leading up to and following the 2020 Uprisings.[23] They also tilled the soil for recommendations of the Oakland Reimagining Public Safety Task Force convened in response to the Uprisings, which reflect abolitionist principles and practices of community care.[24]

These iterations illustrate how mapping our relationships, building our skills, and strengthening our networks are examples of fractal approaches to surviving and transforming violence.[25] They can in turn contribute to building robust ecosystems of support for entire communities and potentially spiral structures, ethics, and practices of collective care outward. Mimi Kim, founder of Creative Interventions, writes that "as social movements and, indeed, humankind seek new visions to steer us beyond the current context of crisis, a turn to small, local, and flexible formations has been ubiquitous."[26]

But not all fractals are exactly the same. Policymakers, philanthropists, and even some organizers often fall into the trap of believing that we just need to find one singular model that "works" and replicate it all over the country. In this context, it is important to remember that no single experiment, organizing project, or practice is "*the* answer."

Focusing on critical conversations, pod mapping, creative interventions, and practicing emergent strategies doesn't mean that we don't need to create intentional containers in which to do so—what Wheatley and emergent strategists call communities of practice—that become part of networks with the potential to shape complex systems. By definition, organizing requires organizations, spaces in which critical connections are fostered and deepened; places where we can study and learn from each other to develop a shared analysis of the world around us; and practice grounds for new social, economic, or political relations. In "Building Resilient Organizations," Maurice Mitchell reminds us: "Organizations and institutions are political vehicles. They are also spaces where individuals develop skills, connection, and ideological alignment. Institutions transmit knowledge, hold strategy, and cultivate power. Atomized individuals that loosely assemble cannot do this at the scale needed to take on entrenched power."[27] After relationships to yourself and others, neighborhood and community-based programs, organizations represent the next level of fractals that cycle upward to shape society.

API Chaya is a Seattle-based organization that works primarily with migrant communities, including South Asian, Asian, and Pacific Islander migrants.[28] Like OPP and Build the Block, its Natural Helpers program operates at a fractal level above individual madmapping and pod mapping by training and resourcing the folks that people experiencing violence are already likely to turn to in their communities—faith leaders, health care providers, neighbors, community members—to respond to, intervene in, and prevent violence. Kalayo Pestaño, who serves as the co-director of API Chaya, described the program's evolution to me: "We were able to really mobilize our volunteers. Aunties were showing up in all of these places and really pushing people to have conversations about sexual assault, about domestic violence, that were deeply uncomfortable. Our work is to be having really uncomfortable conversations all the time. If you're not uncomfortable you're probably not doing the work." Over the past three years, the program has iterated and adapted in response to the pandemic:

> The pandemic has really tested some of the foundational things that we had been doing around building up pods or community networks of care. They definitely solidified during the beginning of the pandemic, and, for the most part, really held a lot of our communities in place. For some people who were surviving violence or who were stuck in a house with their abusers, the only felt sense of safety or belonging they had was over Zoom with a group of people that have had a similar experience. A lot of our natural helpers plugged into the mutual aid work that was going on overall, in addition to having their own pod that they were checking in with frequently.
>
> Now we're challenging people to do more, to imagine what else we can create as a group now that we've established that we're good at supporting each other through a hard time. . . . There are other people who don't have this, who have never heard of API Chaya, who are still continuing to survive without any connection to resources. How do we then invite more people into these networks of care? We can't lose sight of the fact that our communities are huge.

Two additional organizations that use fractal approaches to generating greater safety and well-being—Relationships Evolving Possibilities (REP) and the Young Women's Empowerment Project (YWEP)—are described in greater detail in the Visionary Practice section following this chapter.

Mutual Aid

Beyond individual and community-level experiments in creating safety and responding to crises, in our conversation Woods

Ervin reflected on the fractal nature of meeting people's material needs. "I think about what a dramatic shift it is for people to go from not having a safe place to be and three nutritious meals a day to having that . . . That produces a dramatic qualitative leap. Their experience of time, agency, capacity is just so dramatically changed by having those basic needs secured for an extended period of time." This, in turn, creates new possibilities for change they can make in their own lives, and in the lives of the people around them.

This is why abolitionists practice mutual aid to meet each other's needs when the state does not, enacting the slogan "We keep us safe" in concrete terms, and creating more possibilities through imagining and building something different and beyond survival. As organizer and writer Kelly Hayes says, "There simply is no future of resistance without mutual aid."[29] Mutual aid is also essential to contesting with the Right for power and fighting fascism. Fascism grows under conditions of scarcity and deprivation created by racial capitalism by creating familiar scapegoats for hardship. And, part of how the Right builds critical connections and networks is by meeting those conditions by showing up when people are in need, offering spiritual and material support and community. We cannot build power to resist their vision of society without doing the same. As Shane Burley writes, "Mutual aid plays a key role in this; it is what makes it possible for us to survive accelerating crises while simultaneously planting the seeds of a new kind of social relationship . . ."[30] Kelly Hayes agrees, saying, "Mutual aid offers us an opportunity to reconnect at the most basic human level with our potential co-strugglers in a fight against fascism."[31]

Recognizing mutual aid as a strategy and tool to meet a moment that was unfathomable, unprecedented, and catastrophic, communities across the country launched a multitude of mutual aid projects in 2020.[32] These initiatives created opportunities to meet the overwhelming sense of powerlessness I and so many others felt, in the face of the magnitude of the coronavirus pandemic and the economic crisis that it precipitated, and to embody abolitionist politics. To share just a few examples from my own experience, in the early days of the pandemic, when personal protective equipment (PPE) was scarce in the US, I delivered masks manufactured by my nephew in Jamaica to my neighbors and broader community as well as to health care workers and unhoused people. I posted information about financial, food, and other resources in my building lobby. As a queer person of color, migrant, Black New Yorker, person in community with people impacted by incarceration, and former restaurant worker, I contributed to pooled funds to sustain people in each of these communities and beyond. I joined others in my neighborhood in distributing clothing and warming kits to unhoused people who were being evicted from shut-down subways. We also checked in on and offered support to elders and disabled people. Existing organizations in my neighborhood built and maintained full-on grocery delivery and eviction defense operations, while new mutual aid projects sprang up and subsided as needs shifted. Each of these actions not only provided for people's immediate material needs, they strengthened analysis and relationships locally, nationally, and transnationally.

As adrienne writes in *Emergent Strategy*, "We must become the systems we need. No one is going to create them for us, we have to remember how to care for each other."[33] Through mutual aid projects, Dean Spade argues, "we are both building the world we want and becoming the kind of people who could live in such a world together."[34] Mutual aid projects allowed us to take actions consistent with the world we wanted to emerge from the pandemic portal—a world in which we collectively took responsibility for each other's health and well-being. Prefiguring and projecting the world we are building, we overcame overwhelm and responded to the crisis that was precipitated by structural racism, ableism, neoliberalism, and abandonment by the state by responding to each other.

Emergent strategies highlight the tremendous potential that exists in mutual aid efforts. Mutual aid creates opportunities to focus on the fractal by building and strengthening relationships and changing individual material conditions to create more possibilities for people to act. They also facilitate critical connections and conversation about the systemic conditions that contribute to the dire situations we find ourselves in and how we might organize to shift them. At Interrupting Criminalization, we worked to create tools to further catalyze conversations like these—for instance, Mariame collaborated with Congresswoman Alexandra Ocasio-Cortez to create a mutual aid toolkit under the theme of #WeGotOurBlock.[35] Woods and I worked with artists to develop posters and postcards that could be included in mutual aid kits and outreach about masking, isolation, housing, health care, structural supports, and social solidarity.[36] As Mariame concludes,

> I think one of the most important parts about mutual aid has to do with changing the social relationships that we have among each other, in order to be able to fight beyond this current moment, beyond the current crisis, beyond the current form of a disaster that we're trying to overcome. And so, one of the beautiful aspects is that you really don't know where the connections are going to take you. You're going to make and build new relationships that will lead to new projects and will lead to new understandings, that will shape the potential future of your community and beyond.[37]

Mutual aid projects offer opportunities to start small without getting stuck. The conversations, relationships, infrastructure, practices of governance, and assessments of root causes of crisis they can foster make more change possible. They also have impacts on larger systems—by highlighting their failures, building consensus toward new ways of being and doing, and pushing for institutional change. Some of the more well-known examples of this are the Head Start program, which was initiated by the US government after the Black Panthers highlighted the crisis and impacts of poverty in Black communities through their free breakfast programs, or the provision of community-based health care rooted in harm reduction at Lincoln Hospital in the Bronx after the Young

Lords' takeover of the facility.[38] More recently, Black Mama's Bail Out called attention to the rapidly growing population of Black women incarcerated in jails pre-trial, the majority of whom are caregivers for their families and communities, by collecting resources annually to pay their bail and secure their release in time for Mother's Day. Moving beyond charity to mutual aid, the National Bail Out organization, which coordinated Black-led localized, decentralized Black Mama's Bail Out efforts, hosted fellowships for women who were bailed out through the project to join organizing efforts to end money bail and pre-trial detention and support others returning to their communities through the bail outs.[39]

Importantly, as Dean writes, "scaling up" mutual aid projects,

> doesn't mean making groups bigger or merging them into one organization across a region, state, or country. Locally operated mutual aid projects work better . . . because our needs are best met by those with the most local knowledge, and we are the ones making the decisions affecting us. Scaling up our mutual aid work means building more and more mutual aid groups, copying each other's best practices, and adapting them to work for particular neighborhoods, subcultures, and enclaves. It means intergroup coordination, the sharing of resources and information, having each other's backs, and coming together in coalitions to take bigger actions like rent strikes, labor strikes, or the toppling of corrupt governments or industries.[40]

In other words, it is important to keep our focus on the fractal level, whether through mutual aid or interrupting harm in relationship. But that doesn't mean we are relieved of the responsibility to work toward structural change. Like Maurice Mitchell, Ejeris Dixon points out that the phrase "small is all" should not be used in defense of a refusal to think and act at a larger scale that can shift the structures that produce and perpetuate harm. Fractal changes at the level of individuals are necessary to shift structural relations of power, but they are far from sufficient. Woods describes what can emerge from individual transformation and shifts in everyday interactions as qualitative at the individual level but not necessarily quantitative change at the structural level. Just as it's not enough for individuals to recycle or make different choices around driving or flying when industrial capitalism is devastating the planet at a massive scale, it's not enough for us to simply work to meet each other's needs or find ways to address harm beyond policing and punishment in our everyday lives without an intention to shift larger systems. We need to do both, replicating fractals at all scales.

Critical Resistance offers the abolitionist framework of "Dismantle, Change, Build." Each of these pillars requires shifts at the fractal level, which must also be multiplied to a structural level. We need to dismantle both the cop in our head *and* the precinct down the block by organizing to defund and divest from policing. We need to tear down the prison—and the things that look and feel like prisons that come to replace them, including prisons we construct in our minds and in our interactions. We need to change our ways of relating to ourselves and each other *and* the way society organizes and distributes resources to meet everyone's basic needs without conditions. We need to build new ways of being—and build institutions that reflect them, whether through mutual aid, safety pods, transformative justice hubs, conflict mediation centers, and so much more.

We need to multiply, support, and project these interactions and values onto the larger structures that shape our world, take action to dismantle the institutions and structures of power that perpetuate them, and build the power to defend our experiments and shape the future into the world we want. As shea howell put it, changes in larger structures become possible when transformation and action at the fractal level coalesces into collective practices and institutions that shift power. When the water crystals coalesce into a snowflake and then into an avalanche or a glacier, their power becomes undeniable.

Make It Mycelial

Like any of the principles of emergent strategy, the quality of being fractal doesn't work in isolation. The key is connection. Self-talk, efforts to deepen relationships, and local experiments can't exist in isolation. They must be networked with each other, and undertaken with shared values and visions, and an intention to impact and shift larger systems.

For instance, Kelly Hayes and I talked about how, in the face of the growing criminalization of abortion, becoming an abortion doula to support people seeking abortions is a concrete action at the individual level that can also shift what is possible on a larger scale. Like Dean, Kelly believes that "creating very small units of folks who are in communication with each other about what we're doing is critical." Kelly and I both were able to participate in abortion doula trainings by Ash Williams of the Mountain Area Abortion Doula Collective and become part of a network of doulas in loose communities of practice in the wake of the Supreme Court's decision to overturn *Roe v. Wade* in the summer of 2022.[41] Each of us is attuned to local conditions and the people we serve; together we are knitting together a fabric of care.

The National Network of Abortion Funds (NNAF) is a large network of close to a hundred autonomous grassroots organizations working to ensure that people can access abortion without logistic, economic, political, and cultural barriers, organizing at the intersections of racial, economic, and reproductive justice.[42] Adaku Utah is the network's former organizing director, and described NNAF's work on the *Emergent Strategy Podcast*:

> These are folks who live in our communities who are taking folks across state lines to receive the care that they need. They are banding together to gather millions of dollars raised from the community to make sure that folks are not having to use their rent to cover a procedure. Abortion funds are folks who are meeting people

who need abortions at gas stations to fill up their tanks and offering transportation across state lines to the nearest clinics so people can get access to care. They are also opening up their homes for folks who've been forced out of their communities—queer and trans folks who've been forced out of their communities, and housing people so that before, during, and after their care, they have a place to land. They're also translating medical information and babysitting people's children as they're going through their procedure. And I think one of the most fundamental and powerful things that abortion funds do is offering just deeply compassionate care to people when they need it the most.

The network has also recognized that only doing direct service alone does not get us to the liberation and justice that we need, particularly for Black, Indigenous, and people of color. So folks are also organizing for thriving wages and abolishing ICE at borders, and making sure that our people have gender-affirming care and safer conditions for sex workers, and land sovereignty.[43]

Both in conversation with me and on the *Emergent Strategy Podcast*, Adaku highlights the ways NNAF draws on the lessons of emergent strategies to prepare for and weather moments of crisis, including the one we are currently living. Understanding individual abortion funds as fractals and weaving them into a network rooted in interdependence creates practical opportunities for partnerships within and across regions to share resources and fill gaps. It also makes way for adaptation under increasingly adverse conditions-based on decades of practice in coordination and trust building. The network of abortion funds, along with abortion doulas and courageous care providers, are coalescing into a system that is preserving and even expanding access to abortion care through widespread, decentralized resistance, instead of the top-down, law- and policy-based strategies large national organizations are exclusively relying on. According to Adaku, "taking action and preparing for a future that isn't just focused on securing legality but really cultivating these networks of care that will support folks outside of the state" enables communities to both build resilience and transform conditions.[44] This is what it takes to shift systemic conditions under pressure:

> Because we know that in the absence of systemic care—in the presence of systemic violence—we are the ones that are going to keep creating safety and care and security for our people. That is why we exist. That's why this network was built. That's why we do the work that we do. Another world is possible, and we're proof of that. We don't have to rely on or contract ourselves to only look to the state or governmental institutions to give us what we need. For close to three decades now, we've been connecting hundreds of thousands of people to compassionate care and making abortion a reality beyond the state and federal barriers and really reclaiming our own autonomy and sovereignty.[45]

What these examples demonstrate, drawing on one of the Complex Movements emblems, is that our organizing must be mycelial. *Mycelium* is the Latin name for the underground network of fungal root-like structures that bear "fruits," such as mushrooms, above ground. Networks are made up of single spores (fungal "seeds") that sprout filaments that connect into an underground mat, spanning areas ranging from a square inch to square miles. These networks can, in turn, connect with others, sharing information in a highly decentralized way. Mycelial networks play important roles in decomposing plant material and soil into nutrients for the fungus itself, as well as neighboring plants and soil micro-organisms, releasing carbon monoxide, transporting water, and conducting electricity. In some cases, mycelia can detoxify soils by breaking down organic compounds such as oil and pesticides, filtering water, and composting.

It is important to note that some of the characteristics attributed to mycelium in emergent strategy frameworks are allegorical, and only loosely connected to the science of mush-rooms. For instance, while mycelium does break down toxins, it can take hundreds of thousands of years to do; it's not an instantaneous process. But what we know about mycelium can serve as a powerful catalyst to imagining what connecting single acts, relationships, networks, and communities of practice to each other over time and space might generate and heal.

ill weaver offers an example of how fractal organizing that is an inch wide but a mile deep can be networked to effect more widespread change than efforts that engage more people at a shallower level, in the ways that mass-mobilization strat-egies often do. Pointing to the Detroit Future Youth Network they co-founded, a network of twelve Detroit-based youth organizations focused on investing in place-based organizing in a deep-rooted way over time at a smaller scale in relation-ship with similar organizing efforts elsewhere, ill describes the impact of connecting fractal organizing in mycelial ways.[46]

> If there are twelve youth organizations that each only work with twelve youth, but they're doing such deep transformative work with those twelve youth, and then we're in relationship with each other through regu-lar gatherings where we're thinking about strategy and exchanging and learning through practice together and building shared political understandings and building relationship, sharing resources, building cooperative things so we're not pitted against each other, now we have 140 deeply engaged youth versus one organization that works with 140 youth at such a shallow level that they're not actually building the radical depth.

Emergent strategies teach us that placing small-scale abolitionist organizing in relationship through networks and communities of practice is essential to producing large-scale systems change. This has given me greater clarity around my own work, which has increasingly focused on translocal organizing. I was introduced to this practice by INCITE!, a national network of radical feminists of color working to end violence in all its forms. INCITE! was made up of independent local chapters and affiliates that came together through convenings, campaigns, and resource creation to share analysis, successes, lessons, practices, and dreams for abolitionist, feminist futures. *Abolition. Feminism. Now.*, cowritten by INCITE! cofounder Beth Richie, chronicles how these small, often volunteer projects, acting at the local level in a coordinated fashion, were able to shift collective understandings of violence, and of the state as central organizer of gender-based violence rather than as a source of protection through policing and punishment, at the national level. As exemplified by the ongoing work of the cofounders, national collective members, and leaders of local affiliates described throughout *Practicing New Worlds*, INCITE!'s nodes have created new, interconnected networks and continue to shape current efforts to build toward greater safety for women and trans people of color through community-based interventions. Critical Resistance operates in a similar fashion, hosting and nurturing a network of abolitionist campaigns and chapters while creating spaces for shared learning, resource creation, strategizing, and disseminating lessons learned in these spaces more broadly.

Informed and inspired by this work, I have increasingly practiced convening and resourcing translocal networks that create spaces for shared analysis and build relationships and connections among organizers working to divest from policing and build safer communities across geographies and movements. That has taken the form of building a network of people and projects working to end police violence against Black women, girls, trans, and gender nonconforming people through the In Our Names Network;[47] coordinating a collaborative process of updating, deepening, and expanding the Vision for Black Lives, a shared analysis and platform for action for the ecosystem of organizations that make up the Movement for Black Lives; hosting learning communities, fellowships, and gatherings connecting organizers across the country working to divest from policing and invest in community-based safety strategies in partnership with the Community Resource Hub; facilitating Interrupting Criminalization's Building Coordinated Community Crisis Response learning space;[48] initiating a cross-movement Beyond Do No Harm Network of health care providers committed to interrupting the harm of criminalization in the context of accessing care;[49] and building a cohort of organizations working to weave together community ecosystems of collective care. Each of these efforts makes more sense as a mechanism for affecting systemic change when understood as an effort to connect fractals into abolitionist networks, communities of practice, and, ultimately, systems of influence.

Translocal organizing, rather than any singular top-down strategy, was a primary mechanism of the 2020 Uprisings and the shifts they generated. Locally initiated decentralized formations across Turtle Island engaged members of their communities using a diversity of tactics tailored to local capacities and conditions. These fractal efforts were strengthened by sharing information, experiences, skills, demands, analysis, strategies, intelligence, toolkits, messaging, communications, and community through networks and by amplifying each other's work and taking action in solidarity with each other.[50] Ultimately, local campaigns coalesced into a system of influence that has fundamentally altered public perceptions of policing and safety, prompting intensifying backlash.[51] Our task is to continue to deepen and further this work through kitchen-table conversations and canvassing, citywide assemblies, study groups, and by building skills and infrastructure for mutual aid and community crisis response, while strengthening our mycelial connections to broaden our power and influence as well as our capacity to withstand the backlash.[52] Daniel Kisslinger, a Chicago-based organizer and co-host of the *AirGo* podcast, points out that once we conceive of our organizing as mycelial, our attention shifts from trying to convince people who currently hold power to do what we want to building power with each other to create the world we want.

As we do so, we need to tend to the conditions in which our networks operate to maximize opportunities for them to flourish like the spread of mycelial mats across square miles and the mushrooms that pop up from them under the right conditions. In other words, we also have to tend the soil. We need to seek to affect material conditions such that what is being cultivated inside our networks will have the space and resources necessary to grow into something with the power to shift larger systems. This can take the shape of organizing to extract resources from the state or capital through efforts to #DefundPolice, engage in participatory budgeting, organize for community benefit agreements, or raise revenue through corporate and wealth taxation.[53] And, we must recognize that the soil in which we are growing our futures is also a space of contention and be careful not to create conditions in which fractals and networks being built by the Right can also thrive. For instance, abolitionist scholar Craig Gilmore urges caution when creating conditions for community groups to take up the work of public institutions like schools, which also makes way for private institutions advancing Right-wing agendas to step in.

Building strong mycelial networks of abolitionist projects and campaigns is critical to defending fractal experiments in the face of threats. As Woods and others highlight, at some point the state—or Right-wing forces beyond the state—will recognize the relationships, practices, institutions, and formations we are building as challenges to their power. "When the state sees the hegemonic shift and the experiments that it spurs as a threat, it will decide to crush it. If we have not anticipated that and don't organize in a way that doesn't just place us on the defensive but actively tries to prevent the state from being able to do that, then we're going to get crushed," Woods said. My beloved Interrupting Criminalization co-worker Maria Thomas similarly writes when reflecting on the role of the state in abolitionist futures, "I don't see how life-affirming experiments won't be crushed without some support. Everything that helps people and gives them some leverage to fight capitalism's stranglehold is threatening to the capitalist state—it's why people are criminalized for building shelters for unhoused people, providing water to migrants crossing the desert, and engaging in harm reduction and self-managed care, and why the carceral state criminalizes protest and dissent. Fascism's go-to move is to criminalize all experiments that give the people more life chances."[54]

In light of this, Woods argues that we need to balance expanding our imagination about making change using emergent strategies with clear-eyed assessments of how we contend for, and with, power. We need to ask ourselves whose interests our abolitionist organizing experiment threatens? What action are they likely to take to protect their interests? How can we build greater power, resilience, and resistance to efforts to absorb or destroy it? Otherwise, our small-scale experiments risk being obliterated, undermined, or co-opted by those in power. We can't simply count on the power of fractals in those moments to push back against an effort to neutralize our organizing at every level, whether it's by stoking our fears, capturing our imaginations, disrupting individual relationships and connections, or capturing or destroying network hubs.[55] But by building the muscles of our imagination, deepening and strengthening our relationships, and proliferating and connecting them into wide, decentralized networks with strong connectivity through shared values, we can find more successful and resilient ways to resist and withstand the inevitable attacks, particularly where the imbalance of power is great. Our ability to coalesce action at the fractal level into structures that can counter and survive beyond these threats is essential to shaping the world we want.

Relationships Evolving Possibilities

.

> "The hypothesis is simple. We can do it better and we know that
> the state's been doing it horribly."
>
> —SIGNE VICTORIA HARRIDAY, REP COFOUNDER

Relationships Evolving Possibilities (REP) is an initiative that emerged from the crucible of the 2020 Uprisings in Minneapolis after the murder of George Floyd and describes itself as one "node in an interconnected network of projects created by communities to manifest safety and center Black life, liberation, and joy." REP's origin story began "during the uprising in late May and early June 2020, when Jason Sole and Signe Harriday worked together on crisis response in Minneapolis and St. Paul. They saw a need to make it more sustainable and envisioned strategies and communications technology that could support the incredible work community members were doing (and have been doing for generations)." REP's work is rooted in three main values: "Black love and liberation, radical consent, and ancestral knowledge."

REP Core Member Josina Manu Maltzman described REP as a tree: "The trunk is relationships evolving possibilities, the pedagogy from which all the work stems. One branch is Radical Ecosystem Pods, and that's a project where we teach up community members in the skills needed to turn to each other in moments of crisis. The other, Revolutionary Emergency

Partners, is a secure hotline that community members can call or text in moments of acute crisis or during ongoing struggle to be met with a community member skilled in crisis intervention, de-escalation, mental health first aid, and equipped with a resource list of vetted community partners that can love the person to the next step."[1]

In her beautiful essay "At Least Two Layers of Support: An Anatomy of Collective Care" in *Liberated to the Bone: Histories. Bodies. Futures.* (part of the Emergent Strategy Series), abolitionist healer and organizer Susan Raffo shares the lessons from nature that inform this structure and operation of REP.[2] Looking to the fractal level of our cellular membranes, wombs, and skin and of tree bark, she notes that each of these benefits from at least two layers of care and protection. Mirroring this, REP focuses on "building/supporting two overlapping circles. One circle focuses on honoring, building, and deepening interdependent intimate infrastructures of protection and support. Some call it pod mapping or collective care or mutual aid. It's moving into community as a concrete commitment."[3]

Through ongoing trainings and "studios," REP invites people into Radical Ecosystem Pods, "a group of people who have come together (based on geography, identity, values, a time-specific need, or a combination of the above) to support each other through crises, either unforeseen or anticipated. Pods have agreed-upon parameters and expectations, and have established consent-based communication around how to support each other."[4] Beginning with a series of questions intended to identify who people are already turning to for support, as well as what skills might be needed to care for each other more deeply and what is needed for us to show up for a larger community, pod members work to increase their capacity to support those they are already in relationship with—neighbors, friends, family—by participating in trainings in de-escalation, mental health support, and conflict resolution.[5] They commit to showing up, to being there for each other, and to continue learning together. Raffo writes, "With this first circle we say, here is the innermost membrane."[6]

"The second overlapping circle," she goes on to describe, "is the one that asks: what do you do when none of the close-in relationships are available or can hold this moment of crisis or vulnerability?"[7] REP's answer is a hotline people can call to be connected with a community resourcer trained in mental health and de-escalation who will either send a community responder or resource team to provide immediate support, or connect someone with trusted existing resources, depending on the caller's need.[8]

> These are the two circles of support. The first circle is those who know you, who already claim you, who remember your life. This is the circle of looking in and support. The second circle is the circle of looking out; the circle of calling someone who does not know you, who is not in your life. That is protection.
>   . . . Two layers of support is connective tissue between an individual life and a larger collective web of mutual aid, of community.[9]

"REP's vision for the future is grounded in relationships," draws on nature's lessons, and reflects emergent strategies' focus on critical connections, networks, and communities of practice. Raffo continues, "Outside our capacity to name and see it, collective care emerges, too big to grasp, too much to fit on a single map. So we start with what we can see and touch, this foundation, these two layers of support. One up close and intimate, the other connecting us to everything."[10]

We can all draw lessons from REP's fractal approach, but it is important to remember that it is rooted in the relationships that formed it and that grow from it, and is therefore not replicable everywhere in the exact same form. Nor is it an approach that must immediately be "proven" to work to be deemed worthy of long-term investment and experimentation. "We claim the right to time," to grow projects like REP at the speed of trust and learning, Raffo states emphatically.

Young Women's Empowerment Project

Former Young Women's Empowerment Project (YWEP) co-director Shira Hassan walked me through the ways in which the structure and work of the organization, a former affiliate of INCITE! where both adrienne and I served on the board at different times, reflect emergent strategies and contributed to the evolution of the principles distilled in *Emergent Strategy*.[1]

As a peer-focused program for youth involved in the sex trades and street economies, YWEP operated at a fractal level—at the scale of one-on-one interactions in the context of street outreach and groups. The organization's leadership, structures, and practices were in a constant state of iteration and adaptation to the particular skills, interests, experiences, and needs of individual members as well as changing political, economic, and social conditions. "We just tried new things all the time and worked with our strengths at any moment. Things didn't need to be the same as the day before. We were in constant conversation and check-ins, redrafting workplans and support plans every week." The annual planning process was a year-long affair, with strategies constantly being assessed, evaluated, and redesigned by youth, staff, board members, and adult allies.

These fractal, decentralized, iterative, and adaptational practices evolved organically from YWEP's roots in what Shira describes in her book *Saving Our Own Lives* as "liberatory harm reduction."[2] Shira points out that "liberatory harm reduction is so organic and so location and condition dependent" that it necessarily operates at a fractal level. By supporting each other in building safety and survival strategies, members manifested interdependence but operated in decentralized peer-to-peer networks. The organization drew on and built the resilience of participants while operating in a transformative justice framework, coining the phrase "resilience and resistance" in the context of its youth-led research on survival strategies embodying both principles.

YWEP's Bad Encounter Line documented youth's experiences of violence and violation when interacting with systems ostensibly set up to help them, which informed the development of the group's organizing and advocacy agenda. The Bad Encounter Line was one possibility inspired by "bad date lists," which were developed through sex worker organizing across the United States. YWEP's work in turn created new possibilities for multiple projects that emerged from or were inspired by it, including youth-led syringe exchange programs, the Street Youth Rise Up campaign, and emi koyama's System Failure Alert.[3] But that doesn't mean YWEP offered a model that could be replicated across the country—it was unique to the people, relationships, place, and conditions that shaped it. As Shira said, "We were asked many times if we could nail down a model and share it, and our answer was always no. We could tell you how we did it so you could use that information to create your own thing."

Abolition Is Decentralized and Rooted in Interdependence

> Decentralization is necessary because everyone's refusal looks different. We can have shared principles, but the functionality is based on relationships.
>
> —JENNY LEE

Decentralization is at the heart of complex systems, in which individual components, acting independently according to a relatively simple set of rules, collaborate and coalesce without top-down direction into something different and more powerful. This process renders the individual components interdependent and capable of surviving and responding to conditions as part of a larger system. Both of these characteristics are also at the heart of emergent strategies: decentralization allows for continuous learning, adaptation, and iteration—of our goals, outcomes, and strategies—to local needs and changing conditions, while interdependence recognizes our connections and shared fate.

Both *Emergent Strategy* and Complex Movements use natural metaphors of starling murmurations and dandelions to represent these concepts. Starling murmurations are breathtaking dances through the sky in which thousands of birds twist and turn in unison. There is no singular leader; instead their tightly coordinated movements are made possible by each bird being attuned to and in a reciprocal relationship with a specific number of birds around it, following simple rules.[1]

Birds flock and fish school for safety and to seek out food, and both learn to move together without any central coordination that we can discern. Likewise, as discussed in the Introduction, ants, bees, and slime mold act in concert without a centralized leader. In each of these systems, both decentralization and interdependence make collective action possible, with impacts greater than individuals can accomplish on their own, while simultaneously offering protection.

Complex systems such as starling murmurations, fish schools, slime mold, and ant and bee societies, are formed through "self-organization," in which

> there is no central or external controller. Rather, the "control" of a self-organizing system is distributed across components and integrated through their interactions.
>
> Self-organization may produce physical/functional structures like crystalline patterns . . . or dynamic/informational behaviors like shoaling behaviors of fish. . . . As the system becomes more organized by this process, new interaction patterns may emerge over time, potentially leading to the production of greater complexity.[2]

Self-organization is the opposite of a top-down, planned strategy developed and executed by a small group of people—and it is essential to nurturing emergence in response to localized conditions and shifts.

Self-organization and decentralization allow abolitionist values and practices to spread through connections, relationships, networks, and communities of practice, much like dandelions spread through the dissemination of hundreds of seeds. Decentralization also enables systems to meet and withstand changing conditions and protect from inevitable attacks. As Shane Burley writes, "Decentralized infrastructure is therefore not just preferable because it gives people more autonomy but also because it provides a form of passive defense by reducing attack surfaces and preventing cascading failures. Decentralization also allows for more redundancy by letting people assess their risk profiles from where they are, instead of having it thrust on them by some authority." In other words, decentralization makes for moving and diffuse targets, limits the impact of attacks, and enables individuals to make their own decisions about the risks they are willing to take.

My first introduction to decentralized organizing came through anti-apartheid movements of the late 1980s. Guided by a call from the African National Congress for global economic, political, and cultural divestment from the apartheid regime in South Africa, groups across the US and around the world began to engage in self-organized localized actions, which were shaped by how their particular targets were connected to the apartheid government or economy. Cornell University, which I attended as an undergrad, was led by President Frank Rhodes, descended from none other that Cecil Rhodes, the "father" of the neighboring apartheid state of Rhodesia (now Zimbabwe). He made an easy target. In fact, anti-apartheid organizing was part of the reason I decided to attend Cornell: in the Spring of 1985 when I visited the campus, it was in the throes of a huge anti-apartheid student occupation. I remember getting off the bus at the center of campus, surveying the quad, which was filled by thousands of protesting students, and deciding on the spot that this was a place for me. Throughout my time at Cornell, I was an active participant, and later a leader, in the South Africa Divestment Coalition. Through constant protests and occupations, we succeeded in reducing the university's investments in corporations doing business in South Africa from $146 million to $42 million.[3]

The divestment movement was highly decentralized, operating by a simple set of rules and with a singular goal: stop investment in corporations doing business in South Africa. Students on campuses across the country joined in a loose network that shared strategies and successes. I rarely met anyone from other schools, but we shared information about trustees' corporate ties, replicated each other's tactics, monitored each other's actions, demands, and victories, moving locally, in a decentralized fashion, toward a common goal.[4]

Like anti-apartheid movements, anti-globalization uprisings and Occupy adopted decentralized structures, in which a
multitude of localized affinity groups, occupations, and formations emerged as part of what has been described as "leaderful"
movements. As a legal observer during the 2004 Republican
National Convention in New York City who later represented
organizers in criminal and civil actions, and an occasional visitor
to Occupy's headquarters at Zuccotti Park, I gained a deeper
understanding of the mechanics and power of decentralized
strategies.

Abolitionist organizing I have been part of or observed has
similarly operated in decentralized ways, connected through
networks such as Critical Resistance, INCITE!, and Survived
and Punished. And, as discussed in the Introduction, increasingly so are Right-wing formations.

Woods Ervin emphasizes that decentralized approaches are
essential to abolitionist organizing because the way that the
prison industrial complex (PIC) has cohered is in itself decentralized—there isn't a singular "Department of Carcerality" that
we can make our target and abolish. In fact, no such department is required because policing and punishment are so deeply
embedded in virtually every institution of society and in our
imaginations about what society is and requires. Therefore, our
efforts to dismantle the PIC must also include decentralized
strategies focused on unraveling this web and extracting ourselves from carceral mindsets, economies, and polities through
decentralized action everywhere, simultaneously.

Woods describes this work of abolition as "creating the
conditions that make abolition possible. There is not some
other magical thing that is the work. I think that's what emergent strategy principles get at, which is that it's small structures.
I don't think a focus on creating a giant US Department of
Abolition would achieve the goals of the abolitionist project—
that's not actually going to create abolition, especially in the
current context." Instead, we need to build toward abolition by
unlearning and unraveling the ways that carcerality is embedded in each of us and our relations, and in the programs and

institutions around us. We need to resist and dismantle through decentralized formations, in ways that are specific and appropriate to each of our communities, to each situation and set of conditions, and in a way that can be kept to the scale of relationships and accountability.

Importantly, decentralization doesn't mean an absence of a shared politic, connection, or coordination—effective decentralized movements are guided by a shared analysis and practice. Abolitionist principles and calls to action—like the demand to #DefundPolice that emerged onto the national stage in 2020—can provide the rules that shape our decentralized individual and collective actions and enable them to coalesce into formations that can impact structures at a larger scale, provide for our individual and collective needs, and create abolitionist cultures through which we are able to prevent, address, and transform harm.

Decentralized also doesn't mean disorganized or that everyone has to do everything. Former AMC co-director, organizer, and multimedia artist Diana Nucera, also known as Mother Cyborg, points out the importance of knowing what you bring to the table, honing those skills and competencies, and identifying the specific role(s) you can play based on those assessments. Deepa Iyer's *Social Change Now: A Guide for Reflection and Connection* invites readers to explore which role they are best suited to play in the moment: storyteller, guide, healer, disrupter, experimenter, frontline responder, visionary, builder.[5] Decentralized movements in Hong Kong have inspired people around the world with carefully coordinated decentralized direct action strategies in which protesters play different roles—holding shields, pointing lasers, setting up tear gas washing stations, acting as lookouts and decoys, participating in "legal" protest activities—with considerable impact.[6] Often decentralized movements require elaboration of complex structures to make decentralized decision-making possible, like the spokescouncils and assemblies used during anti-globalization protests, in Occupy encampments, and Global South movements. They also require naming, recognizing, and if necessary, dismantling the informal rules we operate by—whether it's deference to elders or people with more experience, anti-Blackness, colorism, patriarchy, or the ableist notion that "the people who do the most work should have the most power."

Abolitionist organizers are increasingly gravitating toward practicing new worlds through decentralized participatory governance in the form of people's movement assemblies inspired by Global South movements and modeled in the US by Project South's Southern Movement Assembly. Organized around principles of community governance, organizational self-determination, local leadership, community defense, a multiplicity of strategies, principled dialogue, and rest and regeneration, Southern Movement Assembly is "a multi-racial, multi-issue, multigenerational movement alliance of grassroots organizations across the South that practices democratic governance, coordinates shared actions, and convenes peoples' movement assemblies of frontline communities to grow bottom-up power and build infrastructure for long-term liberation."[7] The Project South People's Movement Assembly organizer handbook and framework gathers wisdom from the Jackson People's Movement Assembly, the 2007 and 2010 US Social Forums, World Social Forums, and a Black Women's People's Movement Assembly held in conjunction with the release of criminalized survivor Marissa Alexander, among others, and has been used in the context of the 2020 Uprisings and beyond by organizers from Minneapolis to Nashville.[8]

Decentralization also doesn't mean diminished impact—particularly when decentralized movements converge around a set of demands or target. The decentralized 2020 Uprisings have been described as the largest movement in US history—based on the estimated twenty-six million people who protested across the US on a single day in June 2020—unified by a demand to end police violence against Black people, with calls to defund police rapidly replicating across communities through new and existing formations. Despite the backlash, their impacts should not be underestimated; they profoundly shifted the landscape of possibility for abolitionist futures.

Fewer people in the US were aware of massive protests that took place elsewhere in 2020, including those led by Indigenous peoples and farmers across the globe in India, who were challenging laws that corporatized an agricultural sector already rife with inequities so severe that farmers were dying by suicide every seventeen minutes on average. Through decentralized, coordinated collective decision-making among 500 organizations gathered in an unprecedented "alliance of alliances," hundreds of thousands of farmers traveled and laid siege to the Indian capital of New Delhi. At one point there were over 100,000 sites of protest across India; on one day in November 2020, over 250 million people participated in a general strike in support of the farmers. They blocked roads and railways and set up encampments that would persist—sustained by collective values and practices rooted in Sikh faith, which "fed and clothed thousands of people daily and provided clean water, sanitation and even barber shops and tailors" for a year until the farmers' demands were met.[9] What has been referred to as the single largest protest in human history was not the product of a top-down call to action but emerged through decentralized organizing as dozens then hundreds and then thousands and then millions of people coalesced around a single set of demands.[10]

Many of us organizing in the 1990s and 2000s were inspired by similarly impactful large, decentralized movements in Central and South America, including the 1994 Zapatista Uprising, the *piquetero* movement in Argentina, and the landless workers' movements in Brazil.[11] More recently, decentralized but highly effective Chilean Uprisings, mobilizing hundreds of thousands into the streets, forcing a conversations about sexual violence and abortion, and ultimately, a constitutional convention, have captured imaginations.[12] While uniquely shaped by time, place, and conditions, what felt significant about each of these movements was the absence of the top-down strategies many of us were familiar with. All of them were decades in the making, rooted in relationships and small decentralized formations that coalesced into action, with profound impacts on larger systems of oppression and resilience to repression.

Decentralization is not only a quality to explore in our movements, it's also one to look for and practice in our organizations. Amanda Alexander describes *Emergent Strategy* as the "bible" of the Detroit Justice Center, a hub for legal advocacy and community building to transform Detroit into a "just city" that she founded soon after the book came out. Just a few months after the center's launch, Amanda led the staff of lawyers in an exercise inspired by *Emergent Strategy*:

> We were being pulled in all these directions, in ways that we could not have anticipated, toward abolitionist ends. The exercise that I put together at the staff meeting was based on the passage in *Emergent Strategy* about birds flocking. Instead of making a plan to migrate and mapping out their exact route, birds are very attuned to the six birds around them. They remain aligned as they respond to a call from destiny inside of them.

In other words, instead of following the traditional non-profit trajectory of creating a mission, a strategic plan, and expanding into a structure in which each person in the hierarchy is assigned to a very specific role to move toward the mission according to this plan, Amanda invited the staff to consider how they might better operate as a flock by understanding what each of them brought to the table, how the work they had already done together had changed them, and how their needs were shifting based on the ways they were stretching and changing. According to Amanda, the exercise

> did some beautiful work in helping us to synthesize really rapid change. It helped us to ask and understand: how can we move as a flock, or as a starling murmuration? This was important because things are going to shift all the time, in terms of how we are stretched, what we will be asked to do, what we are called to do, what's demanded of us, and what the moment presents. But what we can

stay attuned to is what we bring and how we're changing in our relationships with each other.

Staying connected through constant communication and alignment with shared values is important to working in a decentralized way. As the Detroit Justice Center grew and evolved, the challenge became how to avoid becoming siloed, and how to foster more connection, communication, and coordinated action rooted in shared values among teams operating independently. These potential pitfalls of decentralized organizing are critical to keep in mind, whether operating at an organizational or movement level, and require us to practice decentralization with a clear understanding and commitment to interdependence.

> We are living in a world in which everybody
> and everything is interdependent.
>
> —JAMES BALDWIN, NATIONAL PRESS CLUB SPEECH,
> DECEMBER 10, 1986

In order for complex decentralized systems to function well, they must be structured around interdependence: if one ant, bee, or slime mold cell starts to operate by its own rules or only in its self-interest, the collective benefits of operating as a complex system diminish. If every individual does it, the system collapses. In addition to constant communication and connection, recognition of interdependence provides necessary cohesion to decentralized organizing.

The same is true of abolitionist organizing. As Sage Crump put it, "The relationships necessary to create an abolition culture . . . [must] be interdependent. Abolition can't exist without a sense of connectedness." Ruth Wilson Gilmore describes this as "radical dependence," inviting "a sense or sensibility of how interpersonal abolition must be."[13]

In *The Future Is Disabled: Prophesies, Love Notes, and Mourning Songs*, Leah Lakshmi Piepzna-Samarasinha defines interdependence as the simple notion that "all people have needs, that none of us can get through the world solely on our own."[14] Leah highlights the centrality of *inter*dependence to disability justice frameworks—which are essential to abolitionist organizing.[15] She contrasts this with the disability rights movement's focus on "independence," a defining feature of neoliberalism.[16] Acknowledging our interdependence and learning to identify, express, and meet our needs in relationship to each other and our environment are a precondition to effective operation of decentralized abolitionist networks of collective care.[17] One of the simplest yet most critical examples of recognizing our interdependence involves COVID-19 pandemic precautions, including masking. Acting based on our interdependence would mean that wherever decentralized abolitionist networks gather—whether in meetings, at conferences and convenings, or in social gatherings—we prioritize precautions that protect all of us—including those at greater risk—over personal comfort or choices as a method of practicing emergent strategies and abolitionist politics.

As Leah points out, interdependence requires all of us to show up for each other: "Interdependence is not some superhero that's going to fly in and fix it. We—with all our unearthed care lineages, desires, boundaries, and care languages—are the very messy, beautiful, everyday care heroes who are building the new world."[18] Interdependence requires attention to what Leah calls "the nitty gritty of what it looks like to give and receive care," deploying a "diversity of care tactics."[19] What Leah describes as "care work" and "care mapping" operate at the fractal level of relationships and involve developing what fellow disability justice scholar Teukie Martin calls "care fluency" as both givers and receivers of care through emergent and iterative interactions.[20] Martin writes, "Every care interaction is an opportunity for deeper learning and understanding—we become more skilled and more confident in navigating our needs and the needs of others."[21]

Creating care webs—"networks of often unpaid people caring for each other through mutual aid and collective care"—once again implicates elements of emergent strategies: a focus on relationships, critical connections, networks, and communities of practice.[22] And, as we do so, like many others I spoke with, Leah emphasizes the need to keep an eye and intention on systemic change: "I also believe in the need to create societies where everyone has access to care that is safe and skilled, whether or not they have relationships or community. Community care offers a lot, and I've also witnessed mutual aid and disability justice organizers buckle under the strain. . . . Care can be that individual act to an individual person, but it's also about creating systems that benefit everyone."[23] Decentralized networks, made up of interdependent fractals, guided by abolitionist values and practices, are part of how we get there.

Abolition Is Adaptive and Intentional

Emergence to me, in some ways, is about surfing
the edge of change.

—ALTA STARR, "DECLARING THE SELF YOU WANT TO BE,"
THE EMERGENT STRATEGY PODCAST

Emergent strategies remind us that change is actually the
only constant.[1] The key is to recognize that change is already
happening, that we are already experiencing it, that it is more
exhausting to fight change than to move with it, and most
importantly, that we can shape it. No matter where we look,
the world around us is rapidly changing. We are truly at an
inflection point, in the midst of a massive shift, the collapse of
all things familiar, a sense of hopelessness and powerlessness in
the face of rapid change—these days, it seems for the most part
for the worst. Given these realities, our only hope is to lean into
the possibility of shaping change rather than resisting it and
clinging to what we know. We can meet change with intention
and with the knowledge that if something is not working, it
can change again, and if it is, we can continue to innovate and
experiment with it.[2]

This is something I find challenging. I am someone who
often jokes that I am a revolutionary who hates change, conflict, and getting up early in the morning—all of which seem

to be required to bring the world I long for into being. My relationship to mornings has shifted—I now like nothing more than to watch the sun rise, preferably over water. I am learning to understand and practice principled struggle and conflict as generative—of clarity, boundaries, of new ideas and paths forward. My relationship to change is shifting as I embrace both its inevitability and necessity and as emergent strategies teach me more about the possibilities of shaping it rather than just reacting to it.

I know I am not alone in discomfort with change; *Emergent Strategy* discusses how people experience change as crisis and respond with fear rather than meeting it with the knowledge that it is inevitable—and we are already doing it, and we can choose to do so in connection with each other, with intention toward our vision. Efforts to change the ways we meet our needs and generate safety particularly trigger our deepest fears. This is true even in the face of the fact that the systems we currently invest in and rely on cause untold harm and actually prevent us from experiencing genuine safety in our daily lives. Yet, in spite of ourselves, we cling to what we know. Current systems are the devil we are familiar with, the parameters we know how to operate in—even though they wreak devastation and deny safety. Kat Aaron points out that part of the challenge is "being able to sit with the truth of how profoundly our needs are currently unmet, how deeply unsafe we are—with the degrees of varying safety bestowed by varying privileges, and the collective unsafety created by the fact that all of our fates are bound up together." As a result, she says, "We not only live in fear of change but also fear of seeing the truth of the present." Emergent strategies offer a means of meeting these fears through connection and the felt experience of being held in communities and networks of support and by increasing our capacity for adaptation with the intent of shifting systems in favor of our collective safety and survival.

Adaptation is a core feature of complex systems. As Stephen Johnson explains in *Emergence*, "complexity without adaptation is like the intricate crystals formed by a snowflake:

it's a beautiful pattern, but it has no function."[3] According to #ComplexityExplained,

> Rather than just moving toward a steady state, complex systems are often active and responding to the environment—the difference between a ball that rolls to the bottom of a hill and stops and a bird that adapts to wind currents while flying.
>
> This adaptation can happen at multiple scales: cognitive, through learning and psychological development; social, via sharing information through social ties; or even evolutionary, through genetic variation and natural selection. When the components are damaged or removed, these systems are often able to adapt and recover their previous functionality, and sometimes they become even better than before. This can be achieved by robustness, the ability to withstand perturbations; resilience, the ability to go back to the original state after a large perturbation; or adaptation, the ability to change the system itself to remain functional and survive. Complex systems with these properties are known as complex adaptive systems.[4]

The principle of adaptation also teaches that the quicker you can let go of a viewpoint, the quicker you can shift to meet new conditions and become more supple and nimble in meeting your needs and those of others.[5] Contrary to planned strategies that incentivize and reward pursuing a plan from start to finish, even when it is clearly not working or conditions change, emergent strategies prioritize constant adaptation.

To build new futures under current conditions and those we are creating, we need to practice adaptation guided by abolitionist principles, in service of fundamental, deep, unprecedented, structural change. In other words, the adaptive practices at the core of emergent strategies—"move like starlings," "be like water"—may feel unrelated to the structural change I want to see but actually point toward the road to get there. Dismantling oppression requires us to let go of existing structures and find our way to new ones through adaptation. Adaptation alone is not the road to the worlds we are building, but it helps us navigate it.

One of the ways that *Emergent Strategy* explores the principle of adaptation is through the maxim "less prep, more presence." While intended as a counterbalance to the highly detailed and often inflexible approach of planned strategies and agendas that founder when conditions change, like "small is all," this principle has been taken out of context to mean that practicing emergent strategies require no preparation or intention whatsoever. As though we just show up and see what happens. Of course, this drives those of us who, like me, need or believe planning, structure, and some strategic options are necessary to responsibly address material conditions, wild. It also leaves behind people who need structure and advance notice to be able to fully show up—like parents who need to know how long they will need childcare or people who are planning around failing transportation infrastructure. Leah Lakshmi Piepzna-Samarasinha similarly points out that practicing disability justice and making spaces truly accessible requires a great deal of both preparation and adaptation.

Walidah Imarisha emphasizes that practicing adaptation doesn't mean that no planning is required; in fact, planning is essential to create conditions that make adaptation more possible. For instance, she points to the protagonist of the Octavia Butler *Parables* trilogy, Lauren Olamina, whose commitment to adaptation and change is often highlighted by emergent strategists. Lauren, Walidah reminds us, adapted with a clear intention and strategy for survival that led her to prepare for the conditions she saw coming, planning for as many eventualities as possible, and creating as many possibilities for herself and her family as she could by gathering and hiding knowledge and resources, memorizing maps, practicing skills, and building relationships.

Like any of the principles of emergent strategy, adaptation doesn't work in isolation. Walidah highlights that adaptation must be accompanied by intention for visionary change to materialize. In other words, the intention and practice of adaptation must be rooted in a politic—an understanding of the structures of the world, the spaces where we will contest for power, the material changes we want to see. This enables us "to find the flexibility in it without being liberal," as Walidah put it. Practicing emergent strategies toward abolition therefore requires us to engage in adaptation with intention guided by rigorous engagement with abolitionist values.[6]

To illustrate this idea, Walidah cites an example from the Black Panther Party, who adapted their work to meet the needs of the community but with intentions guided by commitment to a politic of Black liberation and self-determination. She describes how the community self-defense programs the Party was most known for at its inception adapted, iterated, and expanded, in the context of a larger revolutionary purpose, to meet the needs of the people they served, including the development of free breakfast, school, clinic, and community clean-up programs. Walidah describes one instance at a community meeting in New York City when Panthers proposed setting up an armed community patrol and community members said they also wanted the Panthers to clean up the trash because people were getting sick from the vermin running rampant through the projects. Similar feedback in Seattle led individual Panthers to get fumigation certifications and set up a program to meet community needs. Walidah points out that these adaptations were possible because the Party wasn't "beholden to some externally influenced five-year plan." Importantly, the adaptation was guided by an overarching vision: building relationships, networks of care, and practice of the world they were fighting for, along with a base that could muster the power to demand structural changes in public housing and sanitation. The revolutionary intention with which they adapted prevented the process from devolving into a community clean up or volunteer-service program.

Adaptation with intention also offers protection under adverse conditions. Walidah cites organizing among incarcerated people, who are constantly navigating changing and repressive conditions, as an example. She describes how incarcerated people she organizes with set up leadership structures that support emerging leaders by having two people play the same leadership role and at the same time create organizational resilience by ensuring that the structure can withstand a leader's transfer to another facility or to solitary confinement. Importantly, the intention of adaptation here is not acceptance of the conditions that require it but to build a network that is more effectively able to fight them.

Similarly, Adaku Utah emphasizes that the National Network of Abortion Funds continuously had to adapt through constant revision of protocols and practices, first in the wake of the 2016 election and again following the Supreme Court ruling in *Dobbs*.[7] They did so with the clear intention of ensuring abortion access for the greatest number of people—which was "made more possible by being in the nimbleness of so much change." As Adaku shared, "So much of this is about people figuring out a strategy that is decentralized and unique to space and place and the protocols that most align with conditions and contexts," even as the conditions and contexts are constantly changing.

Adaptation with intention is also essential to avoiding what Kelly Hayes and I discussed on an episode of *Movement Memos*: "normalization bias" or the very human tendency to normalize even the most devastating oppressive conditions.[8] Examples abound: our normalization of death on an incomprehensible scale since the inception of the COVID-19 pandemic—over 1 million dead in the US alone—and its impacts as an ongoing mass disabling event; our normalization of the violence of policing; of the accelerating march of fascism through white-supremacist, anti-trans, and reproductive violence; of endless war; of climate catastrophes. adrienne maree brown recently posted a meme about this phenomenon on her Instagram page, which, ironically, made fun of the fact that humans are so adaptable that it would take only three days in hell for someone to start making memes about it. I am often struck by how quickly something I experienced as devastating the day before—a war, a flood, a map of the places global capital has already consigned to climate catastrophe (if you haven't seen it,

I'm sure you can imagine it), or an inhuman instance of police violence—recedes from my consciousness, either because I have moved on to the next crisis or simply because I have had to adapt quickly to survive. Intention helps us recognize when the adaptation is leading us away from our values, visions, and politics or causing us to normalize conditions to avoid the discomfort of confronting them. Building abolitionist futures means we cannot allow ourselves to adapt to ever-increasing suffering, surveillance, deprivation, abandonment, policing, punishment. Instead, like the incarcerated leaders Walidah described, we must adapt to resist and transform our conditions.

Abolition Is Nonlinear And Iterative

Imagine a world without prisons, police, and borders. Then imagine what you can do to make that happen. Then try it. Repeat, repeat, repeat.

—MONICA TRINIDAD

As I said in the Introduction, I like a linear, step-by-step, ten-point plan that I can methodically work through until I get to the desired outcome, at which point I will move on to the next ten-point plan. For most of my life, this was how I understood change happens.

In 2016, I was invited to participate on a panel as part of the *Do Not Resist?* exhibit mounted by the For the People Artists Collective in Chicago, of which Monica is a founding member, to highlight the violence of policing. There, I shared my seven-point policy platform (not sure why there weren't ten points) to reduce police violence against Black women, girls, and trans people. Minneapolis-based artist and abolition-ist organizer Ricardo Levins Morales was also on the panel, sharing the MPD150 report, a historical review and evaluation of the Minneapolis Police Department over its 150 years of existence.[1] The report was not developed as part of a campaign but as a cultural strategy to shift thinking around policing by using an evaluation tool similar to one that would be used to evaluate any governmental department. The question they asked was simple: does the police department do what it says it does? The answer, of course, was no. The report concluded that the department was irredeemable and must be abolished. I remember being struck by both the innovativeness and the power of the report and its conclusions and by the absence of policy demands. I remember thinking, yes, this is amazing, but what are you all *doing* with it? What's *your* ten-point policy agenda?

Fast forward four years, and I had to say to myself, "See that powerful Uprising you are following and supporting in Minneapolis? That came in part out of the culture shift made possible by MPD150, along with other organizing efforts that prepared the soil and shifted culture in ways you couldn't understand, not out of any ten-point policy agenda you or anyone else advanced." It was the MPD150 report that we turned to at Interrupting Criminalization as we reached for messaging and resources to amplify and support what was happening on the ground in 2020 and to invite more people into conversations about policing, safety, and abolition, not my seven-point plan.

The thing about complex systems is that they are somewhat unpredictable, and change doesn't unfold in predictable, step-by-step ways. According to #ComplexityExplained, "complex systems are typically nonlinear, changing at different rates depending on their states and their environment."[2] They may remain relatively stable for long periods of time, even if perturbed—much like systems of policing in the US over centuries, despite periods of intensified uprising or protest. Conversely, if complex systems become unstable, they may experience significant disruptions as a result of relatively small disturbances. A tipping point may exist within a complex system where "small environmental changes can completely change the system behavior."[3] And chaotic systems are "extremely sensitive to small perturbations and unpredictable in the long run, showing the so-called *butterfly effect*," referring to the notion that tiny shifts—such as the movement in the air produced by a butterfly wing—can have tremendous impacts—like setting off a chain reaction that produces a typhoon thousands of miles away. Interestingly, shifts may result from present conditions but also from past history.[4]

In other words, change doesn't always happen the same way in complex systems, depending on conditions both within and outside the system—it may fluctuate between two poles, it may be cyclical, or it may be chaotic. *Emergent Strategy* points out that regardless of whether it actually *is* chaotic, acknowledging that change is nonlinear and often cyclical can certainly *feel* chaotic.

Understanding that we are operating within complex systems helps us to better see where our actions might have the greatest impact. Describing one of the gorgeous quilts she creates, Diana Nucera explained that it represented a digital surveillance system, and pointed to one patch that deviated from the overall pattern. She put it there to remind us that our task when seeking to shift complex systems is to find the anomalies and places where our actions can have greater impacts than we can imagine. Or, as Sage Crump put it, focusing on nonlinear change widens our fields of vision and helps us see that things are constantly evolving and harness patterns of change. From this perspective, the notion that systems are constantly changing in nonlinear ways offers "both a tether and a way forward." It's important to remember, as Sage emphasizes:

> It's not: "First we change how we are with ourselves, then each other, in our homes, on our block, in our communities." . . . These things are actually simultaneously being shifted and interacting with each other. . . . It's an invitation to think about them all happening at the same time.

Mariame Kaba makes a similar point, "I am not a progress narrative person—it's all happening at the same time, we are winning and being crushed at the same time. So the question is what's the next best thing you can do—not the next best seventeen." This is why she often reminds us we don't need to know where we are going or what's next in order to move toward abolitionist horizons, we just need to practice something different now, moving with the urgency of the moment and the patience of 1,000 years. In the *One Million Experiments Discussion Guide*, which invites us to imagine organizing on a 500-year clock, Mariame writes, "The temporality of organizing and the temporality of living should condition you to be humble because you don't know how what you're doing today will impact the future, or if it will impact the future."[5] While this may seem discouraging, for Mariame, the uncertainty of the future is a source of hope. "You never know what will happen," Mariame says. "Let go of your deep desire to want to control that. Focus on your next right step and the one after that."[6] As Diana says, "When we refuse inevitability, we gain multiplicity. That's what organizing is." For Tiffany Lenoi, a New York–based Harriet's Apothecary healer, visual artist, and educator, the fact that "abolition is nonlinear" is "why we're able to be changing the present while living in the future now."[7]

Iteration is one of the ways nonlinear change progresses, by repeating actions in a way that produce change with each cycle. Another way of describing the process is practice with adaptation. For the sailors like me out there, the way I understand being nonlinear and iterative is like tacking (zig-zagging) back and forth across the wind over and over as you move in the direction of your vision—you are both constantly repeating the move and constantly adjusting your course with the wind while holding the intention of your destination, and eventually, you get there. There are principles of physics that shape what you are doing (material conditions) and a multitude of ways to engage with the complex system you are operating within (wind, water, current, sails, individual weight, and strength) to steer the boat.

While not completely overlapping, the principle of iteration also resonates with the theory of dialectical materialism—the notion that society evolves based on identification and resolution of contradictions, which in turn produces new contradictions to be resolved through contestation. For instance, classical Marxism posits that under conditions where wealth is created by the interaction between land, labor, and capital, the opposition of interests between labor (whose interests lie in not being exploited) and capital (whose interests lie in exploitation) as the primary contradiction—meaning that is where the main fight is. Of course, it's more complicated than that when you factor in colonialism, imperialism, race, gender, sexuality, and ableism, to name just a few interlocking systems of oppression. In any event, once that contradiction is resolved (ideally through workers gaining power over the means of production), a new contradiction will emerge. Each cycle brings with it an evolution—theorize, practice, theorize, practice, repeat.

Sage explained to me that applying the emergent strategy principle of iteration is "not that different—you are in this idea that's not static; these things are in relationship to each other. They're not just an either/or. I find as a socialist that these things work hand in hand." shea concurs: "They're just different names for a process that's observable." She also ascribes (and contributed to) James and Grace Lee Boggs's theory that dialectical materialism has itself iterated into dialectical humanism—or the notion that individuals are dialectical units, and we have to identify and resolve contradictions within ourselves through the organization of our lives. In other words, "We have to transform ourselves to be more human in order to create a more human state. What *Emergent Strategy* does is help us think about who we need to become in order to resolve the contradictions in a way that will enable us to create something new. That's part of the dialectical. It's not just 'Change yourself and then change the world.' It's that in the process of struggle, you should change," shea expounds. In other words, as Mary Hooks says in the Mandate for Black people in this time, we need "to be willing to be transformed in the service of the work."

The principle that emergent strategies are iterative also teaches us that conditions are not fixed, and what we do in one moment shapes and opens up a multiplicity of possibilities available in the next. As Kat Aaron puts it,

> The thing I love about iteration is that it helps us to avoid becoming fixated on finding "the right" solution or

answer because it assumes and implies that right is only right for right now, and that right now is ephemeral. For me, that helps create space for close to, or aspirational, or better-than-current-conditions solutions—a grappling, a reaching, rather than a landing, an ending, a tying up in a bow. Bernice Johnson Reagon talks about "the ongoing-ness" of the work.

As our struggles unfold, conditions will continually change, requiring our approaches to constantly change as well. This allows us to release a search for perfection and increases the options available to us.

Shira Hassan describes abolition as an iterative process at its core—a call and response of shaping new worlds and ways of being. Walidah Imarisha describes this as a practice of "a constant re-examining and saying, 'Let's run this experiment again. What did we miss? Now we have new information. Does that change the outcome?'" That doesn't mean we release rigorous commitment to abolitionist principles or that we don't exercise care in the process. As the hosts of the *One Million Experiments* podcast point out, experimentation is a rigorous process: it requires that we be clear about our hypothesis and pay close attention to both conditions and outcomes.

The principle of nonlinearity and iteration also means that everything is part of our learning, growth, and change.[8] That requires seeing the gifts in failure and committing to learning from them—this is what underlies the *Emergent Strategy* maxim: "Never a failure, always a lesson." Yet many of us who are engaged in or supporting abolitionist organizing on the ground have experienced or observed a kind of immobilization with respect to practicing possibilities for new worlds that opened up in the wake of the Uprising. People are afraid to try new things—whether it's building non-police crisis response or other community-based safety strategies—for fear of failing in the face of the scope and vastness of the needs in communities ravaged by racial capitalism. Of course, it is important to experiment responsibly—we can't simply write off failures in abolitionist organizing and the people harmed by them as collateral damage. We need to give each experiment our best thinking and effort and do our best to prevent harm and to make amends and repair to those we fail as we learn.

But we cannot let the fear of failure or its consequences stop us from continuing to try, or we will never learn what is needed to create the world we want. It is important to remember that the current system is failing catastrophically, without any intention to learn, grow, adapt, improve, or even acknowledge failures or offer accountability to the vast numbers of people it is harming. We cannot be daunted by the prospect of failure; we are already living a failure of catastrophic proportions that threatens our very survival. Our failures as much as our successes will give us crucial information to shape the next iteration. The key is to enter into right relationship with the cycles of experimentation, failure, learning, and adaptation. This also means we can't hold on to experiments past their expiration date. As Shannon Perez-Darby puts it, we need to be able to commit to our experiments but also "hold loosely to their success." Iteration requires us also to be able to release experiments when they are no longer serving a purpose or have run their course. adrienne and Mariame both modeled this process by announcing that they will be sunsetting the Emergent Strategy Ideation Institute and Project Nia in 2023.

Lastly, understanding change as nonlinear and iterative means we need to learn to discern whether we are moving on a spiral where the loop is very tight, making the change with each iteration almost imperceptible unless we expand our view on a multigenerational scale to see it blossom into systemic change over time. And we need to recognize when we are just going in circles—in the ways that iterations of efforts to reform the police continue to lead back to the same place, because the purpose of policing is to do exactly what it does. We must heed the charge to "repeat, repeat, repeat"—paying attention to both the shifts our actions are producing over time and the retrenchment they may be enabling—while recognizing that ultimately, practice is what makes change possible.

Harm Free Zones

Harm Free Zones are one abolitionist experiment that has been iterating over the past two decades. I first met kai lumumba barrow, a Black feminist revolutionary and the main architect of the Harm Free Zone experiment, in 2005, after a raid at a Critical Resistance fundraising party in Brooklyn when I joined a team of lawyers working to defend the organizers against criminal charges and bring civil rights cases against the cops for brutalizing people in attendance. At the launch of Interrupting Criminalization's Creating Collective Ecosystems of Care Cohort in 2022, kai retold the story of how Harm Free Zones were born out of the struggle that followed the raid:

> At the same time, we were on the ground organizing to make police violence a citywide political issue. Our point of departure was to look at how can we shut down the precinct that had been tailing us, provoking us, and then moved on us. So, we formed a coalition of organizations and individuals. The goal was to make the Fort Greene–Clinton Hill area and Atlantic Avenue area harm free—free of police, intercommunal violence, free of harm. Our first goal was to shut down the 77th Precinct. We started organizing to do that but were not successful.
>
> This was in 2004, in post-9/11 Brooklyn. We were facing an escalated police force in Brooklyn that had

increased in power and equipment and numbers. It was
a very large charge to think that we were going to shut
down a precinct, even though that precinct had a long
history of violence in Black/Caribbean communities. We
realized how difficult that was in terms of the context and
in a period of fear in the city.

We went back to the drawing table and developed
a project rooted in exploring what an urban geography
looks like in terms of community wellness and mutual aid.

I remember kai sharing the Harm Free Zone model with a
group of us who were engaged in translocal organizing through
INCITE!'s 2005–2008 national campaign to end law enforcement violence against women and trans people of color. The
vision—similar to Rachel Herzing's Build the Block project and
the Oakland Power Projects—was that organizers would work
with existing community institutions, such as block or tenant
associations, identify the harms communities were experiencing—noise complaints, garbage, fights, domestic violence—and
build consensus within those communities not to call the cops
and instead to work to create community-based responses, with
the goal of rendering the cops irrelevant. kai describes the lessons gleaned from this experiment:

> We tried to meet with school board folks and commu-
> nity folks and neighborhood folks, and we got a lot of
> push back—there was no stable community that had a
> shared interest because of gentrification, because people
> were getting locked up and out of community, because
> people like us were transient. We were trying to move a
> community-driven project without having a root in com-
> munity. This was happening across the city—everywhere
> people were struggling to build that kind of community
> organizing.

The difficulty organizing communities disproportionately
impacted by incarceration, transience, and gentrification wasn't

unique to Harm Free Zones. As former Black Panther and member of the Black Liberation Army Assata Shakur asks, "How do you organize a community that does not exist?"[1]

There were several iterations of initiatives inspired by the Harm Free Zone model in New York City: Youth Ministries for Peace and Justice began a Harm Free Zone experiment in the Bronx; the Audre Lorde Project, an organizing center for lesbian, gay, trans, Two-Spirit and gender nonconforming people of color, inspired by the Harm Free Zone vision, launched the Safe Outside the System (SOS) initiative under Ejeris Dixon's leadership; and Sista II Sista, a group of young Black and Brown women in another Brooklyn neighborhood co-founded by Paula X. Rojas, later envisioned a Sistas Liberated Ground.[2]

SOS, which I was a member of for several years, worked with local business owners to interrupt and create safe spaces for people experiencing homophobic and transphobic violence, including by police; invited people to form neighborhood pods; and conducted regular trainings on violence prevention, de-escalation, calling for medical assistance in ways that would not lead cops to respond, hosting safe parties, and rights and realities during police encounters. Sistas Liberated Ground worked to create safe spaces for young women in Bushwick, training businesses, community organizations, and institutions on gender-based violence. These groups shared resources, strategies, lessons, and challenges through informal networks and relationships, through the INCITE! campaign, which served as a kind of network and community of practice between 2005 and 2008, and during a gathering hosted in 2010 by the Audre Lorde Project.

As kai moved around the country, she sowed seeds of practice leading to new iterations of Harm Free Zones in New Orleans, Berkeley, and Durham. She describes facing similar challenges rooted in community transience in Berkeley as in New York—and in her own practice. When we spoke about this book, she described how, in the early days of the pandemic, her world and that of her neighbors shrank to just her block: six houses. When kai first moved in, when people on the block were in what kai called "varying states of consciousness" due to drug use, one of the neighbors, who served as the "mayor of the block," would call the police. Applying Harm Free Zone principles, kai would suggest that instead they start by asking people if they needed water, food, or anything else. Eventually, kai said,

> We got it to the point where the neighbor stopped calling the police and we would actually go and care for the person who passed out on the block. Now mind you, I lived there for five years. It took about two and a half or three years to get there. Then I moved. A lot of what happens with activists is that we don't stay for the length of time it takes to shift practices over the long term. I don't know if the neighbors are calling the police again or if they're still giving water to people. How much can we actually impact people's day-to-day thinking if we're not in a day-to-day engagement? If we're trying to reconstruct our day-to-day experiences, then we have to make a commitment to stay in a community, build in that community. It's not just about initiating ideas, it's about a relationship.

Or, as Assata put it, "A lot of us are going to have to go back to block-to-block door-to-door people-to-people 'how you doin?' ways of organizing, and not just organizing 'the masses' but organizing human beings and learning from those human beings. Because we have a lot to learn."[3] In emergent strategy terms, we need to build critical connections and be willing to learn as we iterate in response to what we hear from people in community.

That doesn't mean everyone has to play the same role; in this instance, kai, who practices what she calls "radical nomadism" can serve as a pollinator or dandelion seed, bringing the idea of Harm Free Zones to the communities where she lives and organizes, while others can be the builders who practice them as they take root. For instance, when kai introduced the idea of Harm Free Zones in Durham, Spirit House, a Black feminist abolitionist organization, was already committed to building community and relationships to interrupt violence. The presence of a more secure and solid community created conditions in which a Harm Free Zone is better able to thrive. kai recounts, "In Durham we constructed strategies and models to interrupt violence. Sometimes we would go in and interrupt domestic violence happening in the home. The bigger and broader we got, the more expansive the need became." One instance of violence interruption during this time was documented by STOP.[4] In it, a survivor described the impact of this approach on her experience:

> That made it possible for me to feel like I could come into the space and say what I needed, which at that time really included not being someone who was perpetrating harm against him by engaging the power of the state, or by, you know, which, whether or not it would have benefited me in that moment, could only have had negative effects on him. And then I got to make a decision about like, what do I really need right now to do my work, to take care of my kids, to get through this day, to heal? You know?
>
> We need to trust people to be the experts on their own lives and to take them seriously and have faith in people to set the course for working from harm to transformation. I think that comes . . . best from people who are experiencing harm and have a vision for themselves about what they want. And to give people time to identify what that is and be willing to sit with the discomfort of not being able to rescue somebody in a, in a simple or quick way. I think that those values were ultimately the most healing for me.[5]

Writer, poet, and beloved Black feminist love evangelist Alexis Pauline Gumbs names the question of who makes up the "community" at the heart of Harm Free Zones as critical to their operation as successful fractals: is it geographical, relational, ideological? "We mean so many different things by our community. What's the zoning of a Harm Free Zone?" She answers her own question by saying, "Community exists on so many different levels. It's certainly a mixed zoning situation."

Alexis was part of the organizing that took place in Durham around the time of the Duke University lacrosse team's 2006 sexual assault of a young Black woman. The organizing led to the foundation of UBUNTU, an abolitionist coalition initiated by kai with the goal of generating strategies and actions to prevent, disrupt, transform, and heal sexual violence, which ultimately led to Spirit House's adoption of the Harm Free Zone framework.[6]

When Alexis and I spoke about emergent strategies and abolition, I shared a story I heard at a gathering of community accountability and transformative justice practitioners hosted by the Audre Lorde Project in 2010 that I have frequently shared as an example of abolition in practice. A member of Spirit House was called to someone's house because a survivor was being harmed. When she arrived, she saw the person who was doing the harm standing outside. Angry as she was at him, she went up to him, hugged him, told him she loved him but that what he was doing was making it impossible for her to remain in community with him. Then she went into the house to support the survivor in making a plan for safety while others stayed outside to continue the dialogue with the person who was doing harm. When I think of abolition in practice, this story is often what I think of.

Alexis told me moments like these were made possible by the community created by UBUNTU meetings held in people's houses, as a community of survivors, opening private spaces to do work that was "difficult and intimate, because our own healing was at stake and our vulnerability was where we were fighting," in a way that broke down the walls between public and private space. This is also what laid the groundwork for Spirit House's Harm Free Zone work. It "created a context where we could hold each other accountable in a different way than if we were just convened by one organization, in an institutional space." Alexis and I talked about how much more possibility this approach creates for prevention, interruption, and healing of violence. As survivors, we are much more likely to call someone we know than a stranger when we are being harmed. Violence does not happen outside the context of our relationships and communities—in other words, the zones we create in which to practice worlds free of harm.

Through Critical Resistance (where kai served as a national organizer) and INCITE! (where she was both a member and coordinator of the 2007 Sisterfire Tour), all of these projects were in conversation with each other and with groups around the world. kai points to the importance of Black feminist theory in offering guiding principles for shaping Harm Free Zones into what she calls "petit Maroon" communities. "This movement is very much rooted in Black feminist theory and practice, Black feminist praxis. Globally there are a bunch of us who are thinking around similar ideas and then practicing them in however those communities come together, whether it's neighborhood or community of identity."

Along with other members of the New York City Harm Free Zones Working Group, kai summarized her assessment and learnings of the evolution and iteration of Harm Free Zones over the past two decades in a document reproduced at the end of this chapter.[7] In the Spring of 2022, she reflected:

> The challenges haven't gone anywhere. Organizing toward community accountability requires us to get clear about who we are within the community, what is our accountability within that community, and does the community know that we are accountable to them. How is that dialogue happening, what are the shared values that you can all agree to? Like, if we want real safety, we agree not to call the police.
>
> We also need to ask ourselves, what are the points of entry, how do you sustain these communities, how do they expand, how far do they need to expand, are you needing to be transparent or opaque? There's a lot planning work that needs to happen in this age of surveillance

and this age of disruption, that doesn't call for paranoia but calls for clarity about your theories of change and how your communities are engaged in that knowledge . . . That's how you're going to construct accountability. Who is helping to develop the values because you're trying to shift, get up in people's heads in a consensual way, really engage our people with these ideas of what can we do beyond what is here? That's the challenge.

NYC HARM FREE ZONE WORKING GROUP

(The following document and principles of agreement were created by the NYC Harm Free Zone Working Group.[8])

The Harm Free Zone project aims to work with communities to encourage strategies and practices that reduce harm—without the use of police or prisons. The abolition of the PIC grounds the Harm Free Zone project. Because the PIC is not an isolated system, abolition is a broad strategy. It is not just about getting rid of buildings full of cages but also transforming relationships and transforming our own "cops in the head/cops in the heart" ethos. A PIC ethos dissolves complexity and functions in binaries: guilt vs. innocence, good vs. evil, pain vs. pleasure. It denies collective responsibility and favors rugged individualism. It is a system that takes away our power and our self-determination—our ability to resolve conflict and unease.

The Harm Free Zone project emphasizes community autonomy, independent and self-directing communities, as a necessary step toward abolition. Our focus is *within* communities of the oppressed, placing the oppressed at the center of our vision.

By communities of the oppressed we mean communities of shared daily living or history, shared identity or struggle, or of shared visions. As we affirm and seek to transform ourselves and our communities, we contend with communities that are often fragmented, dispersed, and individualistic. However, despite these obstacles, there are also numerous strengths. People have an investment in their communities. There is a sense of place, of belonging, support, companionship, shared strategies for survival, and not infrequently, a shared identity. Building on these strengths is where we begin.

Community Accountability

To establish a Harm Free Zone is a complex and long-term endeavor. Prior to encouraging people within our communities to deny the PIC, to embrace abolition and strive for community autonomy, we must first uncover or encourage **community accountability**. Community accountability is defined as the ability and desire of communities of the oppressed to adopt a "harm free" way of thinking and to construct processes and mechanisms that broadly address harm.

Community accountability demands certain conditions:

- Community investment—commitment to the past, present, and future of the community.
- Ongoing democratic dialogue—shared power and decision-making and an appreciation for difference within the community.
- Systemic analyses of oppression—evolving and inclusive critical analyses that does not place rank or hierarchy on oppression.
- Agreed-upon principles and practices— community-specific, integrating the history and cultures of its members.
- Clear boundaries and roles—stated and respected limitations, rotating positions of power.
- Vision and hope—desire for liberation, a belief that fundamental social change is possible.

The more autonomous the community becomes, the greater the degree to which these conditions will be fulfilled. The larger oppressive society inflicts constant, pervasive, and systemic harm on our communities without acknowledging itself as accountable. Therefore, in order to reduce harm within our communities, we must be accountable to ourselves.

A Harm Free Zone requires that communities of the oppressed adopt a harm free way of thinking—imagining ourselves outside of the limitations imposed by the state. We are challenged to struggle with our internalized oppression and envision ourselves and each other as people who have the ability and the responsibility to create, implement, and benefit from our own liberation.

Processes of Community Accountability

Once the conditions for community accountability are identified, we can initiate practices that directly address harm. These practices, defined here as processes of community accountability, describe the methods used to address harm as complex, fluid, and interconnected. These processes will take on different characteristics and present different challenges, depending upon the conditions. We have identified four processes:

- **Processes of prevention—the act of preventing harm within the community.** Prevention ensures that basic needs are met for all community members and that information is available and accessible for all.
- **Processes of intervention—the act of directly intervening when harm occurs.** Intervention values all community members and emphasizes active care and compassion.
- **Processes of reparation—the act of repairing harm among all community members.** Reparation analyzes the root causes of harm. It enhances individual and collective investment in the well-being of the community to secure healing, trust, forgiveness, and responsibility for all community members.
- **Processes of transformation—the act of completely transforming individual and collective power relationships.** Transformation honors and encourages individual and group imagination,

critical thought, communal reliance, self-determination, and democratic decision-making.

Just as these processes are not static, they are also non-sequential. They are linked with each other in such a way that separating one from the others changes its meaning and force. The spirit animating intervention and reparation is not punitive but healing; it both requires and creates vision and hope. Thus, there is an important reciprocal relationship between the processes through which a community is accountable and the conditions that make accountability possible.

We have seen numerous attempts to reduce "crime" in our communities where these critical steps are bypassed in favor of immediate "solutions." Community Policing or Neighborhood Watch programs may intervene and seek reparation for crime but neither prevent nor transform harm. These types of programs are generally state defined (or collaborate with the state) and do not present a discourse around systemic oppression or a critical analysis that seeks to understand the conditions in which many acts of harm take place. Nor are the long-range goals of community autonomy central to the goals of reducing crime. Inevitably, these models bolster and encourage the prison industrial complex.

Why Are Community Accountability and Interconnected Processes Necessary to the Development of a Harm Free Zone?

Take, for example, the act of intervention. When there is conflict or violence among community members, intervention would likely be rejected if there was no transparent accountability. A Harm Free Zone would be unrealizable unless the person inflicting harm (the "Actor") and the people involved in the process of intervention had an investment in the community, a systemic analysis of why harms occur, clear boundaries and roles to determine what constitutes harm and who has a right to intervene, agreed-upon principles and practices (including principles for handling harm) that govern the community and are borne from democratic dialogue, and vision and hope that the people within the community and the community itself can be fundamentally changed. Without these components, why would someone let other people "meddle" in their affairs? Why would someone put themselves in the hands of "outsiders"?

When a person harms other people, the processes of community accountability allow the Actor, the person harmed, and the community members to be taken seriously.

Recognizing that we are answerable to each other, the community must see the Actor as:

1. Inseparable from the community;
2. Affected by a historical and present-day reality of oppression that influences the beliefs, character, desires, sense of self, and relationships;
3. Not passive with respect to oppression. Capable of acting, desiring, believing differently, and thus capable of resisting oppression;
4. A mirror for and of the community;
5. Holding promise for the community.

Because the Actor is not a passive receptor of oppression, the Actor can be held accountable for the harmful act. The community can also hold itself accountable for its role in creating an alternative set of social practices, relations, and institutions.

The community's intervention stops the harm. It also enables the Actor to acknowledge the act as harmful, to take responsibility for the act in the face of oppressive conditions, to understand the relationship between the act and its oppressive social context, and to participate in the rebuilding of the community as an active member of the community.

After a harmful act, the person harmed must recognize the changes that have occurred and cannot simply recover without altering their perspective and conditions. The connection between intervention and reparation means that the person harmed must also be viewed by the community as a mirror for itself, inseparable from the community, as holding promise for the community, and as someone who can be made whole and placed in a healthier interpersonal and communal condition.

The work of repair is a communal process of change. In this sense, a transformation of the community accompanies a transformation of the Actor and a transformation of the person harmed. This is one of the most vivid forms of community education available and key to the prevention of additional harm.

All of these processes reaffirm and strengthen the community, which paves the way for a community to resolve its own conflict without prisons or police.

HFZ Principles of Agreement

Collective Action. When an individual is injured or threatened, it is a problem for the community, not just for the individual or individuals involved. We take collective responsibility for addressing problems that arise.

Examples: Commitment to collective responsibility; accountability and reciprocity; relationship building; checking in if someone is consistently missing from meetings/events; clarity about our expectations of each other.

Understanding Power. Transforming violence and conflict requires an understanding of power and how it shapes our lives. We are willing to challenge multiple oppressions on a broad scale, internally and externally.

Examples: Commitment to communicate about domination in the group (taking up space); willingness to educate ourselves about power and privilege; willingness to consider [and challenge?] our power and privilege in communities that we are not from.

Commitment to Prevention and Intervention. We are prepared to intervene in acts of state violence (such as law enforcement violence, evictions, medical neglect, etc.) and interpersonal conflicts (domestic violence, intra-racial violence, queer violence, etc.). We regularly work on developing the individuals' and the group's trust, conflict transformation skills, resistance to state power, and commitment to building community.

Examples: Coincides with the principle of collective action; active participation; commitment to staying in the room—even when conflict arises and things get difficult; commitment to being on the front lines—flexibility with our strategies.

Abolition. We share a political vision that seeks to reduce and eventually eliminate the need for prisons, policing, and surveillance by creating sustainable alternatives to punishment and imprisonment. We aim to live our vision for a better world.

Examples: Commitment to acting toward and addressing each other with less harm; not behaving in a punitive or isolating manner with one another; not watching each other for mistakes, errors—seeking to alienate one another.

How might these principles come into play in our work with each other?

Where do we agree/disagree/need more dialogue?

What concerns do we bring about these principles?

Freedom Square

The Freedom Square Occupation took place in Chicago, Illinois in 2016. This section is based on an interview with Damon Williams and Daniel Kisslinger and an episode on "Freedom Square" from the AirGo *podcast they co-host.*[1]

A different iteration of a harm free zone sprang up in Chicago a decade after that fateful raid on the Critical Resistance party. The Freedom Square Occupation in Chicago, which took place in 2016, represents another experiment in abolitionist organizing. Damon Williams, a cofounder of #LetUsBreathe, the Breathing Room, and Freedom Square, talked about the occupation on an episode of the *AirGo* podcast he co-hosts with Daniel Kisslinger. He described it as, "a forty-one-day live-in occupation across the street from the CPD [Chicago Police Department] torture facility and 'black site' known as Homan Square. We took an abandoned, gravelly, rock-filled, mud-filled lot and turned it into our little attempt at a utopian city that models the freedom we want to see in opposition to the violence and torture and carceral systems that dominate and diminish our lives."

Although the organizers hadn't read *Emergent Strategy*, Freedom Square was an experiment shaped by emergent strategies. But it didn't start out that way. Freedom Square started as a spot—near a police facility—where BYP100 organizers called for a protest during a national day of action. Organizers envisioned the square as a community space for protesters who chose not to be arrested, a place to chill for the afternoon, and for supporters to wait for people who did choose arrest to be released. The decision to create a space of joy, nourishment, and celebration as protesters were arrested and hopefully released was itself an iteration based on lessons learned from an action the previous year at the International Association of Chiefs of Police convention, where organizers found themselves isolated and surrounded by police as they were arrested over a forty-five-minute period.

As the afternoon of food and performances continued, organizers set up tents that represented what would exist in a world without police but were never intended to be used to practice that new world. As conversation following the protest wore into the evening, a group of neighborhood children asked if organizers were going to stay the night. While the organizers originally said they weren't and couldn't, one eventually agreed to, and then others followed. What emerged was a month-and-a-half-long experiment in building a community without police. Damon recalls,

> That wasn't a plan that we came in with, but we made space for adaptation. But it also made things really challenging, to be frank, to not have infrastructure set up to do this and to have to create the systems to sustain it while doing the work of sustaining it. That was a lesson learned: things can emerge, and there's still structure that can emerge. Adaptive doesn't mean always changing. It means building.

When being interviewed on site at Freedom Square, Damon described what emerged as follows:

> We are out here standing for love, fighting for freedom, and building community . . . What we are out here doing is challenging the radical imagination to envision a world

without police, to envision a world without prisons. So we know that there are a lot of things that need to be built, a lot of things that need to be done in order to make that a potential reality. So what we're out here doing is trying to model what system building looks like. Because we know that the "system," with the big air quotes, does not keep us safe and has been hurting us, and we've been talking about it for the last fifty years. We have to accept that we need to start to create the systems in order to get up under the one that has had a boot on our neck since its creation. So that's what we've been doing, we've been engaging the community and putting love into action and moving the political to the human.

Over forty-one days, organizers and community members cooked together, played together, organized the space together, learned together, lived together, and struggled together. They were supported by hundreds of people who brought food, supplies, came to offer programming or support, or simply dropped off cash.

I remember when Freedom Square began—I was at a Soros Justice Fellows conference with a bunch of other criminal justice policy advocates. Several of us talked about the action and occupation—and the absence of a fully formed plan, set of demands, or exit strategy that traditional organizing principles would deem essential. I was one of the many people who sent financial support, dropped off food maybe once, but didn't engage beyond that—because I was off building and advancing national policy agendas I thought would help create conditions that would make abolition possible, instead of participating in a live experiment in the city I was living in.

It's not that Freedom Square was unrelated to policy demands or that demands didn't emerge from that space. They just weren't at the center of what was happening. What *was* happening was an attempt to practice abolitionist principles—which *could* include making policy demands that would create more space to practice abolition and make material change in communities so that more people can practice. But policy demands were not the main driving force.

Damon and Daniel shared ways organizers adapted to changing conditions—including how they handled an influx of media attention that drained time and energy from organizers struggling to hold together an unplanned community, in which only a few people were able to maintain a twenty-four-hour presence. At one point, the group created a policy requiring anyone seeking an interview to contribute to the maintenance of the space in some way. Daniel points out that the policy was not only an adaptation but also reflected the principle of inter-dependence; journalists don't have a story without an interview, and people who want to share their work with the world need journalists. Recognition of this interdependence created space to negotiate a more equitable exchange and boundaries.

As Damon points out, even the demand to close down Homan Square was emergent.

> BYP100 was doing a national day of action . . . . It was an uprising moment . . . Locally, we were opposing a "Blue Lives Matter" ordinance . . . That was what our entry point was, and then largely trying to amplify a divest–invest platform, but it was still very much abstract.
>
> The first couple of days, as a point of engagement, we had all these barbecue grills, music playing. People would just walk up, and the question of "Why are you here?" would be a lot of the starting point. In response I would point to the building and ask, "Do you know what that is?" . . . Particularly people who were in walking distance, they were like, "I know exactly what that is. My cousin was in there. My uncle was in there. My brother was in there. I was in there." Time and time again. There was one day, it was a seventeen-year-old was like, "Yes, I was in there this summer." A guy who looked thirty-five, forty who was helping on the grill, was like, "Yes, I was in there when I was like seventeen."

At that point, Damon says, focusing conversation on the original BYP100 protest demand opposing an ordinance that would impose higher penalties on protesters, but might not have consequences for most people in the community, would have centered the organizers over the people who were directly impacted by the police facility that was the site of the protest. So, the Freedom Square demand became to close Homan Square and invest in the North Lawndale community around it. The organizers made this demand despite the fact that, in Damon's words,

> We didn't have the capacity to do a five-year campaign that demands this thing gets done, and then we win, and blah, blah, blah. But we decided we're going to say it anyway. We are going to amplify it. We are going to talk to the community about it . . . we are going to talk to as many people as we can to make this a thing that people still talk about. It wasn't until this year, during the defund movement, which also was an emergent moment, that Alderman Rosa proposed closing Homan Square and reinvestment into North Lawndale, which was the Freedom Square platform. It was really full circle.

Freedom Square was in many ways an iteration of earlier protests and looked to prior events for lessons and mistakes to avoid. The forty-one-day encampment was an iteration of a fifty-four day encampment on West Florissant, near where Mike Brown was killed, organized by Ferguson group Lost Voices, who were joined there by members of the #LetUsBreathe collective Damon co-founded. In 2016, members of Lost Voices were going to be in Chicago over the same weekend the action at Homan Square was happening, and a cookout was planned—which ended up taking place at Freedom Square. Two members of Lost Voices never left, and one spoke on *AirGo* about how their experience of organizing one occupation informed their involvement in this one. He then described Freedom Square as "a stepping stone to getting a bigger square and putting freedom inside of that and then building that square out to the highest extent we can." In other words, a fractal.

The shape of Freedom Square adapted and iterated throughout the summer. In 2016 the State of Illinois failed to pass a budget, leaving neighborhood youth without summer school or summer programs. Damon described the resulting deprivation the children were experiencing as one of the greatest forms of violence in the community that summer. By the second week, organizers realized Freedom Square had essentially become an overnight summer camp. So they committed to keep it up and running through Labor Day, until the first day of school. "It was not our intention to have this abolitionist summer camp. I've said many times: we couldn't have done it if we wanted to plan it, and I don't think we would have," Damon laughs.

The absence of a plan wasn't without consequences: maintaining a forty-one-day occupation with little infrastructure and growing expectations around meeting the needs of a community deep in the throes of organized abandonment took a deep toll on organizers, frayed relationships, and led to circumstances and harms the organizers didn't have the capacity to prevent or respond to. In this way, the occupation differed from the Harm Free Zone model, where community members come together in advance to develop infrastructure and practices for when conflict, violence, and harm occur. At Freedom Square, responses were emergent, with varying degrees of success depending on the skills and experience of the people holding the space at any given time. In other words, more prep in addition to presence and adaptation would have been helpful.

The Freedom Square experience further iterated to inform the structures of the #LetUsBreathe collective, which take a more circular, nonlinear approach to organizing and power, allowing cooperative work to emerge, and promoting interdependence. Daniel talked about the kind of organizing that makes the emergence of Freedom Square and projects like it possible:

Rather than moving toward a goal, you can move based on principle. You say, "I don't know exactly what this will look like, but I know that all the decisions, or as many as possible of the decisions in the meantime, can be guided by the set of community agreed-upon values, and that whatever that leads to, we'll know the values that got us there."

That's a lot easier for people to—not easier, but it's a more tangible thing for people to understand that than: "Describe this future to me." So, describe how we do things now.

In other words, emergent strategies aren't the plan or strategy but can lead to one and guide the practices that bring us there. Daniel continued,

The other thing, I think for many of those policy people, and just in our general sense of imagination, we're so product focused. That's that capitalist logic of, "What am I buying? What am I signing up for? What am I subscribing to?" That's a product, not a process. It's going to be really hard for people to accept something that isn't a finished product.

But that's not one of our principles, to say, "Oh, no, we got it all figured out. Everything's going to be fine." We can't do that same dance. What we can say is, "Here's what we believe. Here are the examples. Here's the lineage we're in. Here's how we're trying to move." It makes room for the principles rather than the product.

Damon describes finding out about emergent strategies a year after the occupation, at a conference at the Boggs Center. Later. He later read *Emergent Strategy* and thought, "Oh, this is describing what we are doing and can help us be grounded in that intention. In many ways, *Emergent* Strategy is a literary example of what we were talking about embodying. I think a lot of that comes from the fact that a lot of our philosophy is built out of the tradition of James and Grace Lee Boggs . . . like we come from the same root, and why it connected so perfectly."

Damon now describes Freedom Square as a fractal, an attempt at a small level to build practices and systems that could be reflected at a larger level. But, he cautions, we have to resist the urge to say, "OK, now the plan is everybody replicate spaces like Freedom Square everywhere to practice abolition." That wasn't even the #FreedomSquare organizers' plan—it was more emergent than that. The key is to be adaptable enough to seize on opportunities and portals to practice abolition where they appear.

Abolition Is Cooperative and Focused on Collective Sustainability

The Complex Movements collective iconography includes two emblems that don't find an exact counterpart among the *Emergent Strategy* principles. One features an ant, symbolizing cooperative and collectively sustainable organizing. The other is "wave-particle duality," which is discussed in a later chapter.

Cooperatives and solidarity economies represent an important aspect of emergent strategies in action toward abolition. As discussed in the "Abolition Is Fractal" chapter, while we can take individualized and collective action to prevent and interrupt harm without policing, ensuring people's material needs are met is an essential part of the process. Cooperatives and solidarity economies represent critical ways to do so that prefigure new economic relations based on fostering collective sustainability and disrupting economic systems that produce and require policing.

According to Steven Johnson's *Emergence*, "The intelligence of ant colonies may be the . . . most compelling argument for the power of the collective."[1] Ants form complex, decentralized societies that "are capable of remarkably coordinated feats," making them one of the most successful species on the planet.[2] Importantly, ants do not, as commonly believed, operate on orders from a "queen."[3] Individual ants play specific roles, interacting in multiple ways guided by relatively simple rules. Like slime mold, they communicate and coordinate by adjusting the levels of chemicals they release.⁴ In combination, their actions shape patterns one level above individuals, at the scale of the colony—enabling them to collectively locate food and dispose of their dead and debris in an organized fashion that prioritizes collective well-being. While individually limited in skills and cognitive capacity, "they are able to collectively engage in nuanced and improvisational problem solving."⁵ As a result, "ant species have a massive environmental impact, moving immense amounts of soil and distributing nutrients even in the most hostile environments."⁶

In *Undrowned: Black Feminist Lessons from Marine Mammals*, Alexis Pauline Gumbs also invites us to learn from collectives, focusing on flocks and schools of dolphins and rays. She describes schools as collaborative "organizational structures for learning, nurturance, and survival," and calls us all "back to school."⁷ She asks us to consider what it means to function as a group in a changing environment, "when where you live becomes inhospitable to your living."⁸ She invites us to intentionally organize ourselves cooperatively "to combat the embedded isolation of late capitalism," to "trade the image of 'family' for the practice of school, a unit of care where we are learning and relearning how to honor each other, how to go deep, how to take turns, and how to find nourishing light again and again."⁹

Just as Alexis reminds us in *Undrowned* of how Ida B. Wells called the Black residents of Memphis to collectively flee white terror, cooperatively ensuring collective survival, Dr. Jessica Gordon Nembhard, an expert on cooperatives and solidarity economies, describes the essential role of ecosystems of collective sustainability in Black communities. Both before and after the end of legalized chattel slavery, the Underground Railroad, social clubs, benevolent societies, barter, gifting, mutual aid, and buying each other's freedom were practices of cooperative economics. Later, Black farmers and workers excluded from both labor and government protections also formed their own cooperatives and credit unions.¹⁰

In an episode of the *Solidarity Is This* podcast, Deepa Iyer describes solidarity economies as those which prioritize people and the planet over profit and growth, in which our needs are met without or harm or exploitation of people or planet. "Solidarity economies are bound together by core values such as participation, cooperation, community ownership, respect for the Earth, and reciprocity," Deepa emphasizes. Importantly, as Julia Ho of the New Economy Coalition points out, solidarity economies are intended to be adaptable to crisis, to provide a space for people to survive, and to rebuild the way that we want society to look. According to the Solidarity Economy Principles website:

> Common solidarity economy (SE) tools on Turtle Island often include: Low-income credit unions, housing cooperatives, community land trusts, food and consumer cooperatives, community supported agriculture (CSA) programs, worker and producer cooperatives, fair trade networks, community gardens, susus, buying clubs, barter networks, timebanks, and even complementary currencies and open source software.
>
> Movement-building strategies and practices used by SE organizers include solidarity supply chain creation, anchor institution strategies, joint marketing or certification initiatives, peer-to-peer technical assistance and knowledge sharing, educational projects, democratic and cooperative financing, policy campaigns, and forums, assemblies, and participatory budgeting spaces to build vision and strategy together for SE development. Many of these elements working together can create powerful solidarity economy systems.[11]

In some cases, cooperative formations perform more than one of these functions. For instance, Queer the Land (QTL) is "a collaborative project grounded in the self-determination of queer, transgender, and Two-Spirit Black/Indigenous/people of color (QT2BIPOC) and the vision of collectively owning our land and labor." Founded in 2016 by two Seattle-based

QT2BIPOC community-based organizations, QTL is "working to establish a cooperative network anchored by a community center and transitional and semi-permanent housing that meets the needs of working-class QT2BIPOC in the greater Seattle area. Our mission is to create a movement-building space that can generate income and become a political hub for QT2BIPOC and our community organizing." The membership-based organization acquired a twelve-bedroom house that can serve as a home to aging organizers or queer and trans youth experiencing homelessness or returning from incarceration, as well as a space for income generation and mobilization. Members are able to access funds to support housing and leadership and can participate in self-defense classes or gather quarterly to plan for emergency preparedness. Non-members are also able to access resources depending on availability.[12]

QTL cofounder Kalayo Pestaño told me that emergent strategies played a pivotal role in how the cooperative was founded and has evolved. Kalayo began attending the Allied Media Conference around the same time I did, where they were introduced to ideas about visionary and prefigurative organizing by Grace Lee Boggs and the zine that became *Emergent Strategy*. Once they returned home, conversations over food with fellow queer and trans organizers surfaced shared experiences of scarcity and absence of care. Together, they decided to collectively gather resources that would make it possible to build collective sustainability through a shared space and practice. We were "really envisioning both place and work that we could grow old doing and be cared for in, and a very deep sense of interdependence," Kalayo says. Practicing emergent strategies made it possible to enter and move through conversations that generated big abolitionist visions of creating and living otherwise, and to try different approaches aligned with a core set of principles that brought the vision to life in a nonlinear way over time. While they are now entering a more formal planning process to shape the next phase of their work, Kalayo credits emergent strategies with providing important signposts and methodologies to move from identifying a need to dreaming a structure to fill it that can serve as a fractal for shaping a world where Black and Brown queer and trans people can thrive.

As is the case with practicing new ways of preventing, inter-rupting, and healing from violence, the formations that make up solidarity economies are shaped by unique relationships and conditions. They are rooted in interdependence, and practice experimentation and adaptation guided by shared values. For solidarity economies to maximize their transformative poten-tial, these formations must be connected through networks, communities of practice, coalitions, and federations. For exam-ple, the US Federation of Worker Cooperatives is a network of cooperatives that creates communities of practice through which members share resources, lessons, and support.[13]

Cooperatives and cooperative movements have served as engines of system transformation globally—including in the context of the Argentinian *piquetero* movement and the Brazilian Landless People's Movement referenced in earlier sec-tions. My beloved comrade and Interrupting Criminalization coworker Maria Thomas, who coordinates the Beyond Do No Harm Network at Interrupting Criminalization, writes about the power of decentralized cooperatives in one of her homes of Kerala, India.[14] She highlights the fact that 4.5 million of the 17 million women living in Kerala are members of a statewide cooperative movement, Kudumbashree, that was sparked and supported by elected communist governments. Decentralized economic production at this scale has had significant systemic impacts, both in times of relative calm and times of crisis. Maria writes, "When the pandemic hit, with just a light touch everything was able to hum into action, and they were able to mass-produce masks, meals, and everything else that was needed to take care of the population. Strong trade unions took the initiative to build handwashing stations next to bus stops without waiting for any government directive." The coopera-tives provided decentralized social and economic infrastructures that aided pandemic response on a massive scale, as they served as vehicles through which to distribute loans, food, and aid. And, in contrast to mutual aid efforts in the US that emerged from organized abandonment, those in Kerala were supported by a state that created conditions for them to thrive.[15]

Drawing lessons from cooperative societies of ants and bees and embodying emergent strategy principles of fractal formations and decentralized power, solidarity economies enable us to practice a world beyond racial capitalism, experimenting with new economic structures and relationships in which we collectively control the means of production in service of sustainability. As Julia Ho put it, "Essentially, the solidarity economy movement is an invitation for people to practice liberation now. We don't have to wait until everything is perfect in the world. We can start to plant those seeds now, and this is the time to do it."[16]

Abolition Builds Resilience and Fosters Transformation

Complexity science teaches that resilience and transformation are nurtured through critical connections, adaptation to environmental conditions, and iteration, often operating in relationship.[1] As defined by beloved friend and teacher Alta Starr, resilience is moving toward that which affirms life. Sage elaborates that resilience is "how we are able to identify and build more places, build things that give us life." While individual practices of resilience are necessary, Sage emphasizes the importance of the collective cultural aspect to growing resilience, which includes building capacity to expand our imaginations.

Emergent Strategy posits that "one core practice of resilience is transformative justice, transforming the conditions that made injustice possible."[2] According to adrienne, "Transformative justice, in the context of emergent strategy, asks us to consider how to transform toxic energy, hurt, legitimate pain, and conflict into solutions. To get under the wrong, to find a way to coexist, be energy moving toward life, together."[3] In other words, the goal is not to celebrate or build resilience through adaptation to deteriorating conditions—normalization bias—but to nurture resilience through "positive adaptation"—transforming the world around us to reduce and eliminate the conditions that produce harm.[4] True resilience requires transformation of conditions, not simply adapting to conditions as they move from bad to worse.

Transformative justice is a central pillar of PIC abolition. In an article on anti-carceral feminism, Creative Interventions founder Mimi Kim defined transformative justice as "a flexible set of politics and practices committed to collective and community-based mobilization, nonpunitive practices of accountability, and a theory and practice of violence prevention and intervention that addresses the context of historic and systemic oppression."[5] In other words, instead of delegating power and resources to police to respond to violence after the fact while reinforcing existing structures of power and consuming resources that would support prevention, we focus on creating conditions under which violence is reduced and ample resources are available for healing. Transformative justice requires us to imagine and practice responses to conflict, harm, and need that don't replicate policing, punishment, and exile, while simultaneously holding boundaries around harm and inviting accountability and transformation.

As a longtime transformative justice practitioner, Mimi beautifully describes how emergent strategies nourish the process:

> The feminist wisdom of emergent strategies urges a slowness but not a hesitation—a reflection on what feels connected and right rather than a reaction to what is going wrong. For those of us who have participated in collective processes to intervene in violence, we know that there is a balancing of reflection, compassion, trust, and action that can move human beings in conflict forward toward connection or spin them further into despair. It is true that this balance feels more like nature than the mechanics of machinery. The logic of fractals suggests that it is this wisdom found in the microworld of human connection in response to harm and violence that can be expanded into the wider world of organizations and efforts to scale up. It may be that finding this rhythm and moving our collective footsteps forward will keep resonating and persisting even as containers fall away.[6]

Mimi adds that a focus on "small interactions tie emergent strategy to transformative justice as an orientation to conflict, relationships, and community."[7] As a result, "transformative justice remains locally driven, anti-state, and anti-institutional; therein lies its strength—and its possible limitations."[8] As Mia Herndon put it in emergent strategy terms, "Transformative justice asks us to recognize our interdependence, the ways we impact each other, and to practice adaptivity and constant learning."

The fractal and foundational process of pod mapping, popularized by Mia Mingus during her time with the Bay Area Transformative Justice Collective, invites mapping the relationships and connections we can rely on to interrupt and transform harm. It is one way of charting the fractal "microworld of human connection." More recently, Mia founded SOIL, an initiative focused on creating the conditions for transformative justice to thrive through political education, skills building, formation, development, and strategic partnerships. Mia explains SOIL as a metaphor:

> SOIL was the concept because what I saw happening, again and again, was even skilled TJ [Transformative Justice] practitioners were doing interventions or processes and they were being dropped into communities that were either barren in terms of resources or understanding or toxic and hostile. Even for the best TJ practitioners, it can set up an intervention or a process for failure or just to be unsuccessful. They may be able to achieve a couple of goals, but it would be so much different if we had better soil.
>
> The concept of SOIL, the organization is, really: how do we build the soil for transformative justice, and how do we do that in a way that sets TJ up so that it can actually be practiced? We have to stop planting plants in barren or toxic soil, period, and expecting huge harvests and a healthy plant. We have to stop expecting interventions where everybody is healed, there's full accountability, and

it's all wonderful when we are starting with nothing. Any farmer or gardener worth their salt will tell you, you need to take the time to build up your soil. Building soil could take years before you even plant your first seed.

Of course, that doesn't mean we just wait for it to happen. Practice is part of the process of building soil—or, as Mia puts it, "planting plants is also part of how you can grow and build the soil . . . . the roots help to feed the soil and create conditions for the mycelium." She, too, points to the importance of mycelial connections. "One of the properties of mycelia is that it dissolves organic material found in soil—including some toxins—into nutrients. So building mycelial networks is part of building the soil for transformation," she says.

Through SOIL, Mia is creating richer conditions for transformative justice work by offering basic skill-building and political-education workshops around the basics of transformative justice for large groups. Individuals are recruited to the program through a group or organization as well as directly through the community. A much smaller group of fifteen to twenty-seven who are open to greater involvement will go on to participate in intensive, multi-year workshops offering skills to facilitate transformative justice processes. In the SOIL metaphor, these individuals represent plants. The hope is that they will remain connected through a mycelial network through which they can continue to share skills, strategies, and support. SOIL also supports an existing mycelial network of abolitionist parents looking for ways to interrupt cycles of harm, discipline, and punishment, and to explore how to build cycles of joy, healing, accountability, and transformation instead. Operating at a fractal level above individuals as families, parents from across the country connect and support each other in parenting that is rooted in accountability and transformation when harm occurs, whether it's intervening in a generative way in fights between siblings, physical harm to children, or child sexual abuse.

Mia describes this process of training and practice as a drill. "We are building the soil now in these trainings so that when that rupture happens, when that house catches on fire, we have done fire drills, we know where the hose is, we know how to get the fire out quicker than if the fire happened and we had no idea what to do," she said. "I mean, I'm sure we could eventually put the fire out, but the amount of damage that it would have done would be much more devastating." Thinking of SOIL as a fractal leads Mia to ask, "How can I help to seed transformative justice in as many places as possible? Because that all helps the other collective abolition work that's happening."

It's important to emphasize, as the SOIL program demonstrates, that it's not enough to watch one webinar or read one book to be skilled enough in transformative justice to lead a healing circle or accountability process. It requires years of training, engagement in communities of practice, and learning through experimentation. And you don't have to be an expert to start practicing transformative justice in small ways, to begin to build your skills to practice and foster transformative justice on a larger scale in your life and community.

Just Practice Collaborative (JPC) is a Chicago-based formation that has been tilling the soil for transformative justice through a community of practice since 2015. Cofounded by Rachel Caïdor, Shira Hassan, Ana Mercado, Deana Lewis, Mariame Kaba, and Keisa Reynolds, JPC is a training and mentoring group focused on sustaining a community of practitioners who can provide community-based accountability and support structures for all parties involved with incidents and patterns of sexual, domestic, relationship, and intimate partner violence. Serving as a resource and a model for people who want to address violence without reliance on the criminal legal system and traditional social services, JPC's goals are to build our communities' capacity to effectively and empathically respond to intimate partner violence and sexual assault without relying on police or other state-based systems. JPC has trained thousands of people from around the world and provide resources and structures of support for facilitators of restorative and transformative processes. They also created a "Transformative Justice Mixtape" for the general public and developed a workbook titled *Fumbling Toward Repair: A Workbook for Community Accountability Practitioners.*[9]

For people looking to learn more about and practice transformative justice at the fractal level, Mimi Kim, Shira Hassan, Mariame Kaba, Shannon Perez-Darby, Hyejin Shim, and a host of others have created a plethora of tools, many of which can be found at transformharm.org. Through the Build Your Abolitionist Toolbox Series, Interrupting Criminalization and Project Nia have hosted trainings and practice labs and created multiple videos, workbooks, and curricula focused on building skills and capacity so that more people can engage with and practice transformative justice responsibly and skillfully.[10]

Beyond building skills and communities of transformative justice practice, abolition requires that we continuously exercise creativity, consistently work to evict the cops in our heads and hearts, and use our imaginations to generate new possibilities under changing conditions for worlds without policing. Visionary fiction, described in greater detail in the Introduction and in Walidah's essay, "To Build a Future Without Police and Prisons, We Have to Imagine It First," offers one way of imagining different ways to address violence and harm—and testing whether cops' colonization of our imaginations keeps us recreating new structures and practices of policing in different forms.

The following two visionary fiction stories from the Wakanda Dream Lab anthology *Black Freedom Beyond Borders: Memories of Abolition Day* explore structures to address violence and conflict in a world where prisons no longer exist.[11] The first, Shawn Taylor's "Tending the Acre," imagines one way people who have done harm could be invited into accountability and transformation in relationship with the people they have harmed. "Albina Zone" by Lisa Bates explores the pitfalls of institutionalized transformative justice.

As you read each of these pieces, ask yourself:

- *Are these responses truly transformative?*
- *Do they shift the conditions that make violence possible?*

- *Are they fully aligned with abolitionist politics and practices?*
- *Are they an iteration toward abolitionist horizon or a testament to the continuing hold that policing and punishment have on our imaginations?*

Tending the Acre
by Shawn Taylor

Former prisoner V12874, now back to being Marquise Hanks, choked down the vomit that threatened to launch out of him. He hadn't been on, or in, anything that moved for seventeen years, four months—damn the minutes and seconds. The nausea was so strong it was hard to think. Before prison, he never got carsick. He loved driving more than anything. He loved cars more than anything, aside from his (former) girl. A whole lot had changed since his incarceration.

Marquise still couldn't get over the fact that Abolition Day was real. He couldn't believe that all 123,000 inmates of the California Department of Corrections and Rehabilitation were just let go. San Quentin was the last to close and release. The warden fought and fought, using every legal technicality at her disposal, but ultimately, she had to give up. The tide was too big and too powerful. Prison abolition was no longer a thought experiment of over-eager activists. It was real. It was happening. Hell, it happened.

He thought about this as the bus bumped and swayed down the 101. They were going to Oakland, why in the hell didn't they just take the Richmond Bridge? The driver was talking about taking the "scenic route" and chose to go over the Golden Gate and all the way through San Francisco instead. Marquise tried to focus on being outside, beyond the walls of San Quentin, but his stomach wouldn't let him. He tried to turn on his tablet, but its power was drained. His tablet was in pristine condition. Most of the other inmates—former inmates—their tablets were nicked or scratched, cracked screens and discolored housings. Not his. The tablet, and what was on it, was the only thing that gave him hope the last sixteen months of his bid. He clutched the tablet to his chest and laid his head against the cool glass of the bus's window and drifted off—hopefully he wouldn't vomit in his sleep.

Marquise felt himself being shaken and bolted awake. He started swinging. In a handful of seconds his arms were trapped against his body, and his body was trapped against the bus seat. He'd never felt anything so strong before.

"Easy, bruh," he heard a man say. "You don't have to do that here. I get it, but you're safe. Take a few breaths. I'm Lonnie, bruh. Welcome home."

Taking several huge breaths, Marquise cleared his head and saw the enormous mountain of a man Lonnie was. Well over his own 6' 2", neck damn near as thick as his arms but with a childlike smile that was as inviting as it was unnerving.

"My bad. I'm Marquise. Sorry. I still got them prison reflexes."

"Don't ever lose those, family. Just know where and when to use them. Might come in handy at some point. I know who you are. We were worried when you didn't check in. We thought something happened. But here you were, sleep, and they just left your ass on here. Let's go. Now. Carmelita is the last person you want to be late on."

Lonnie led Marquise off the bus and onto the campus of the Yuri Kochiyama Receiving Center. He hesitated, tears welling in his eyes. He dropped to his knees as the sobs racked his body. Lonnie gave him the space to adjust, but then gently placed his gigantic hand on Marquise's shoulders. "Bruh, let's go. Carmelita will get in both our asses. There's time to deal with the energy later. You about to go through . . . a whole ass process, bruh."

The Yuri Kochiyama Receiving Center (or YURKO Campus, as the employees called it) sat on the northeastern side of Lake Merritt, overlooking the lake, a newly renovated bird sanctuary connected to one of the most diverse botanical gardens in Northern California. Marquise had never been in a place that was so beautiful or so clean. Before he went away, the lake and its surroundings were filthy as hell. Now? It looked like some kind of sterile resort.

"Lots of things have changed, haven't they, Marquise?" The voice, accented but Marquise had no idea from where, calmed him. He turned around to see a woman in her—well, she was Black so she could be anywhere from thirty-five to sixty years old. She was nearly as tall as him. She carried herself with the ease of someone who knew how their body worked and was in perfect concert with it.

"Damn. They grow y'all big out here." Marquise couldn't help but stare.

"I'm Carmelita. I don't have all day to mess with your late behind, come on. I will give you a little slack. The first sleep of a free man is nothing to discount. But we have a lot of work to do. Please give your tablet to Lonnie."

Lonnie held out his hand, but Marquise hesitated. This thing and what was on it had kept him whole. It saved his mind, his heart.

"Bruh. I'm just going to charge it and put some more on it. You'll have it back by the time you two are done. Nothing to fear here. We got you." Lonnie held out his hand and waited. He then snapped his fingers, "Bruh."

Reluctantly, Marquise handed the tablet to him.

"Thank you. Carmelita? Do something with this boy."

Carmelita's laugh was musical. "You want me to start talking about your first day here? How about your first week? Get your big ass out of here, and let me get to work."

They shared a long hug and Lonnie went about his business.

"Inside or outside?" Carmelita asked. "Some returnees don't like being confined by walls, and some aren't used to suddenly being in wide-open spaces and want the security of walls and a roof. Which do you prefer?"

"Outside, please." Marquise felt like a little kid as he followed Carmelita into the botanical garden and into a clearing. There were two chairs, a table with fruit and water, and another table with a headset on it.

Carmelita sat down in a chair that had some kind of controls on the armrests. She motioned for him to sit across from her. She poured a glass of water for him and gave him a handful of grapes. Her fingers flitted across the buttons in her armrests.

"I'm recording this," she informed him. "Video and audio . . . and a few other things. Now, tell me why you got locked up."

This shook Marquise. Here he was, chilling, getting used to it all, and she went and messed all that up.

"Not sure why you're so hesitant. You did the crime. It wasn't an accident. You did it. Now tell me about it." Her voice was firmer than it had been.

He told the tale, getting into more details when she asked. He had killed a man—Juan Sanchez—over some money. Over some money owed for drugs. Shot him twice. Once in the chest and once in the face. He wanted to throw up. He felt sweaty and dizzy.

Carmelita changed the tone of her voice. Compassionate. Loving. "How do you feel about what you did?" He stuffed his mouth full of grapes, stalling. She smiled. She'd seen it dozens of times. "How did killing Juan Sanchez make you feel?"

Hard swallow. "I didn't want to kill him, but . . ." Carmelita interrupted him.

"No buts. You say you didn't want to kill him but haven't told me how you feel about taking Juan's life."

He felt anger and sadness and confusion and fear. He tried to keep the tears out of his eyes but couldn't do it. "I've had nightmares every single day since I killed him. I hate myself for it. It was the drugs and the money."

"Are you sure that's all it was? From reviewing the case, your testimony, and conversations with your therapist, it seemed like there was a whole lot of ego and reputation maintenance involved. You look confused. Let me rephrase. It seems like you didn't want to be known as a punk that wasn't about his money, and so you had to let the streets know you weren't the one. Sound about right?" Marquise nodded. "That kind of outlook comes from somewhere. Do you know where you got that from? That all-or-nothing thing? How did you form your view of the world? Tell me your life story. Start at the beginning."

Marquise gave her waves of trauma and retraumatization. Abandoned by his father. Abused by his mother and her lovers. His mother was always in financial and emotional trouble. He had to steal at an early age just to eat. Started as a lookout for some dealers and then became one. After a while, the streets seemed safer than home, so he stopped going home. Right before he got locked up, he met Ana. That was his girl. He thought that they would be together forever—forever how twenty-year-olds think about it. Just when it got really serious, he got locked up.

"What about the good times?" Carmelita pressed.

"What good times?"

"Boy, you've had that tablet for almost a year and a half and you're asking me this question? Put that headset on. Now, please."

He did. It was dark for a few seconds and then it was bright with floating images of the video clips that were on his tablet. He turned his head and there were more clips. He tried to reach out and he heard Carmelita laugh.

"Virtual and Augmented Reality. Strange, huh? When you're ready, you'll have full control as part of your advancement in the re-homing process. But for now, I'm the boss. Now, tell me what you see."

"All the stuff on my tablet, wait, and some new stuff. Is this what Lonnie put on?"

"Yes. I don't want to belittle or ignore the horrors you've been through. You've had a really rough life, and I'm genuinely sorry that you weren't loved and looked after as you deserved to be. Your momma and her momma before her, and according to our research, your great-great grandmother were all horribly abused, mistreated, and neglected. And all that's in you. It's probably why you had some difficulty concentrating in school and were more skittish than your friends and classmates. You've inherited your family's trauma. It left a kind of chemical stain on your genes. Aside from this, you experienced trauma at the hands of your mother and all the people that where in and out of your house when you were a kid. But know what else gets passed down? Joy. The research is new, but joy seems to be locked in our genes as well, but our bodies aren't oriented toward it like it is for trauma. It's like our bodies—Black bodies are almost primed for the worst. The growing consensus is that, for Black Americans, slavery's legacy has messed us up so badly that our body is a physical and genetic miracle of maladaptive coping. Sorry for all the jargon. Now what do you see? See and hear?"

The images coalesced into one image. It was a film clip of him and his auntie, Lavenia, dancing. He openly cried.

"Me and my Auntie Levi. I was trying to teach her a dance. I used to be a real good dancer."

"I'm sure you still are. What do you hear?"

"Music. Loud music. I remember her neighbors banging on her door, telling us to turn it down. Does hip-hop still sound like this?"

"Some. What else do you hear?"

Marquise listened. Laughter. Auntie Levi, Uncle Ray. Him and his mom all laughing at how uncoordinated Lavenia was. She just could not get it. This was the only time in his life he could think of that all three of the siblings had been in the same room with him there. Lavenia sat down. "I can't do that shit. Show me how it's done, nephew." Marquise watched his younger self dance his ass off. His mom, auntie, and uncle yelling, "Aaayyyyyyy," cheering him on. The video faded to black.

"Don't move," Carmelita instructed. Put your arms on the armrests of your chair." He did as he was told. "You're going to feel a pinch and a shock."

"Owww!"

"Be quiet, big baby. Now tell me what you see."

It was a photo this time. He was on a bicycle, his Uncle Ray looked like he was pushing him.

Carmelita's voice intruded. "Describe that day to me."

He tried, but he couldn't. "I don't remember."

Another pinch and shock. He barely flinched.

"Okay. How about now?" The picture came to life. Not fully, but he distinctly experienced movement of the bicycle and the clouds moving across the sky. Uncle Ray's legs moved, like he was running—he felt the sun beating down on him.

"My first and only bike. Uncle Ray got it for me for my birthday."

"Who is that in the background, looking at you two? To the left, on the porch?"

"Momma?" Marquise's mom was sitting on the porch, the ever-present cigarette hung from her lips. She pointed and laughed at her brother and her son. She seemed to move, but how was that possible? He distinctly heard her laughter. It was something unfamiliar but sorely missed.

"Look at her face, her eyes, Marquise. What do you see?" He felt another shock. Longer and sharper than the last one. "Really pay attention."

He searched his mother's face, a face he hadn't seen in person for over twenty years. He had one visitor, Ana, in all the time he was locked up. She told him while she did love him, she wasn't going to wait for him. He was angry, but he understood. You can't wait for a life sentence to be over. But his mom not coming to visit? That was something he didn't think he could forgive.

"You're distracted. Stay focused, Marquise. Look at your mother's face."

She looked different somehow. Not at all how he remembered her. There was something about her that looked easy, free, like she didn't have a care in the world.

"She looks happy," he said.

"And that happiness is in you, too, Marquise. We just have to find the correct key to unlock it so it has as much influence and impact as the trauma. Take the headset off, please."

His eyes were filled with tears. They ran down his cheeks uninhibited. Damn. He'd been crying all day. In front of people.

It was seventeen years, four months—damn the minutes and seconds—since he had let anyone see him cry. Yeah . . . Crying in prison was not the move.

He wiped his face and noticed that it was dark out. The hell?

"Yes, it's dark. And it's late. It's close to 11 o'clock at night. This part of your therapy messes with your perception of the passage of time. How do you feel?"

He felt a little dizzy, but the earlier nausea was gone. And he was tired. Not sleepy tired but tired like after you've just exercised.

"Worn out but not sleepy."

Lonnie interrupted them to return Marquise's tablet. He also gave him a key card. "You have some choices you gotta make. You can have a private room, or you can share."

"Private room, please." He hadn't a real moment to himself in almost two decades. Damned if he shared anything with anyone for a long while. Lonnie took out his phone and programmed the key card.

"You're on the third floor, number 327," pointing to a high-rise a half-mile in the distance. There's food, clothes, and ways to stream your tablet to see it and operate it on a much bigger screen. Just follow the map on your tablet and you'll get there. See you tomorrow, family." Lonnie skipped off into the darkness.

"How do you feel, Marquise?" Carmelita put a little extra emphasis in her voice. "Emotionally. How are you coping with all this?"

"Can I get out this chair?"

Carmelita nodded.

He stood and shook out his legs and arms, noticing bumps where the pinch and shocks happened. "I'm worried. I don't have nowhere to go. I don't have a job. I'm just . . . out here." He waved his arms.

"Valid concerns but unnecessary. Work and housing are covered for the next year. You'll have work and housing for as long as the re-homing process takes. After you've completed everything, we work with you to obtain housing that's sustainable and work that will help you to rebuild. Now, it's late, and I'm going to bed."

"Thank you, Carmelita. I mean that. F'real. Thank you."

"My pleasure. Now, go. This was only day one. Hundreds more to go."

***

Marquise woke himself up with his laughter. He was free, goddammit. He was actually free. He jumped up and down on the bed, giggling like a kid. It wasn't a dream. He somersaulted and bounced off the bed, dinging his head on a chair. It hurt, but he didn't care. He was about to do another one when his tablet buzzed. He saw a photo of Lonnie on the screen but didn't know what else to do. What has he supposed to do? He tapped the green icon. Lonnie's gigantic face and head filled the screen.

"What up, caveman? Took you long enough to answer. Be downstairs in thirty minutes. You got a big day."

Marquise took a shower and reveled in its warmth. He put on non-prison-issued clothing and shoes. He found a shoulder bag hanging by the front door. He put his tablet in in and went to meet Lonnie.

Lonnie met him in an electric golf cart that looked like a toy under his muscular frame. "Let's go, bruh. You always late."

Marquise hopped in. The cart was surprisingly fast.

"Um . . . . What was this like for you?"

Lonnie looked at Marquise and gave him that smile. "It sucked, bruh. Gillian—she's like Carmelita but meaner—put me through it. Made me face some shit that I had to bury to survive in the doghouse. But it was necessary. And here I am. I'm employed. I got a place to stay. I'm in love. I'm chillin'. But I wasn't in nearly as long as you. I did a cool five before Calbolition. That's what folks be callin' California's Abolition Day. I hate to say it, but you were gone so long that adjusting to all this new shit is going to be hard. You've missed a gang of stuff."

Lonnie hit the brakes, hard, causing the cart's rear end to lift up and crash back down. "Here you go, bruh. Second room on the left. Day two always sucks." Marquise hopped out as Lonnie sped away.

He was in a different part of the campus than yesterday. This didn't look like an Ikea-mixed-with-a-Clearasil commercial. This part looked lived in, like it was functional and not just built to impress people.

He made his way to the designated room and saw Carmelita there. She motioned him in and directed him to sit, facing a huge screen.

A moment later a face appeared on the screen. A woman. Some kind of Latina. Old.

"Is this the one who killed my Juan?"

"Yes, Miss Sanchez," Carmelita acknowledged. "His name is Marquise Hanks."

Marquise felt heated anger rush through his body. He was about to get up, but a look from Carmelita assured him that leaving wasn't a possibility.

Miss Sanchez didn't blink as she stared at Marquise. "Doesn't really look like a murderer, does he?"

"I'm not sure there's a look, ma'am."

"True. My Juan didn't look like he could do the things he did, but he did them."

Miss Sanchez steadied herself. "Mr. Hanks. You killed my son. I didn't go to the trial, I couldn't, but Juan's father said you didn't have much remorse. He said you and your attorney tried to make excuses; basically, saying that my son deserved it. Make no mistake. I knew my son was into some bad things. Some very bad things. But as a mother, we forgive this. He did bad things, got himself into bad situations, but he was my son and I miss him every single day. Want to know something? You and him shared a birthday, April 8th. Same year. Same hospital. When you killed him, we lived about five blocks from you and your mom."

Marquise felt ambushed. He would be damned if he'd cry right now. He shot Carmelita a dirty look.

Miss Sanchez cleared her throat. "I forgive you, Mr. Hanks. So does Juan's father and his brothers and sisters. We know Juan . . . *no era un ángel*, but he was our family and we loved him. We loved him. Thank you for this, Miss Carmelita. I guess we'll be talking in a couple of weeks?"

"Yes, Miss Sanchez. We'll see you then."

As soon as the screen went blank, Marquise exploded. "What the hell was that? You set me up. What are you talking about 'We'll see you then'?"

"You killed her son. You think everyone has forgotten about that? You are returning to a world that you have to be prepared for. Part of that preparation is you facing what you've done. You need to make amends. Part of doing this is to apologize as many times as necessary for the apology to be true. Not as a punishment but as a way to make the people you hurt feel, even if it is only a tiny bit, somewhat better about their loss. Juan isn't here to process with you, so his family will. His mother needed to see you, to forgive you for taking her son's life. Just because you're free does not mean that your crimes evaporate. We won't bludgeon you with them, but you won't be allowed to pretend that you didn't commit them. You are earning your way back into society. We're helping you. You're welcome."

He didn't know what to feel. He was angry. He didn't know at who. He was sad. Looking at Miss Sanchez, seeing the pain in her eyes and hearing it in her voice, wrecked him. He did kill her son, and it is something he would have to live with. If he were locked up, it would be easier. He'd only be seeing other inmates and guards. But out in the world? Of course, he was going to run into people who knew what he'd done. He might even run into folks who might want to get back at him.

While lost in thought, Carmelita had put a headset in his hand. "Put it on."

He hesitated. What other shit was she about to pull?

"This only works if you cooperate. Put the headset on."

He did as he was told and settled into the chair, fully expecting the electric pain to shoot through him. He meant to ask her about that.

"Marquise, what do you see?"

The blank tan of the virtual environment swirled, changing color until there was an ethnically ambiguous baby floating in his field of vision. He sighed. Loudly. One of his therapists in Quentin, the blond wack one, tried this with him before. She told him to pretend to be a baby so he could be rebirthed into a healthy reality.

"I see a big-ass, bald baby."

He heard Carmelita chuckle. "Keep watching and listening."

The virtual environment changed again. He felt like he was at the movies but a mix of still and moving images. The baby grew and matured. He saw the baby attempt and then master crawling. He saw it, her, take her first tentative steps, followed by her running and laughing and climbing on things she wasn't supposed to. He then heard a voice that caught his ears and a brief glimpse of something that caught his eye. "Carmelita, go back. Please. Please."

"We don't go back here, Mr. Hanks. Unless it serves a healing purpose. Please keep that in mind."

"Was that Ana?" Marquise thought to himself. It couldn't have been.

The baby was now a little girl. Her skin had darkened slightly, and her once-bald head was full of bouncing curls. He saw her doing gymnastics, swimming, winning spelling bees—the little girl was nothing but smiles, laughter, joy. He saw her at school dances. He must've witnessed sixteen or seventeen of her birthdays. By the time the video faded out, he was smiling ear to ear. It was beautiful to see. But his heart ached. He had an idea why he was shown this, but he wasn't sure, only that he felt it was cruel.

He took off the headset and tossed it unceremoniously on the floor. "Y'all are kind of cold-blooded here. What was this supposed to be? That was Ana, wasn't it? Why would you show me her kid like that? I don't want to see her with another man, having a life."

"You're projecting, Marquise. There was no other man in any of that footage. You have a good eye, though. We tried to scrub any footage of Ana, as it wasn't about her. Wasn't about you and her. She's moved on with her life. She doesn't owe you anything. Please understand this, Mr. Hanks. You will have to make amends with her as well. That time will not be about you pining over her, wondering what would have been. However, that girl is your business. Your shared daughter is your business."

Carmelita tapped the screen of her watch, and a moment later Lonnie escorted the girl from the VR session into the room. She looked dead-on Ana. Same forehead. Same too-long eyelashes. Her hair was crazy curly and rust colored, while her mom's was jet black and straight.

Lonnie was very gentle with the girl, whispering to her. After she nodded, he left.

Marquise and the girl stared at each other until she broke the silence. "I'm Grace. Gracie. Graciela. But no one, aside from my abuela, calls me that. Hi, dad."

He didn't know what to do. He'd never met her before. He felt guilty because he didn't have a rush of paternal feelings, only feelings of confusion and anger at Ana for not telling him she was pregnant when they last saw each other.

Gracie reached out to hug him but decided against it. What was he supposed to say?

"I'm Marquise. Hanks. I guess I'm your dad. If I would've known . . ."

Carmelita interrupted. "Marquise. Hanks. I told you that we don't go back unless it will help you or someone else heal. What you were about to do would only hurt the both of you. That's not why we're here." She touched her watch again and Lonnie appeared with another headset. Carmelita motioned for Marquise to pick his off the floor and put it on. She then instructed Grace to don hers. "Please sit down," she commanded. "Are you two comfortable enough?"

Marquise and his daughter affirmed. Grace giggled. The sound of it was beautiful to Marquise.

"Good," Carmelita said. "Now we can get to the real work."

VISIONARY PRACTICE

Albina Zone
by Lisa Bates

Portland, Oregon 2036

> It holds a possibility of deep remembrance of the
> freedom dreams of our ancestors, those who worked
> before us and walk beside us, and those yet to
> come. Freedom dreams don't live in real time.

—ZENZELE ISOLDE, "BLACK ETHNOGRAPHY,
BLACK (FEMALE) AESTHETICS"

"I don't even LIKE marshmallows!!" I yell and push away from
the table, rattling the latte cups and almost knocking over my
chair. I'm storming out as Mx. Garner calls out, "This isn't like
you, Tayshia, I'm *concerned*."

I think back to the past couple of days—I've been slamming
my way out of just about everywhere, and it isn't like me . . . but
this week hasn't been like anything I've experienced before. . .

***

It all started when I went through the attic and found a bunch
of my mom's old stuff, including her high school gear from
before the AZ, back when the school was named after Thomas

Jefferson. Obviously, with abolition, the old slave-owning founders were canceled and so was the mascot. Our school doesn't really have a dress code because those are gender oppressive, but we're definitely not allowed to wear Jeff High stuff, even it it's just the mascot like this, a sweatshirt she had cut off as a crop. "This is too cute . . . and if anyone can get away with it, I can," I thought to myself as I checked it out in the mirror. I was in good standing with all my teachers, star students, blah blah. The person who would stop me was my mom, and she was definitely gone for work already—or so I thought.

As I thundered down the stairs, I saw her come back in through the front door because she had forgotten her badges. I froze on the landing, but it was too late. Definitely busted. "What . . . are you thinking?" she said in a strained voice. I tried to think up a story about a retro day or a costume or—"You know what, I can see you're about to get cute, but don't even try it. Give it to me now."

I wished my mom would say something, anything—or even just roll her eyes and laugh a little, but she doesn't even look in my face. My mom held out her hand while I took off the sweatshirt. She practically ripped it out of my grasp, tightened her lips, and turned away—"I've got to get on the road, I'll probably be late for work now."

I didn't mention that I had also found her old phone and earbuds, and I've been listening to her music. My mom never plays music—honestly, my mom never does anything fun. She just works and . . . works. I figured she'd just take that, too, and I might have lost the battle, but I wasn't going to lose the vintage tech or these beats!—"Did my mom used to dance???" I wondered as I headed out, bass thumping in my ears.

* * *

My mom is usually gone way before I am ready to leave in the morning. Mom's commute is super long because she has to pass through the AZ exit checkpoint. She wears like seven different badges around her neck and has papers in the glove box because she never knows when she'll get asked for proof of employment. Most people who live in the AZ have jobs through the Trust that include classes and trainings, but my mom has a regular job, out in what we call Occupied Oswego. But the AZ . . . the Albina Zone, that's where we've lived since before the abolition.

The AZ—for a time it was Black, and then it was like really Black, but it got gentrified when my mom was young. That's when all these apartments came in, and the houses got fixed up super cutesy. This was before I was born, but when I was a baby, the city was trying to make up for it by reserving apartments for Black families who had gotten pushed out. My mom got one because her family had always lived around here, and that's when we were living when the Uprising happened. I was really small and I don't remember it. Sometimes I think I saw flashing lights and heard sirens, but probably that's just from what I've heard about. Not from my mom—she never talks about the Uprising—but just around the Zone.

After Abolition Day, a whole bunch of Black and Brown people showed up, released out of the old prisons. We call them the Returned Family. At first they moved into the fancy empty apartments. Then the white folks started leaving—all through elementary school, my classes were emptying. White classmates would get up to say goodbye and solemnly pronounce, "We're giving you reparations"—a word they stumbled over, and none of us really knew what that even meant. What it meant was that they left their houses, and some Returned Family started moving into those instead of staying in the buildings.

My mom was always really quiet and really strict. In the buildings, all the moms had to go to classes and programs. I think they had them all along, but when the Trust took over governing the Albina Zone, it was like every night. I remember sitting in the back of a room coloring while someone would drone on about family dynamics or saving and budgets or whatever. Anytime I whined about it my mom totally ignored me, so I figured she didn't mind. But one night when I was in middle school, a bunch of Returned Family uncles came to our apartment and packed everything up. I didn't even know my mom knew any of those guys! She didn't say a word to me about what was going on, but when we went down in the elevator she grabbed my hand—I started to twist away because I was way too old for that, but she gripped hard.

The Community Coordinator on duty came across the lobby when she saw my mom was rolling a suitcase, but as soon as she saw who was carrying our boxes, she plastered a huge smile on her face. Everyone was very, very polite. But I could tell she was terrified by how fast she was blinking. We moved into a house that night, and now I'm the only one who has to do the Trust programs. My mom just said it's because she needs to work, but it's totally unfair. I have to sit through all the workshops, and all she says is, "Just do what you have to do"—usually while she's on her way out the door. Which, like I said, she always is.

"At least she had decent musical taste," I thought as I trudged up the stairs at AZ High. As the chorus "we gon' be alright!" started up, I thought I saw a flicker out of the corner of my eye at the empty stone base that used to have a statue of Thomas Jefferson sitting on it. Was that yelling part of the song?

I took out the earbuds to join my BFFs on the steps. "Heyyy what's—ooh you look mad!" yelled Bea, pretty gleefully in fact, but even though I rolled my eyes, I can't be annoyed, she just loves any drama she can vicariously experience. "Yeah, my mom caught me trying to come in this old t-shirt I found . . ."

"BORRRING, was it ratty or something? Your mom stays pressed over . . . staying pressed!" she cracked herself up. Kendra looked at me a little more closely—she's quiet and way more sensitive. "Wait, no, what was it?"

"Welll . . . it was an old Jeff High shirt with the mascot on it." Bea's attention snapped back—"WHAT! Oh my gawd, where did you even get that! Your mom probably launched you into the sun, forget all those anti-spanking seminars!"

Kendra looked really nervous, glancing over her shoulder as she asked quietly, "What were you thinking. . ."

"It was HER shirt," I said defensively, "and anyway, it didn't have the name, just the mascot. I just wanted to . . . I don't know . . . anyway, she took it. But she didn't take this!" I showed them the phone—"It's loaded with music, and y'all . . . was my mom at some point . . . coool?? Hip? What is it you teens say?" I laughed, trying to reassure Kendra with a swift hug. "Listen to THIS one"—I skipped ahead to a track by an artist called KayelaJ and turned it way up so we could share the earbuds among all three of us.

Over the music I could hear some girls' voices—one so loudly it started drowning out the music, but I only had one earbud in so maybe they were nearby? I looked up curiously. I hadn't seen anyone else out here—and there wasn't anyone out on the steps . . . I blinked at the statue base—could they be behind it? Some weird acoustics because I could clearly hear this voice proclaiming, "I will be the crazy black girl and I will carry it with pride. I'm sorry I'm so radical that I believe that we are all equals."

—"*What is this, a poetry reading?*" I thought as it went on—
"and I'm sorry that I tear the weak bindings of your system because I believe in education and no, not this institution we send our children to now."—other girls' voices were yelling, "Yo girl you're gonna kill it! Yess!"[1]

I still didn't see anyone. I craned my neck around, and out of the corner of my eye I saw a tall brown girl in a head wrap and what looked like three or four more around her and . . . wait, what? I could have sworn I also saw . . . a statue? I blinked harder and it was gone. Kendra was standing up, extending her hand to me, "Ok, Earth to Tayshia, we gotta go—the music is great but we've got naming committee!"

The naming committee. When the Trust took over governance of the Albina Zone, everyone agreed that we shouldn't have a school named after a slave-owning, raping president. But this renaming thing has gone on forever—years! We've been on the youth committee since ninth grade, and sometimes it seems like there's no way we're going to have a name when we graduate next year. The Trust brought in some consulting group to set up this process, and every time a new person joins we have to go through all this training and ground rules and consensus process—and when you're in high school, there's new people every year! Honestly, it's been driving me up a wall, but it felt like we were closer than ever to a choice so I was trying to be optimistic.

When we got to class my good feeling was quickly punctured. There was a new Trust Teaching Fellow with Mx. Garner. Me and Bea exchanged a look . . . some of them are cool, I guess, but Mx. Garner is one of the only Teaching Fellows who stuck around after a couple of years. She's leading our group process to rename the school now. A couple minutes after the bell rang, two of the guys came sauntering in laughing. When Mx. Garner gave them her "are you serious?" look, they held up both hands saying, "sorry, Karen, sorry, Karen," with over-the-top puppy dog eyes. As Mx. Garner started to respond, the new Fellow jumped up, saying loudly and way over articulated, "It's okay! *We* called *you*"—here she gestured vaguely, looking a little lost but she plowed on ahead—"we called your *femmes* Shaniqua or Maria or Ling-Ling, so it's only fair that you call us . . . *Karen*. We understand."

This solemn pronouncement was met with total silence for about ten seconds, and then we all just busted out cackling as Mx. Garner briefly covered her face with her hand. I thought she might laugh, too, but she got it together to say gently, "My name is actually Karen . . . it's just a joke. . . " She shot the guys another one of her looks that was remarkably like my mom's "why are you showing out in public like this?" face and pointed to their seats. The new Fellow's face was blotchy pink, and as she sunk down in her chair she was clutching on her teacher's copy of *White Fragility* the hell all these sticky tabs in it, staring straight ahead. I almost felt bad for her, but I also snickered real loudly as Bea flashed me her phone with the video ready to share, captioned "oh no baby what is you doing?" with about a thousand facepalm emojis. We finally got settled down as Mx. Garner called the meeting's attention to the name question.

Bea whispered, "Girl, if you had worn that old slaver sweatshirt in here today you would have killed that lady, and then what?"

"Exile to Oswegooo," we both whisper dramatically, laughing and shivering at the same time.

Kendra glanced over, "Y'all play too much."

Which brought us back to the task at hand. I kind of spaced out while everyone dutifully repeated the ground rules: "one diva, one mic . . . ouch and oops. . ." like a lot of AZ advisory committees, we use a consensus model, and I've started noticing there's plenty of times when we the students are pretty cool with an option until the latest facilitator starts poking at it, asking about problematic issues and asking if anyone wants to call a hold. But finally we've gotten down to the Vanport Resilience or Michelle Obama Senior High School when this brand-new Teaching Fellow comes out of nowhere and even after her totally humiliating start, jumped in to just ask some questions about how we've centered the voices of—and I couldn't even listen anymore because the impatience and frustration was just bubbling up inside me, and I suddenly said out loud, "Demos, I say!"

I know from hearing some of the older Returned Family on our block that this was a cheer; they would break it out later in the evening at cookouts sometimes. But I didn't know who else knew or what they would say back. "Excuse me?" said the Fellow. Kendra was looking at me like I had lost my absolute mind. I put both hands on the desk and repeatedly loudly, "Demos, I say!" Everyone's mouth gaped open, and the guys who came in late were elbowing each other in anticipation that finally someone else was making a scene. I stood up from the table, slapped down my name placard, and positively yelled it again, and I heard something faintly in response—was it coming from outside? The hallway? "You know!"

By that time both teachers were talking very fast and clearly getting mad. The new Trust Fellow was saying, "Okay, okay we need to consider a trauma-informed approach," while Mx. Garner was shaking her head, declaring her disappointment in my desire to violate our collective safe space, but honestly? I was just not having it.

"We've been doing this forever, and you can't even tell us what the whole process includes, there's an organization chart for seventeen different committees that takes up more than three sheets of paper, and I still can't figure out who actually decides anything at all around here!" I picked up my stuff and stomped over to the doorway, then turned at the last moment to yell, "And WTF is a Resilience?!"

I stormed out of the building, and by the time I got to the street, my adrenaline had stopped pumping and I realized I was going to be in trouble. I would probably get booked into a few weeks of after school sessions with one of the Trust Teen Trauma Specialists, daily supervised meditation, and God knows how many one-on-one and group reconciliation sessions with everyone on the naming committee. As I trudged down the street, I just got madder at myself. They would definitely call my mom. UGH! But at least I had some music to listen to. I popped in the earbuds and selected a track off an album called *Worldwide Underground*. The singing was amazing, even when the song's lyrics didn't make total sense—"we like to keep the car running in case the sweeper boys comin'"—maybe police stuff? No wonder my mom's been hiding this, she hates stuff that glorifies the old days.

I was walking down MLK Ave. when the song cut out and was replaced by a whole lot of voices.

"The whole point of this policy is to push us out!"

"Yeah, remember—master's tools. . ." another voice warned.

The first voice again—"What we need to understand about the Tif is. . ." I looked at the phone screen thinking, Tiff? Is this like one of those old album skits? Is Tiff a person like Tiffany . . . Huh? This isn't really funny. . .

"The question is, can we use the master's tools to subvert the system, or do we need a whole new hammer!"

What sounded like an older man's voice broke into the conversation, "Listen, y'all young people, y'all ladies, you want to have these radical ideas of what you need to understand is a business mindset. . ." now this definitely wasn't funny—this was like listening to the old busybodies on our street lecturing my mom about coming to the AZ block association meetings and whatever else they think they know all about. The skip button wasn't working so I had to keep listening. The femme voices got louder.

"We're investigating these policies and how they've worked here . . . we don't have to just ask for crumbs, we can take the whole cake!"

"They can't just placate us"

"They can't just put up pictures of Black people while we can't even live here."

"They need to give this land back!"

Just as I got to the corner of MLK and Alberta, the voices cut out and the music was back. I was jabbing at the screen, trying to figure out if it was broken, but it seemed like it was playing ok.

As I looked up at the mural on the corner, I thought about the last things they were saying. . . . So, the faces are here, but what else did they want? Did they ever find the tools? I shook my head. At that moment, I thought I might really be losing it. . . . Maybe going to some meditation wasn't a bad idea after all. . .

I decided to just go home and try to do a little anticipatory kissing up. I was cleaning the kitchen and keeping my mom's food warm when she got home. It didn't seem like she had gotten any calls from the school yet since she wasn't actually yelling at me, and I quickly grabbed her bag and coat from her saying, "Relax, have dinner." She made a skeptical face but sat down, sighing as I put the plate in front of her. "How was the drive, Mom, what do you want to drink?" She said, "OK, ok, if this is about this morning, let's just move on. Just do—" "What I need to do—I know, Mom, I am."

We ate in silence for a few minutes, and then I asked, "Sooo, Mom, was there something about MLK and Alberta? Where the Trust office is now? Was that like a controversy or anything?"

My mom let out a puff of air. "Tay, the Trust has been there almost your whole life, and they're gonna be there. Does it really matter about what building it is?"

I should have known. My mom never talks about anything that happened before. But she's gotta know about this, it sounded like it was a pretty big deal. "Ok, but, Mom—"

She cut me off. "There was something about a development, and that's how we ended up in the apartment, but it really doesn't matter. Things are how they are." She left the room, and I slumped down on my arms on the table. What I heard sounded like femmes, girls, standing up for themselves. My mom must have known about it when it was happening if it was big enough to get the apartment. . .

The next few days of school I kept feeling annoyed and bored—and on edge wondering when Mx. Garner was going to get a hold of my mom about the meeting and my reconciliation plan. I was slouching through the halls and staring out the window in class, listening to my mom's old music and getting more and more irritable. I got through my Accountability Apology in the naming committee without rolling my eyes, but obviously Bea and Kendra knew something was up. After the meeting, Bea got right in my way and yanked the earbud out of my ear. "Ok, girl, what. Is. Up." Kendra stood next to me, but she was also staring at me, waiting for my reply. "Well . . . I think . . . I'm just sick of all of this! They taught us that Abolition was about ending systems of oppression, but this!! This doesn't feel like freedom! We can't even pick our school name, let alone anything else, and we don't know anything about so much of what happened!" Kendra started pulling us down the steps away from the building, "Come on, we have to talk further away—now, what do you mean about what has happened?"

I took a deep breath. I was about to reveal to my two best friends that I was possibly going totally out of my mind. "I've been . . . learning about some stuff. . . . Stuff that happened in the past, like, stuff in the school and the zone."

"What STUFF?? Girl, use your WORDS," said Bea with exasperation, and Kendra said, "Shh, let her talk, damn!"

"Ok, so . . . I think there's been way more than just the Uprising. I heard there were lots of fights, not just how we learned about the urban renewal and stuff from a long time ago, but like when our moms were kids. I heard there were people . . . girls, femmes. . . . Who were trying to make a lot of revolutions happen. Like, not just to have the Trust come to make programs, but something . . . I don't know, something else." I looked warily at my friends. They exchanged a glance, and Bea said, "What do you mean you heard?"

"Well . . . like, I hear their voices. I hear the music," I said, holding out the phone, "but I also hear . . . them. I hear them talking about what they think and arguing and gassing each other up, talking about what real education could be, and. . ." I trailed off. . . . "You probably think I'm insane."

Bea chewed her lip for a second and said, "I don't know what you're listening to . . . but . . . I have heard about some stuff, like, from before." We all looked around to see if anyone could hear us and instinctively kept walking, arms linked together so we could stick close and hear as we whispered loudly. "I mean, we do all agree that the name committee is some bullshit. And I'm sick of being sent to Teen Trauma what-EVAH just because I'm fully over learning about Oregon's constitution with yet another Trust Fellow on tour to the equity experiment! We get it, they did the racism back then, but what about *now*?"

"Right, exactly!" I exclaimed. "How are we supposed to think we're free in here when there's so much . . . else . . . out there!? My mom won't even take me over to Oswego, and you know she got stopped on her way in to work again this week! She doesn't talk about it, but I could tell because she got home SO late because she has to make up those hours."

I was getting pretty heated, when Kendra chimed in, "I don't know about what happened here . . . but my uncle, like my real uncle, not just Returned Family, but when he came back, he went to Oakland. He talks to my mom sometimes, and it sounds like it's really different there. Like, they don't have the Trust or anything like that. He was talking about cooperatives—I asked my mom if that's like the Advisories, and they just laughed, but they didn't say any more while I was there."

"See?" I said excitedly, "there's gotta be more we need to know! Adults are not gonna tell us—I mean, my mom? She already shut me down. But I don't know how to hear more!" I was swiping the phone screen, and I could tell my friends were exchanging another look. "Oh, man, y'all do think I'm nuts."

"I mean . . . it's not that," Kendra started. Bea interjected, "But yes, girl, you sound cray! The point is whether you're listening to ghosts or whatever, we're with you . . . we have to do something about this no-name-having-ass high school and probably this whole damn zone."

But what? And how? As my friends kept talking, complaining, and sharing their wildest ideas about what might be happening in Oakland, which included different cute femmes to date (Bea) and a real horticulture program (Kendra), I kept idly scrolling on the phone's music list, trying to see if there were hidden tracks and thinking about what I'd heard . . . if the master's tools don't work, then . . . what are the tools we need?

The next day, after yet another derailment at the naming committee—this time, the reintroduction of Senator Solange as a better name than Michelle Obama because she was elected and not just a wife—I was trudging home, listening to music from back when the Senator was singing about trying to dance it away, when . . . it was happening again! This time I was excited and turned up the volume so I could try to hear more.

It was one girl's voice at first, she sounded pretty young. "So, it's about . . . power? That sounds kind of, like, intense . . . like fighting?" An older sounding voice responded, "Yeah, it does sound intense, doesn't it? So let's talk about what power means, so we can talk about why we call ourselves Sisters. . ." the voice started fading out, which was so frustrating! I scrubbed back on the track to see if I could pick it up again . . . no, still music . . . there it was!

"Ok, so we won at the board because we showed that we weren't just a bunch of teens making noise."

"No, we were making noise *and* we knew our stuff!"

There were a bunch of whoops and hollers. The older voice was talking again, "Now, we're taking on something harder because everyone thinks they're doing the right thing for the right reasons . . . so we really have to know our stuff."

"But how can they think it's right to tear down our home?"

"They think they know what's best for our families"

"And they're trying to push us out again!"

"Yeah, we're going to have to find out a lot of information, and get our friends on board."

"My mom is worried that we're going to get in trouble," said one of the younger voices.

Oh man, I could relate, I thought. I saw what looked like a group of young femmes up ahead, kind of shimmering, walking together like my friends and I did, but they were—were they punching each other? No, they were just playing, or practicing maybe?

As I kept walking, the images and voices faded out, and I couldn't get them back. But now I had some more clues to follow, I just had to figure out who to ask.

I was so excited when I walked in the door, I had completely forgotten about the whole waiting for my mom to have heard about my episode at school and basically end my life. But when I busted into the kitchen, my mom was sitting there—damn, it was really early, she must have left work—oh no. She was totally stone-faced and gestured to the chair opposite hers.

"Tayshia, I had to leave my job two hours early today after receiving a phone call from your teacher. That is not what I expect to have to do."

I didn't know what to say, why hadn't I prepared better for this? "Mom, let me explain, I've already done my apology, and—"

She cut me off. "Whatever they've required you to do, do it double. You need to be impeccable. You've never been on a reconciliation list before, and I will *not* have my daughter—"

Then I interrupted her—"Yeah I *know*, Mom, your daughter will not be on any list of any kind, no conflicts, no talkback, do what you have to do and never even think about it! I get it!

You don't want me to question anything! You just want me to do what everyone tells me!"

"You need to sit *down*, young lady . . ." she warned.

"No, you know what? No. I'm sick of this! It's practically like . . . it's like living with . . ." I was so angry, my whole body felt like it was on fire. "It's like you're a COP."

As soon as I said it, I knew I had gone way, way too far. In the Albina Zone, calling someone a cop is the worst thing you can say, we don't even joke about it. Even before my mom started yelling, which she was clearly about to do, she quickly glanced to the window to see if it was open and if anyone heard. Before the Trust took over governance here, it used to be that the Returned Family would expel police and their families from the area, and even though it's been a long time since there were any actual cops around, I knew that's what my mom was worried about.

When she turned back to me, she was clearly furious, and I started to babble an apology. She put up her hand and cut me off. The worst thing was her face was totally blank. She didn't look scared or angry, she looked like nothing. She was staring at a spot on my forehead, no eye contact. Tears were streaming down my face as I kept trying to say I was sorry, but she just got up from the table, turned her back, and walked out of the room.

That's when I called Mx. Garner to see if I could talk to her. I thought she was the only adult I might be able to get some answers from, and she agreed to meet me at the coffee shop the next day, and I got in bed with my nose still stuffy and cried myself to sleep.

By the time I got there, I knew I couldn't come out and tell my teacher that I was hearing voices and maybe even seeing things? So I just talked a little bit about the fight with my mom. Not the whole thing—I couldn't admit what I had called her—but just that I was tired of meeting her and everyone's expectations all the time. I was about to ask if she knew how I could learn more about the Uprising and all the stuff that happened before then, when she went into teacher lecture mode. Inwardly, I sighed, but I guess that's how teachers are, so I could listen and then ask my questions. Anyway, she was being pretty complimentary and after my mom's total disgust with me, it felt reassuring.

"You're having a rough week, but I know you'll snap out of it! Listen, Tayshia, you are one of the special ones . . . You should have seen yourself back in kindergarten, when we were testing.

You just looked at that marshmallow and you didn't grab it, didn't even touch it! We all knew then you were going to be a leader, not like some of the other kids. I mean, I'm sure you can guess your friend Bea gobbled that down right away! She just has never had the grit you do . . ."

My head was spinning. I did remember those days in the room, being told not to touch the marshmallow and thinking, yuck, why would I? I loved sour candy, it's still my favorite. Wait, so that was a *test* for real? And they're still talking about it? They're using something I did when I was a little kid to say I have more potential than my friends?

Mx. Garner was going on and on about how I could come straight into the Trust Fellows program after high school, learn to do family support, and all I could think was—

"I don't even LIKE Marshmallows!!!"

* * *

And the next thing I knew I was here, running. I know my outburst and taking off might trigger someone to call the AZ Street Support team, so I have got to get out of here. I take a left and veer a couple of blocks from my normal route. The music is still playing in my ears—when did I put the earbuds back in?—

Just as I got a massive stitch in my side, I looked around—oh, shit. I was at the old precinct. I never come this way. Most Black folks in the AZ avoid it. The Trust made a reflective garden and a memorial here after Abolition, but there's just way too much bad spirit around here . . . . Unfortunately, I'm cramping up and panting hard, and I have to stop. And then . . . it happens again. This time it's much more—my vision is kaleidoscoping, and I stagger back until I'm leaning against the wall, which feels surprisingly warm—oh my god, what am I seeing, it's like fireworks right in front of my face, loud, sparks. The music is even louder—"OK, ladies, now let's get in formation"—and all of a sudden it drops out, and I hear a new beat, with hundreds of voices calling out in a singsong, "You about to lose yo' jobs"

I'm seeing splinters like a broken mirror—here's the street and the fountain and the grass but also here's concrete and bodies, so many people, all yelling, sweating, and I can hear—it's a voice I know, so well. I can hear *my mom's voice* above everything, the shouts, the bangs, the drumming. I hear my mom so clear, her voice ringing out—"Stay together, stay tight," and I look up and she's right there—locked arm in arm with two other femmes. They all look so young, and they're right up front as the bangs get louder and people are screaming. A robotic voice is saying, "Impact munitions will be deployed," over and over, but my mom's voice is louder and braver, and I can hardly breathe, I'm coughing and I don't know if it's from running or the smoke I can see in the air, and my mom turns her head and I swear we lock eyes, I swear she sees me for one split second as I whisper, "Mom"—and the girl on her right yells, "Dana, GO," and she turns away to run. The moment we break eyes, everything clears, and the music is back in my ears.

I'm bent over with my hands on my knees, still breathing heavily. Everything looks like it normally does—quiet, except the gurgling fountain. I pass the historical markers and walk as fast as I can to get home.

As I burst through the door, my mom is just hanging up her badge in the kitchen. "Mom, Mom, I need you!" She doesn't turn around when I enter the kitchen. She's rubbing her forehead, and I can tell from her back she's still mad and even more tired—"Mom, please! Mom! I'm sorry! I'm sorry for what I said, I didn't mean it!" She sighs and says, "Ok," but she doesn't turn around.

"But, MOM—Mom, I have to know! We have to talk. I know you don't want me to, but I have to do something! We know about Oakland, about the liberated zones, me and my friends, we want to learn, we want to fight—we have to! This place isn't right, it's not what you wanted."

When I say this last part—you—her shoulders go up real tense. "Mom!" I grab her hand and try to turn her around, but she's looking at my ear, past me, blinking faster.

"Mom, I know you know how! I SAW YOU"—she finally snaps her eyes to mine.

"You saw me. And I saw you."

We're gripping each other's arms tightly, and my mom is looking deep in my eyes, like she's never really looked at me before. She breathes in deep as I race ahead,

"Mom, we've got to do it now, please we—"

She interrupts: "We've got time."

Abolition Creates More Possibilities
(That We Can't Currently Imagine)

Both complexity scientists and emergent strategists frequently remind us that emergent strategies create new possibilities that are not always predictable. Abolitionists, Mariame Kaba reminds us, should always be asking generative questions pointing us to what new possibilities might emerge beyond what now exists.

Continuing to ask generative questions can be challenging, to say the least, in the context of escalating instability, which climate justice organization Movement Generation describes as "the defining feature of our times."[1] In this context, change is marked by shocks and slides. Shocks represent "acute moments of disruption," while slides are shaped by incremental change.[2] Both shocks and slides trigger our instincts to reach for certainty, a singular solution, a guaranteed escape hatch. Instead, our goal must be to "harness the shocks and shape the slides" toward achieving the shifts we desire.[3]

In the context of abolitionist organizing, the shock of each new police killing, rape, beating, corruption scandal, cover up, or uprising, and the slides precipitated by neoliberal policies leading to organized abandonment and criminalization of our communities offer us opportunities to create new possibilities, new practices, and new institutions from the wreckage that move us toward the world we want. The coronavirus pandemic, the economic crisis it precipitated, the ongoing epidemic of anti-Black police violence, and intensifying climate crisis represent shocks that reveal the effects of slides over the past half century. They also opened new portals into different conversations about policing, safety, abolition, and new ways of being in relationship.

Sage emphasizes that emergent strategies teach us that "the moments of tension are actually an opportunity for more to be born than the notion that there is a particular destination we are all moving toward." This, Sage says, is where leaning into intentional adaptation, iteration, and exploration of a multitude of possible futures makes way for portals to open. We choose one, enter it, practice, learn, and then find ourselves in the midst of the creation of the next. Rather than find the one possibility that we must all jump on and move toward, abolition requires us to create infinitely more possibilities to manifest futures we cannot yet imagine.

Visionary Fiction (Reprise)

> Harriet Tubman did not wake up one day with a strategy. She woke up from a dream: she saw that her people were free. They were seven or eight generations into slavery at that point? There was no guideline to be like, "We can be free." She imagined it. And then she bent reality. I think we all have to do that.
>
> —ADRIENNE MAREE BROWN,
> "HOW TO BEND REALITY," *PUSHBLACK*

Black feminist abolitionists teach us that abolition is both a project of analysis and a project of imagination. As explored in the Introduction and the "Abolition Builds Resilience and Fosters Transformation" chapter, visionary fiction is one conduit for sparking imagination that can create new possibilities. For Walidah Imarisha, visionary fiction is a way of actualizing emergent strategies by "re-envisioning what already exists, subverting it, and talking back to it, but also creating space for us to start from our own vision, our own imaginations, our own future."[4]

She points out that, like emergent strategies, visionary fiction is nonlinear, moving backward and forward through time and space in order to open more space of possibility beyond worlds structured by policing and punishment. "It is the idea of the past and the future reaching into the present . . . specifically rooted in Black liberatory dreaming."

On an episode of the *Emergent Strategy Podcast*, Walidah emphasizes that visionary fiction is essential to practicing emergent strategies and to the abolitionist project:

> If we don't imagine something different then all we have is this, and we are just going to reconfigure it . . . . We're gonna just keep building the same thing, slightly reconfigured, if we don't take the space and time, make the leap.
>
> And it is a leap, because it is terrifying. It's much easier, because it feels more concrete, to be able to say all the things that are wrong with what's happening now. And that's important. It's not an either/or. We have to analyze, we have to critique, we have to explore, we have to break it down, we have to take that courageous leap to be, to imagine something different and to recognize that may mean that we are wrong or we only have a piece of it.
>
> But I think that's why we have to do this together. It's imperative for us to take up that responsibility, which is both beautiful and terrifying. And doing it collectively not only means we don't have to be so scared of not having the right answer, it means that we are going to create something.
>
> We cannot allow these systems to dictate to us when is our time to dream. We have to claim that for ourselves. From the times when things are in flux, the times when things are in crisis, the time where it feels like everything is changing, that's when systems of oppression tell us to lock down and hold onto the little that we have. But that's every moment, because things will change . . . . this is the time to be as expansive as possible.[5]

Calvin Williams, the editor of the Wakanda Dream Lab anthology *Memories of Abolition Day*, added:

> My highest hope for dreaming while Black is that we create these irresistible spaces to be like, yo, Black liberation gets to look like all of this, and that we don't limit ourselves based on what we think, what's realistic, or what can be done.
>
> And [I don't have to be] so beholden to my beloved power map that I love to do while I'm talking about the materiality of how we organize toward this or that . . . . I don't want it to be done in a vacuum . . . I want it to be done in the spaciousness of where I get to exist this whole universe in, in all the different ways.[6]

adrienne responded by describing Calvin as a "visionary materialist or material visionary."[7]

The introduction to *Memories of Abolition Day* points out that, "As Black organizers call to divest, defund, and abolish the police state—they have recast their roles from movement builders into worldbuilders. . . . These stories not only explore Black Freedom beyond the borders of the prison, police, and surveillance state but also beyond the borders of time. We are being called to dream of liberated futures while also remembering, and repairing, our collective past."[8]

Perhaps the most well-known example of abolitionist visionary fiction is *Octavia's Brood*, the collection coedited by adrienne and Walidah. It literally blew my mind, not only because it helped me realize that all organizing is science fiction but also because I got a glimpse into the imaginations of abolitionist organizers I have struggled alongside—including Alexis Pauline Gumbs, Leah Lakshmi Piepzna-Samarasinha, and Mia Mingus—in ways that unlocked new possibilities. Some of the stories offer glimpses into worlds without police and prisons, others are populated by superheroes, angels, and memory workers. Some stories illuminate new strategies of resistance. Others serve as cautionary tales about the many new forms policing can take, or how exile can serve as a death sentence in new worlds, or how if we're not careful a river might exact revenge in ways that are not at all transformative for her targets. All of the pieces in *Octavia's Brood* invite us to imagine new possibilities for abolition.

Octavia's Brood and other works of visionary fiction (did you know both Mariame and Barbara Ransby have written some too?) have contributed to my own journey of transformation from chronicler of atrocities to nascent visionary fiction writer.[9] At a writing retreat in 2018, I found that I was no longer able to "continue to simply track every crack in the shell," as adrienne once put it, or engage in what Ruth Wilson Gilmore describes as the "recitation of the problem." In other words, for the first time in twenty-five years, I found myself unable to write any more about the harms of policing and criminalization. Instead, no doubt inspired by the copy of Alexis's *Dub: Finding Cere-mony* I brought with me, I imagined and wrote about different worlds instead of this one.

Artist, musician, organizer, and former AMC co-organizer Diana Nucera emphasizes the importance of cultivating curiosity and creativity to practice visions of alternate futures, particularly in the most politically dire moments. And yet, as an artist, she still sometimes asks herself, "People are dying, why am I doing this?" Answering her own question, she responds, "There needs to be at least one crew that is trying to figure out what the tools are to enhance our creative ability," she says. She cites Surrealism as just one example of an artistic movement that provided tools for people to think differently under fascist conditions.[10] "Our creative ability is an immense power that I think this moment really calls for," Diana says. Not surprisingly, she points out, the state recognizes art as a threat, censoring and cutting funding for it at each turn toward the Right. This is part of how, she says, "the state has torn our creativity out of us." Visionary art, like visionary fiction, can show us how to reclaim it to imagine and organize our way through impossible situations.

kai lumumba barrow is a longtime abolitionist organizer whose current primary practice is creating visual and immersive art installations through Gallery of the Streets.[11] Like Complex Movements, Gallery of the Streets fuses public art and community organizing through political education and experiential engagement in solidarity with abolitionist movements, but with Black feminism as an explicit starting point. kai points out that art is not inherently liberatory—"It's not like the art industrial complex isn't carceral and doesn't contribute to a world that is anti-abolition. You're still in a struggle." For kai, the critical questions are: "How are you thinking about abolition art? How are you thinking about art as a strategy to invite a visceral relationship with violences and anti-violence that could change your organizing practices, instead of just an intellectual response? That's the charge of the artist—to construct a visceral relationship with violence that allows us to dismantle it and rebuild something else." Experiential, interactive engagement with abolitionist art—like *Beware of the Dandelions* and Gallery of the Streets, offers a multisensory and multidimensional way to engage the practice of abolition beyond the theoretical.

So too can engagement with popular, non-abolitionist art through an abolitionist lens. Morgan Phillips, a contributor to *Octavia's Brood*, developed a workshop inviting science fiction and fantasy fans to embody the oppressed people of a particular franchise, like *Star Wars* or *Wizard of Oz*, and then create plans for direct action to achieve a goal within the worlds they inhabit.

I participated in a similar exercise at a convening for movement lawyers organized by Law for Black Lives, Detroit Justice Center, and Movement Law Lab at the AMC in 2018. Instead of exploring potential legislative, litigation, and policy "solutions" in the midst of the second year of the Trump administration—an exercise that increasingly felt like tilting rusty pitchforks at a tank—we told stories, played, and line danced. These felt like very unlawyerly activities, which some might find frivolous in the face of the rising tide of fascism. I will admit to thinking on more than one occasion during the day that I should be somewhere else, attending something more "serious" given the conditions we were facing. Then, during the second half of the day, we were invited into the assignment of designing a legal system for a new Wakanda from scratch. Easy, right? We'll make it abolitionist but with fierce and fabulous costumes. We delighted in stretching imaginations broken by law school to envision how an abolitionist, anti-capitalist, and borderless society could be structured that would hopefully give us a better sense of what we are fighting for in the now.

The exercise was profoundly humbling and instructive about where obstacles to abolition lie, including within our own imaginations. Even as we emphatically declared there would be no police, courts, jails, prisons, or immigration detention, we very quickly came to the root of the problem: it's all about the vibranium.[12] As we wrestled with how to ensure equitable distribution of the nation's most valuable and magical resource without policing, the fabulously attired cops in our heads emerged in response to the question of how to address the likelihood that, without borders or citizenship rules, people from around the world would likely migrate to Wakanda to claim a share of its vibranium stores, eventually potentially undermining the value or utility of the resource if Wakanda's stores were divided into the equivalent of nine billion shares.

We let our imaginations run and came up with the principle that only those who shared Wakanda's values could partake in its riches—and, suddenly we had re-created a nation-state. How would we establish who *really* shared our values? Someone proposed that there be a team of witches who could determine whether people "really" embrace our shared values or were just pretending to with their minds bent on vibranium accumulation.

In other words, it took us less than an hour to come back to cops—witch cops, sure, fabulously attired, but cops all the same—as a response to what felt like insurmountable questions around borders, resources, and belonging.

When I told Walidah this story, she quipped, "So, it's border patrol with omniscient surveillance state technology?" She describes the outcome of our imagination experiment as evidence of "the ways we just replicate these systems but don't necessarily realize in real life until we put them in the context of another world, then we're like, 'Oh wait, that sounds terrible.'"

The questions raised on that playful and ostensibly frivolous afternoon five years ago have stayed with me as I continue to wrestle with the role of the state in abolitionist futures and how to envision resource accumulation and distribution without extraction, concentration, and policing in an anti-capitalist, abolitionist future.[13]

Diana also pointed to the power of play as a tool to generate new possibilities. "The Surrealists had games, then these games became very political because they became places where people started questioning fascism, communism in the '20s and '30s . . . Surrealism really took off as this tool to imagine something different." Similarly, the Allied Media Conference and other abolitionist gatherings often host children's spaces or intergenerational tracks where everyone is encouraged to build new worlds through play. In one particularly memorable instance at the 2008 Critical Resistance 10 conference, a group of kids who were playing musical chairs refused the scarcity and competition inherent in the game, began to share chairs and collaborate to keep them from being removed, and ultimately brought the whole thing to a halt.

Diana and AMC's commitments to creating spaces for people to experiment and play reminded me of an event that Mariame Kaba once hosted in Chicago—a "day of play" in memory and honor of Tamir Rice, a twelve-year-old killed by police within seconds of their arrival on a playground because he was playing with a toy gun—ironically a classic prop for kids' games of cops and robbers. I remember being surprised that Mariame was organizing a playday—if you know Mariame, you know she really doesn't play, at least not in public. But the event was rooted in both a deep desire to highlight and resist the notion that Black children can't play without fear of state violence *and* a desire to foster our collective creativity in the face of devastating violence As Adaku observed, "Imagination spaces connected to joy, play, healing, create more space to think outside the box to come up with solutions, to help people access solutions rather than just strategy, workplan, tactics. Centering joy and connection generates more radical ideation about what could be possible and restore staying power in the work."

What's Pleasure Got to Do with It?

Emergent Strategy points out that pleasure invites people to open and grow, to be creative, to stretch beyond our current beliefs, our edges.[14] In other words, it creates more possibilities. Therefore, to really transform society, we will need to make justice one of the most pleasurable experiences we have.[15] adrienne's second book, *Pleasure Activism*, offers a deeper exploration of these concepts.[16]

Black feminists like Audre Lorde and Toni Cade Bambara have waxed poetic and extensively about how the process of radical worldbuilding must be irresistible, joyful, and pleasurable. It's simply not sustainable or effective to live in an endless state of rage, despair, and overwhelm at what is. I have learned this in my own body and by watching others burn themselves out and destroy what possibilities might otherwise exist while doing so. I have also frequently been reminded of this by dear friends. In one instance, I remember sitting socially distanced on Maura Bairley's back porch under orange wildfire skies in October 2020, facing the prospect of Trump's re-election. As I outlined the dire futures I believed lay ahead, Maura looked at me and simply said, "I am just not motivated by fear and rage." I remember initially being irritated by her response, thinking that it meant she was Pollyannaishly dismissing the realities I was describing. But I soon realized the truth of what she was saying; it is profoundly human to want to move toward joy, pleasure, connection, and hope, and it is profoundly demobilizing to operate exclusively from the cold numbness of fear or the quick fire of anger rather than the long, slow burn of love. Love is what gets us to what is transformative, resilient, and helps us creates new possibilities we cannot otherwise imagine.

In other words, building a world without police, prisons, and punishment should be a process that is "abolitious," as Jillian

Grissel, a graduate student who presented at the 2019 ASA conference where I first shared these ideas, described it. And, as panelists speaking to the legacy of Grace Lee Boggs and Jimmy Boggs at the same conference emphasized, it is a process that must be deeply rooted in love, in the ways revolutionaries from Che Guevara ("At the risk of seeming ridiculous, let me say that a great feeling of love guides the true revolutionary") to Assata Shakur ("r/evolution is love") to Detroit water warrior Charity Hicks ("wage love") have taught us. Of course, Black feminist love scholar bell hooks has much to teach us about the healing and transformative properties of more deeply understanding and moving from love. And, I think this is what beloved friend and Just Practice Collaborative cofounder Rachel Caïdor means when she says that emergent strategies require emotional rigor as well as political rigor: both emergent strategies and abolition require us to have the discipline to stay rooted in and to move from love, from the understanding that "justice is what love looks like in practice."[17]

Shannon Perez-Darby talks about the importance of experiencing joy as we do the hard work of abolition: "I want people to be lighter and have more fun. Are you actually enjoying what you are doing? Are you just rolling into your bed at the end of the day with nothing left, exhausted? That is not going to get us to the world we want." I have been leaning into finding joy, pleasure, and ease in the everyday rather than presuming all that will come "after" the never ending revolutionary work of abolition is done. Staff meetings at Interrupting Criminalization often erupt into peals of laughter, and I am increasingly remembering to bring spaciousness, music, scent, light, and pleasure to work. I pause work to play Legos, cards, or games with my next door nibling as often as I can; I am learning to follow the rhythms of my body and nap as I need to; I am saving summer evenings for sailing, gardening, and lying in my hammock watching the sun set and the stars come out.

Leah Lakshmi Piepzna-Samarasinha notes that pleasure activism, which she defines as "a politic that uplifts joy and pleasure in activism and radical life," is often critiqued as uplifting "individual self-care and hedonism as the world burns, without a class analysis of who gets to afford certain pleasures and how we define pleasure with regards to what things cost."[18] Similar critiques have been leveled at politics of radical rest (as Seattle-based organizer Angélica Cházaro quips, "Sure, take a nap, but be sure to set an alarm!"). Leah fiercely claims both pleasure and rest, asserting, "Consciously choosing to create disabled pleasure is a radical act," echoing Audre Lorde's words to the same effect.[19] "Joy and pleasure are key parts of what both helps us make the disabled future we are dreaming of now, in this moment, and in helping us keep going when the work is hard and heartbreaking."[20] And, as Barbara Smith emphatically reminds us, "As important as it is to create positive conditions under which we do our work, to my mind creating these conditions is not the same thing as political organizing to eradicate the socioeconomic conditions that created the need for healing, self-care, and rest in the first place."[21]

Surprise

A key concept of complexity science is that complex systems are more than a sum of their parts, operating through something beyond simple cause and effect. Margaret Wheatley describes this as "surprising." In other words, it can feel like there is an element of magic in how critical connections, small structures, networks, and communities of practice shape and shift larger systems. Part of the reason this may be the case is that it is impossible for individuals in complex systems to perceive or conceptualize the whole system or how it operates—much like individual ants don't fully grasp how their actions coalesce into a colony and the vastness of the universe boggles most human minds. What feels surprising about emergent strategies may simply be the product of forces we cannot measure or understand.[22]

It feels risky and potentially dangerous in this moment of rising fascism, white supremacy, economic, and climate collapse to put something out into the world that essentially says, "Focus on your relationships, build your networks, create spaces to practice abolition every day, learn from your experiments, and trust your efforts will coalesce with those of others, and something surprising will happen that can disrupt these larger, murderous, harmful, and destructive systems." And yet, I am reminded that in *Golden Gulag*, Ruth Wilson Gilmore writes, "The chronicles of revolutions all show how persistent and small changes, and altogether unexpected consolidations, added up to enough weight, over time and space, to cause a break with the old order."[23] My hope is that drawing on emergent strategies will help us to remember and better understand this and to focus on creating the conditions that will make these unexpected consolidations more likely—in which, as shea howell says, "emergence will combine with convergence to make abolition inevitable."

During my conversation with Mia Mingus, we sat with how hard it feels to stay focused on building the soil in the face of urgency—whether it's fascism or the ongoing epidemic of child sexual abuse her work has tackled for decades. We concluded that, hard as it is on both fronts, we just have to accept that we only need to do the work steadily every day and that, at some point, there's going to be an unlock, a tipping point, a shift somehow. We can't forecast or predict exactly when or how it'll happen, but what we can do is keep putting in the work—what Ruthie calls "life in rehearsal."

As gardeners, we know that you just have to constantly keep plowing the soil, aerating it, putting in more fertilizer, bringing more nutrients into the system to make it flourish. Mia added,

> I feel like it's that—just steadily doing the work—but also knowing that you're hopefully priming the pump in the steady work. It's not just steady work for the sake of steady work; we're doing this because we know at some point there's going to be something. Either it's going to completely die and we're going to learn from that, or it's going to explode with life because there are things

happening under its surface that we can't even see or that we can't even understand necessarily.

Diana, who is also a gardener, talks about policy as a way of trying to change the weather (a complex system), which fails because, actually, the weather (the complex system) shapes how policy is implemented. The goal is to shift the system through our actions and the conditions they create. She talks about how the spectacular abundance of her garden, which spills out onto the street, has encouraged her neighbors to garden, and how together they have shifted the microclimate on their block, as well as conditions for everyone who lives there in terms of access to fresh food and for wildlife who now find spaces to flourish even though they are less than a mile from a freeway, without any top-down or policy-based strategy to achieve these outcomes. Of course, that's a long way from averting mass extinctions, climate collapse, and the food shortages and economic upheaval they will produce. But given the failures of current efforts to address these things through law and policy, what new and surprising possibilities might acting in ways consistent with emergent strategies, shaped by a clear politic, with the knowledge and intention to impact and shape larger systems, open up?

Beyond that, as kai lumumba barrow puts it, "There's something about trying to predict the future that is ridiculous." As shea howell points out, "Nobody knows the future. It's created by the choices we make. That's why everybody's little piece matters because it's in the process of making choices that are in distinction from this overall thing that's falling down that we're able to create the new."

There is so much about emergent strategies that requires us to trust and lean into the unknown, uncertainty, unknowability—when, at a time of such rapid and terrifying change, our instincts to grasp for the known, the tried and true, are at their strongest.

The same is true of abolition—we are being asked to dream and practice a world we have never known, and which the cops in our heads and hearts make it impossible to imagine by design, as violence of all kinds rages and rips through communities and ecosystems we care about.

Yet, as I was writing *Practicing New Worlds*, I kept thinking and talking about the first fish who began to grow legs—even though swimming in a primordial ocean many millennia ago, they couldn't possibly conceive of a world where this action (I know it wasn't intentional but bear with me) would have an impact.

And here we are, many millennia later, on land, typing on a computer, reading this book, thinking about the fish. What can it teach us about leaning into uncertainty to create new possibilities?

A Note on Wave-Particle Duality

The wavicle emblem in Complex Movement's iconography signifies the principle of wave-particle duality, which posits that energy moves like a wave until you try to measure it, and then it acts like a particle, for which you can either know speed or location but never both. In other words, for those of us who, like me, failed physics, the act of observation itself changes the nature of the object being observed. Or, as shea howell put it, "What you expect to see changes what you see . . . once you start observing, you actually enter into and affect the observed thing." Or, as Octavia Butler's protagonist Lauren Olamina says in the Parables Series, "All that you touch you change. All that you change changes you."

Complex Movements interprets this principle as an invitation to release both certainty and false binaries. The collective offers it to help organizers understand that we need to continue to reach for what we cannot see—for a world that is as elusive as energy—while we grasp for what shows up as a particle, a fractal, a piece of a larger whole. As soon as we claim to know what abolition is, to point to one step we have taken toward it, the horizon moves further ahead.

Over the past several years—in fact, probably since my involvement with INCITE!—I have been one of many abolitionists grappling with the role of the state in abolitionist futures.[1] ill weaver of Complex Movements suggested that this is a conversation where the wavicle principle might be helpful: is the state something fixed that is incompatible with abolition by definition—or is it something mutable, like a wavicle, that we can't truly put our finger on, whose energy can be reshaped and redirected toward abolitionist futures through our interactions with it, by simultaneously contesting with it and inhabiting it? shea muses, "There is something in that about how when you enter the state, you can change what's there." At a commemoration of the twentieth anniversary of the publication of *Freedom Dreams* during the Socialism 2022 conference, Robin D.G. Kelley describes his book as an invitation to think beyond the binary of state and non-state, to find what lies in the fertile ground between these two poles.[2] Wavicles, like emergent strategies, remind us to recognize and release false binaries, to take hold of a piece of what we are wrestling with while recognizing that it is impossible to measure all of its properties and to remember that the state, like everything else, is part of a larger, imperceptible, complex whole that we are shaping through our interactions.

The wavicle principle also invites us to value process and outcome equally and to understand that each informs the other. That is what emergent strategies is about: focusing on how the processes shapes the outcome. Wave-particle duality also helps us to let go of the need for certainty about what abolitionist futures will look like and see ourselves as part of weaving them into being.

Practice (A Conclusion)

Any theory you got, practice it. And when you practice it, you
make some mistakes. When you make a mistake, you correct that
theory . . . A lot of us read and read and read, but we don't get
any practice.

—FRED HAMPTON

I must look about me and, as a Black feminist, I must
ask myself: how is my own lifework serving to end these
tyrannies, these corrosions of sacred possibility?

—JUNE JORDAN

At the end of 2021, I participated in an online retreat that invited
us to distill a single word from our life maps and visions for
the year ahead. "Practice" is the word that surfaced. Throughout 2022, the year I did the most writing, thinking, and talking
about this book, the word "practice" hovered in front of me on
a stickie on my desk lamp.

Practice is something I became more attuned to through
my participation in Black Organizing for Leadership and Dignity (BOLD), in which we are regularly invited to practice new
ways of being in our bodies, in relationship, in our organizing toward Black liberation—and we are taught that it takes

hundreds, thousands of repetitions to embody something different.[1] Practice can imply many things: a trying something new, honing a skill or competency, a profession, or a daily devotion. I practice singing (something I was always told I couldn't do, but it turns out maybe I can, with practice), yoga (something I found torturous when I first started, but through the pandemic I have practiced my way into a decent relationship with downward facing dog), law (but with a strong intent to undermine the structures and relations of power it manufactures and upholds), and meditation (a practice that has created new possibilities in my life). And I am learning to see and experience love and relationships as practice spaces for healing and transformation.

In addition to organizing with the National Network of Abortion Funds, Adaku Utah is a healer with Harriet's Apothecary and an instructor with BOLD. They emphasize that rigorous practice is essential to individual and systemic transformation: "I really believe that without practice, we move away from what we long for, what we value, and automatically sometimes start to adopt ways of being with ourselves and with each other that have harmed us for generations. Practice is such a vital piece of how we change, and emergent strategy has offered so much shared language and practical tools around how we do that."[2]

The question "What are you practicing?" always brings me back to myself, my values, my intention, my commitments— Am I practicing policing and punishment? Or am I practicing embodying and receiving love, with boundaries, for the sake of ancestral healing and bringing into being the world I long for? Am I practicing doing what I have been taught, what I have always done, what will likely continue to lead to the same results? Or am I practicing being the person I need and want to be and to become to fulfill my purpose—to contribute to building a world where Black women, girls, trans, and nonbinary people can freely love and be fully loved? What is the person, politic, future I am practicing? During a panel at the Highlander Center's Eightieth Homecoming, I mused that I had no idea when I was engaged in anti-apartheid struggles in the

'80s that I was practicing becoming someone who, decades later, would be gathered with hundreds under a tent in Tennessee talking about abolition and preparing for a new world coming—or who would be writing a book like *Practicing New Worlds*.

How do we collectivize this practice of becoming? In *Undrowned* Alexis Pauline Gumbs asks, "What are the intergenerational and evolutionary ways that we become what we practice? How can we navigate oppressive environments with core practices that build community, resistance, and more loving ways of living?" As Adaku wondered on the *Emergent Strategy Podcast*: "How do we sustain the relationships that we need to meet the depth of the changes that we need to make across generations? How do we sustain the relationships we need to make our dreams of interdependence, of liberation, of justice and repair, come true?"[3]

Practice is perhaps another word for what emergent strategists call "iteration" and Ruth Wilson Gilmore calls "life in rehearsal," for the process of transformation. In a session hosted by Interrupting Criminalization about the role of the state in abolitionist futures, I was deeply moved by a series of generative questions offered by South African scholar/organizers Kelly Gillespie and Leigh-Ann Naidoo. Their provocations were rooted in their reflections on the failure of the traditional two-stage approach (seize the state to transform it) to create conditions conducive to a full manifestation of Black liberation in the transition from apartheid to post-apartheid South Africa. They asked:

> How do we prepare for the life we want to live?
>
> What is the work of liberation?
>
> What is the psychic work, the relational work, the institutional processes that need to take place in, around, and between us for that liberation to manifest?
>
> What kind of schooling and skilling or readying is necessary to practice self-governance?
>
> What do we need to make way for liberatory relationships?

I have come to the conclusion that some of the answers to these questions lie in emergent strategies, in pursuing greater understanding of how we transform structures of oppression by transforming ourselves, our relationships, networks, and communities of practice rather than seeking and putting all our faith in top-down approaches that depend on and are of the systems we are fighting. Emergent strategies are far from the totality of the answer, but they are tools for better understanding how change happens. Deployed within the context of a clear set of political commitments, a clear understanding of the relations of power we are contending with and must confront, and a clear grasp of the types of power we are trying to create, they can point us to toward the best of abolitionist organizing as a politic and a practice.

And, as I was working on this book, I expressed to many of the people I spoke with my discomfort with advancing emergent strategies in the face of rising fascism, ecological collapse, and state and white-supremacist violence. I would often say that I worried about offering false or simplistic answers along the lines of "be like mushrooms" in a context where white-supremacist violence is a daily and escalating occurrence, where the very existence of trans people and bodily autonomy of people with the capacity for pregnancy is under attack, in which, as Talia Levin compellingly argues, people and communities I am part of and care about are squarely in the sights of a holy war.[4] While I profoundly believe we need to reach beyond the strategies we know to bring into being abolitionist futures, I can't be unserious in this moment.

Walidah Imarisha resonated with this concern and with a strong sense that explorations of emergent strategies must be grounded in these material realities: "We can't just be like, 'We're birds, we're flying'. . . . People are shooting at us, it's hunting season. . . . We have got to have a strategy. . . . It can be adaptive, but we have to recognize we're in it. We can create freedom, but we don't have freedom."

The more I talked to people, the more I became convinced that emergent strategies do, in fact, offer a critical part of the answer to how we create freedom, even in the most serious of times. During our conversation about the SOIL initiative, Mia Mingus responded to my concerns by saying,

> We need to be the people who are already wrapped around the families and the people in the community who experience these forms of violence, who can help them to collectively heal and strengthen our relationships with one another and build resilience. This helps to create fertile soil for more and more of us to prevent, heal, and transform the conditions that create barren and toxic soil.
>
> That's literally all we can do.
>
> There's no rake or pitchfork or magic law or tool we can take to the situation, and I think that's the hardest thing. I mean, it's what *No Shortcuts* says.[5] That's what all the organizing books that are coming out now are saying, but I think it's particularly rooted in transformative justice. We really just have to figure out how to build resilience and make soil for transformation.

As I worked on this book, I also listened to one of my favorite podcasts, *Movement Memos*, which is produced by Truthout and hosted by Kelly Hayes, longtime organizer and coauthor, with Mariame, of *Let This Radicalize You: Organizing and the Revolution of Reciprocal Care.*[6] In an episode with Chris Begley, author of *The Next Apocalypse: The Art and Science of Survival*, in which they discuss fantasies and realities of societal collapse and rebirth, Kelly says:

> Stories about how pretty much everyone will pose a threat to us during an emergency justify and inspire our cooperation with profound levels of violence dealt out by police, the government, and the capitalist system. This cooperation helps to enable systemic violence against some of the same targets that white supremacists and fascists target in their fantasies and in their real-world violence, such as migrants, Black people, Muslims, and trans people.

This cooperation also helps ensure that the system that is marching us toward destruction is not disrupted in its work, because we have been conditioned to fear the disorder that authority and fiction have foretold more than neoliberalism, fascism, or ecocide.[7]

Kelly and Chris go on to talk about the fact that during a short-term crisis people tend to behave in ways *contrary* to "every man for himself" narratives of collapse, as seen in responses to natural disasters or mutual aid the early months of the coronavirus pandemic. However, it is not a certainty that these tendencies will hold in the face of prolonged stress. As Kelly put it and Chris affirmed based on his anthropological studies and the history of post–World War I Europe, "People do not become progressive, informed, fair, and equitable after they go through a crisis. Often, they look for somebody to blame, and the blame will fall on the least powerful, the marginalized, and those unable to defend themselves."[8]

When elites fan the flames of these tendencies in an effort to hold onto power, the result is what we are seeing: people walking into grocery stores, schools, and clubs that are populated by the people they have been goaded into scapegoating for the fallout of racial capitalism and neoliberalism and enacting devastating anti-Black, anti-Indigenous, anti-trans, anti-Muslim, anti-migrant, anti-Asian, ableist, misogynist violence. Not a single act of collapse, Kelly emphasizes, but an acceleration and ongoing manifestation of the collapse we have been living since the advent of settler colonialism, the transatlantic slave trade, accelerated by industrialism and neoliberalism.[9] As Leanne Betasamosake Simpson writes in *Rehearsals for Living*, "Imperialism and ongoing colonialism have been ending worlds for as long as they have been in existence, and Indigenous and Black peoples have been building worlds and then rebuilding worlds for as long as we have been in existence. Relentlessly building worlds through unspeakable violence and loss."[10]

While many of us (myself included) are frantically preparing "go bags," learning wilderness survival, honing self-defense skills, and plotting our escape in response to our fantasies of the apocalypse, the reality is that the same things that have helped Black and Indigenous people survive the ongoing apocalypses are the things that will serve us best now: discernment and critical thinking skills; our relationships, our networks, our capacity to make and maintain critical connections; our cooperation and commitment to our collective sustainability; our ability to learn from our mistakes and adapt; our interdependence and willingness to collaborate and generatively engage conflict; our resilience and capacity for transformation; and our faith in our ability to create new possibilities.[11] And these are the skills, the connections, that capitalism—and the policing that produces and maintains it—has robbed from us.

They are also the skills that have sustained what kai describes as "marronage—that's how the Maroons and Indigenous communities and radical poor white people who were in struggle around the violences of colonialism and slavery survived." Picking up her questions about the operation of emergent strategies when communities are under direct attack from the state, kai emphasizes that marronage wasn't always about running away, fugitivity. There were points of direct confrontation—like the ones imagined in Kung Li Sun's contribution to the Emergent Strategy Series, *Begin the World Over*.[12] kai elaborates,

> Right now, we deal with direct confrontation through policy, through a public forum that asks or demands the state to change its practices. When it comes to expanding beyond networks and the cells that we're constructing, what are the strategies to shift the way power operates that don't mean taking it to them for their approval or disapproval but taking action that disrupts the system as it is currently operating, that gets to the root of where the problems lie?

kai and I pondered how to reconcile abolitionist organizing guided by emergent strategies with the inevitable need for direct confrontation with the systems that seek to repress the new world emerging through our practices. As we did, I mused about how practicing, deepening, and strengthening our relationships, communities, and networks can help to build connective tissue that grows our capacity to be, as Adaku Utah put it, "hopeful, courageous, and audacious" as we confront the violences of the current moment and contend for our vision of the future.[13]

Speaking of the decade during which they organized with the National Democratic Movement in the Philippines, facing intense state repression, Kalayo Pestaño told me, "When we're facing down the military, it's a very real thought that you may not make it out of this or you may not make it fully intact." They talked about how participants in this mass movement draw strength from being a part of small collectives of people they live with or see daily, build relationships and share resources with, with whom they seek and offer emotional and spiritual support around challenges and hardships: "I would see the same group of three to ten people all the time. I think that is necessary and has always been an effective way to make sure that we have the bonds and trust that it takes to be out on the streets and look out for each other." This is another way that building critical connections rooted in care and shared values matters; while some of us might not be willing to risk our lives, limbs, and livelihoods for an idea, many more of us are absolutely willing to do so for people and communities we love.

People are also motivated by longings for a different future for themselves and their loved ones and emboldened by a felt experience of different possibilities. Abolitionist organizer and BOLD trainer Sendolo Diaminah talks about organizing as "creating lived experiences of exceeding what we were told the present could be . . . and then having the courage to take the risk" to act toward the future we want.[14] Offering people an embodied perception of a world beyond carceral capitalism, a lived experience of otherwise, a perception of a collective ability to generate greater safety and well-being in relationship even under adverse conditions makes it all much more possible for so many of us.

As I was making final edits to this manuscript, the battle to #StopCopCity was raging in Atlanta. At the same time, a different yet familiar battle was being fought over how to respond to yet another brutal, videotaped police killing of a Black man, this time a young skateboarder, father, and amateur photographer named Tyre Nichols. Once again, the vast majority of people reached for policy-based solutions that, for the most part, would prove empty—none would have stopped Tyre from being killed, none offered healing and transformation of the conditions that led the cops to beat him to death. Nevertheless, the people Mariame calls "police preservationists" sought to pass legislation in Tyre's name that would make changes on paper without changing deadly practices of policing—and worse yet, that would pour still more money and legitimacy into the cops. Meanwhile, the Memphis Police Department continues to consume almost half of the city's resources. Thankfully, community organizers in Memphis fought for and continue to fight for legislation that would actually transform the conditions that led to Tyre's killing by ending police involvement in traffic stops and decriminalizing minor traffic offenses.

Less than six hours away, police and politicians are engaged in virulent and violent aggression against people organizing around a demand rooted not in policy but in direct confrontation with police and corporate power: stop construction of a $90 million police training facility designed to skill cops up in urban warfare on land stolen from the Muscogee Creek Nation, on grounds that previously served as a prison farm, in the middle of the Weelaunee Forest, known as one of "the lungs of Atlanta."[15] Thirty million of the construction budget would come from Atlanta's public coffers, while $60 million would come from private corporations' contributions to the Atlanta Police Foundation. The connection between capital and cops could not be more clear.[16] Organizers have effectively targeted city officials preparing to suppress future uprisings against ongoing structural and police violence and the corporations colluding with them to build Cop City and buy police protection as they engage in ever more extractive and destructive practices.[17] In response, protesters have been targeted with deadly violence, taking the life of a beloved, dedicated, and beautiful young queer Indigenous Venezuelan forest defender named Manuel "Tortuguita" Terán during a raid of a forest encampment that also led to arrests of dozens of protesters who were subsequently charged with domestic terrorism.[18] An independent autopsy revealed that, contrary to police accounts, Tortuguita was seated cross-legged with their hands in the air when they were shot. During a heartbreaking press conference, Tortuguita's grieving mother, Belkis Terán, assumed their posture to demonstrate, offering a haunting image of what amounts to the extrajudicial execution of a person resisting a police state.[19]

The full story of the movement to #StopCopCity has already been written and remains to be told by those who are on the front lines.[20] As I joined people across the country in solidarity actions while completing this book, I couldn't help but see the contradictions I am wrestling with here unfolding in real time. There is no question that emergent strategies are at play in the fight to #StopCopCity. Organizers are seeking to shift a global system of policing by targeting a fractal that would replicate to intensify the violence of policing, racial capitalism, and environmental racism on a worldwide scale. By training police from Atlanta, across the US, and around the world in suppression of popular movements and repression of Black, Indigenous, migrant, and low-income communities targeted for elimination and abandonment in the midst of economic and climate collapse, #CopCity would serve as a host for virulent repression. The protesters are fighting to plant and nurture a different seed, to manifest an abolitionist fractal on that land instead.

There is no singular leader or organization directing the highly decentralized movement led by residents of a predominantly Black neighborhood in the throes of organized abandonment located next to the proposed #CopCity site. It is instead composed of anti-police violence and climate justice organizers; school children and outdoor enthusiasts; along with area students and faith leaders. The movement to

#StopCopCity was built from existing networks and has taken an experimental approach, iterating and adapting their tactics in response to internal and external challenges and changing conditions, guided by a simple intention: "Cop City will never be built."[21] They have created multiple roles for people and yet moved as a whole. They have leaned into a tempo of action that allowed for ebbs and flows.[22] Like Freedom Square, forest protest encampments have sought to prefigure abolitionist futures, featuring free food and collective care. Organizers have advanced transformative demands that not only focus on the violence the facility will facilitate but the climate injustice its construction represents and the colonialism that destruction of the forest on the traditional lands of the Muskogee people it would perpetuate. They have cultivated resilience in the face of repression, literally finding each other in nature. And through struggle, they have created new possibilities for people across the country and around the world to join in resistance to the violence of policing and capital and offered a master class in tracing and targeting the shared interests of cops and corporations.

They are facing the very intensifying violence, repression, and punishment intended to crush them that I, and so many of the people I spoke with while writing this book, fear emergent strategies neither prepare us for nor contend with. Certainly deployment of emergent strategy principles did not prevent Tortuguita's killing or the ongoing (at the time of this writing) prosecution of dozens of protesters facing charges that could lead to decades of incarceration. Nor were they able to stop the approval of construction plans—although they were previously successful in getting the first contractor to withdraw its bid for the project.

It is also true that, through critical connections built in and around the struggle, as well as networks of support and practice, decentralized solidarity actions are taking place across the country and around the world. Communities of care are wrapping themselves around Tortuguita's family, each of the protesters facing arrest and draconian charges, and around the communities of Black residents, Indigenous land stewards, climate justice activists, and justice seekers who are leading this movement. Even as my heart breaks for Tortuguita's mother, for everyone who knew and loved them, and for every single person who is being caged and targeted with or living in fear of terrorism charges, I am nevertheless heartened by the possibility that we are once again coalescing into a system of care and influence that can produce yet another radical shift in our collective consciousness and practices toward abolitionist futures.

Writing this book has itself been a practice—of stepping into the unfamiliar, of seeking and relying on critical connections when I felt lost, of embodying something that is profoundly uncomfortable into a muscle memory, of writing about what I don't know instead of what I do, of learning and potentially failing in public, of adaptation as internal and external conditions shifted over time, of cooperation through collectivization of the process of thinking through, of iteration after iteration, of grasping for things I thought I knew and realizing that once I did that they became more unknowable, of finding pleasure in learning, writing, and collaborative exploration, of reveling in the beauty of the cover art, the emblems and the gorgeous visionary art and writing reproduced in its pages, of vulnerability in publicly sharing my creative fiction for the first time, and of a commitment to transformation in the service of the work. And there are ways that it came together that were surprising. In other words, the process of writing *Practicing New Worlds* has been a fractal of the invitation it represents.

This offering represents a practice of study and exploration of what is and what lies beyond, a strengthening of new capacities, an effort to reach past what I was taught about making change in the hopes of finding and perhaps shining some light on a multiplicity of ways forward. What I do know is that we need all the tools we can muster to meet this moment and those to come, that we can no longer afford to keep reaching for those that continue to fail us. What I do know is that we need to fight like hell, using the best of our collective wisdom, for the living and for the futures we long for, in the name of those who have come before us, those stolen from us, and those who will come after us. What I do know is that we are contending for a vision of the future that centers collective care and care for the planet we call home.

What I know is that we are practicing new worlds.

Pandowrimo

What follows are some of my own forays into visionary fiction, in the form of responses to adrienne maree brown's Pandowrimo writing prompts offered in the first months of the pandemic on her Instagram account.

adrienne described the goal of the exercise as "to harness our imaginations to help us survive this pandemic and generate the world we dream of on the other side of it."

These pieces represent some of my first attempts to answer this call through my writing, in which I processed what felt like an overwhelming and incomprehensible reality by dreaming alternate beginnings and endings.

Day 1 Prompt

What if we see COVID-19 as a sentient, even sacred force . . . one that emerged to address an urgent crisis. What is the crisis? Write a conversation between the virus and the crisis.

Humanity: Where did you come from? Why are you here?
COVID-19: How are you even asking me this—isn't it obvious? I am here to make it impossible to turn away from you what you have refused to look at, to bring into the sharpest possible relief the realities you have refused to recognize and respond

to, to make it impossible to unsee the wickedness of your ways, the cost of your capitalism, the inhumanity of your indifference. To make clear that everything must change. To teach you new ways of being.

Humanity: You are a cruel teacher.

COVID-19: I am the teacher that you require. You have refused the lessons of my predecessors—of famine, of flu, of floods, of financial collapse, of earthquakes, storms, volcanic eruptions, tidal waves, of the voices from behind the walls you built and beyond the borders you constructed and inside the cages you locked them in and from the bodies and minds and beings you considered disposable. You have been lazy students, remembering for a minute of crisis then forgetting, submitting sloppy solutions that didn't respond to the questions posed, refusing the deeper lessons, taking advantage of the situation, cheating on the test. You have refused to heed, even as each teacher raised their voices louder and louder and louder. Now you will listen.

Humanity: OK, we got the message—now can we just go back to normal?

COVID-19 [ROARS]: NO. NEVER. WHEN WILL YOU UNDERSTAND??? THERE IS NO NORMAL. THERE IS ONLY THIS. There is only one message. There is only one lesson. Change EVERYTHING. Let go of the idea that you can salvage this system, tweak this, reform that, shift a few things, but continue as before. There is no before. There is only now. This. What comes next . . . . depends on you.

Humanity: . . .

Day 2 Prompt

Many of us are realizing we had premonitions of this moment. Now you are given the opportunity to travel back in time (maybe to that premonition moment) and make one change that prevents the crisis of COVID-19 in your city. Tell the story of your intervention.

They made themselves ungovernable.

They refused to accept the theft, the desperate snatch of power by those bent on destruction, the lies, the grift, the naked hatred, the visceral refusal of humanity, of change, of collectivity, the empty promise of elections, the notion of a singular savior.

They refused.

They marched in the hundreds of thousands, every single day. They went to the borders and airports and stayed there until they couldn't keep anyone out. They went on strike, they disrupted proceedings and business as usual every single day. They put their bodies in between each other and harm, they found ways to freeze the police, the army, the National Guard called on them, to neutralize them, to walk them out of their neighborhoods and communities. They found ways to fill the gaps, to take care of each other, to buy each other's freedom, to link arms around the globe, to become each other's business, to wrestle with the hard things we do to each other, to put forward and live an irresistible vision and reality.

They refused to go back to business as usual, to double down and put their faith in the same tools that had betrayed them, proved themselves useless, proved themselves deadly disappointments.

They tapped in and out as they could, imagined new ways everyone could be part of the resistance, new ways of leading and following and recognizing each of us as an imperfect s/he/queero, of taking care of each other, and of living each moment in love and joy and struggle. They studied and learned from the lessons of the past and celebrated and nurtured the imaginers, the visioners, those who could see beyond all we know to all that can be.

They never let go. They never tried to go back to "normal," to wait it out, they never just hoped that it would go away, they never stuck their head in the sand, they never turned away even when they turned within or turned to rest. They never fell for those who would claim to lead but collude instead. They didn't stop at screaming at them, they unseated them. They didn't waste their time on "reforms" and "elections."

They dreamed the world they wanted while they vehemently shrugged off the one they had created and inherited.

And so, by the time the death throes came, they were ready. With comfort, care, compassion, a deep collective spirit, a blueprint, and the harvest of a multitude of experiments in new ways of being. With power. With strength. With resilience. With the means to cast off the killer carapace once and for all and the courage to step forward into resurrection.

Day 3 Prompt

Tell a story from an alternate timeline that runs parallel to this one, sparked at the beginning of this pandemic. (If we took it seriously from the beginning.)

They loved each other through it.

When the first person landed in New York City, they welcomed her with love and care. They asked her what she needed to feel safe and heal and made sure she had it. They cheered and celebrated her for loving everyone by staying away and eased her time with songs and prayers and laughter and beauty. They asked her to share lessons of how to survive separately and told each other stories that would prepare them all. They loved her families and peoples by immediately lifting the cruel sanctions they had imposed on them for reasons no one could remember and eased her worry for them by sending them love, and supplies.

They loved each other by immediately shifting to new ways of being together and apart. They made sure everyone had a safe place to be. Hotels opened their doors to survivors—of the streets, of violence, of jails, prisons, detention—and people made sure they had clothes, food, care, and connection. They closed schools and in-person communities—and made sure that everyone had everything they needed to stay connected, wiring free, high-speed, and unsurveilled internet into every home, making sure everyone had a way of using it. They set up a loveline staffed by people whose jobs were on pause to share information and strategies—everything from how to stay safe together and apart to how to care for children and elders and home pedicures to safe shopping to safe copping. They loved each other with songs and dance and yoga and poems and love letters. They all carefully learned the distance of six feet and lovingly gave it to each other with smiles as they moved through the world to breathe in the clean air and flowers.

They loved each other by looking for the cracks it crept through and closing them. They canceled rent and mortgages, they made sure everyone had quality, affordable housing, they paid everyone—everyone—what they needed to stay home, they made all health care free, they made tests available to anyone who wanted one—and mandated no one to take one. They told the police to stay away, stay home. They loved the people who had been caged by setting them free and welcoming them home to safe places and inviting them to dream a new life for themselves.

They loved the healthcare workers by giving them everything they needed to stay safe, enough equipment, ventilators, medication, humane schedules, healers for healers, care for their families and ways to come home to them without fearing that they were bringing death with them. They loved them like they were life itself and celebrated them with permanent living wages, protections, and sustaining working conditions. They loved the farm workers by giving them everything they needed to stay safe. They loved them like they were life itself, and they celebrated them with permanent living wages, protections, and sustaining working conditions. They loved the service and delivery workers for making life possible in this time and all times by giving them everything they needed to stay safe, celebrated them with permanent living wages, protections, and sustaining working conditions.

They loved disabled people and gave thanks and gratitude for sharing all the ways they had learned to live together and apart, all the wisdom they had grown about how to care for themselves and each other, and all the brilliance of their beings.

They loved them by prioritizing their care, and by refusing to deem anyone disposable.

They loved survivors by making them safe, by asking what they needed, by understanding when they didn't know or were too scared to step into safety, by loving them fiercely until they were safe, no matter what and how long it took.

They loved each other by spending the quiet time dreaming and imagining new ways of living, being with each other and the Earth, together and apart. They loved each other by grieving and celebrating each one lost and asking themselves what lessons and gifts from each life they would carry forward. They loved each other into the world they couldn't imagine before, which is now the only possibility.

They loved each other safe. They loved each other home. They loved each other free.

Day 4 Prompt:

Tell a story of the (beginning of) our quarantine and long-term isolation from the perspective of plants and/or the non-human world—the day the humans left.

The day the humans left.

At first, we didn't notice the quiet—that the solitary evening hours extended into the days and then past the days into weeks. We were fiercely focused inward on the business of Spring, of gathering all that we had incubated, nursed, nurtured, tended, fed, fueled, imagined, dreamed, concentrating and alchemizing it into leaves of impossible green, brilliant bold blossoms, berries for our bird friends, shining bark, potent and intoxicating fragrances. And slowly, as each of us allowed the beauty we had been cultivating within over the long, dark, gray months to burst forth in an operatic celebration of life sustained, renewed, reborn, reclaimed, reimagined, reinvigorated, reblessed, and brand new all over again, reaching for the bright blue sky and spring sunshine, tall in our radiance and glory, we noticed.

They weren't there.

We caught glimpses of a few here and there—a security guard, an occasional gardener come to tend to us, snapping a photograph or two and then moving on—but none of the crowds who regularly flocked to us at this time of year, pilgrims making sacred rounds, worshipping under our bursting branches, playing and laughing at our feet, crowding around us for photographs, celebrating love, ephemerality, and the truth and glory of life reborn each year. "We made it through another winter!" they would reflect with relief and disbelief, joy and aliveness. "We made it to see the cherries and peaches and almonds bloom, the daffodils sing out, the tulips mesmerize, the azaleas blaze, the wisteria hang redolent from the pergolas, to bathe in the honeysuckle and Oregon grape's sweet scents, the magnolia's spiced fragrance, the grape-flavored glory of the muscari, the heady fumes of the hyacinth, the loving embrace of the lilacs!"

We wondered what had happened. How could so many have forsaken this rite of passage, this ritual of renewal? What else could possibly be calling their attention? Why had they given up on celebrating the glory of life?

Some of us wondered if our lavish displays, curated with such care, so long awaited, our one annual magnum opus, are worth it if no one is there to witness them. Others reminded each other that each of us creates for our own sakes, for our own lives, as an expression of our own unique life force, for our own futures, as our own prayers, pilgrimages, and offerings of thanksgiving to the universe. Nothing more is needed or expected than to burst forth with our own expressions of aliveness.

So we flower on, now more attuned to the feeling of the wind against our bodies, the sun on our leaves, the songs of the birds flying in and out of us, the gifts of silence, cleaner and clearer air, sunshine, rain, and solitude. The grass is grateful to be free of feet and stretches high and green and strong. The water flows freely, no longer channeled to populate this area and that for their pleasure. The geese come and go, the cardinals, jays, finches, and robins have the run of the place. Bunnies busy themselves without fear. Dragonflies and fish begin to stir from their sleep, the turtles sun themselves without interruption.

Occasionally, now, we see one or two at the gates, looking in, straining to partake in our now solitary celebrations, sometimes smiling, sometimes weeping. Someday, they may return, and we will welcome them with open arms and brilliant blooms, we will listen as they whisper their sorrows into the waters, grieve those who will never again witness our miracles—and those who never did—soothe their hearts at our feet, tell tales of their long hibernation under the trees, sob in the hidden corners until they are sated, cautiously approach each celebration of love with the habit of distance, and slowly, slowly, slowly realize that they made it through another winter and remember that no matter what, Spring always comes.

Day 13 Prompt

How will all of these souls get reincarnated and reappear on Earth? (Will they be the souls of the coronials?)

It must be crowded on the next planes.

Not the ones we will rush to as soon as we are told it is safe—and maybe before—in an attempt to escape all the last many months of solitude and staring at the same walls has surfaced, in a desperate effort to cleanse our eyes of the sight of bodies piled up in refrigerated semi-trucks, frantic funeral home directors trying to move caskets to cars as quickly as possible, of mass graves dug by prisoners—of capitalism or Rikers, a distinction without difference—to cleanse our ears of sirens, persistent, wailing, demanding, grieving, to soothe our souls of grief and disbelief and the knowledge that it will come again and again and again, taking so many more until it is satisfied that we have learned, transformed, fully passed through the portal.

On the planes we transition to when we leave these bodies. The lines must be at least as long as the ones at the grocery stores we take for granted or at the food banks we rarely notice, or at the testing sites that prioritize those who can drive and turn away those who can only walk. Perhaps the accommodations are as crowded as the shelters we refuse to empty for fear of soiling pristine hotel rooms with the grime of abandonment, the refugee camps locked down in suffering, the nursing homes without nurses.

Maybe there is an inconceivably raucous celebration, a celestial festival, going on among those who made it through the portal first, who can see what we cannot, the world that lies on the other side. Maybe they are cheering us on like loving coaches, pushing us to get there together.

Maybe they are sitting in endless rows of waiting rooms outside the doors, like the ones at the hospitals where they died alone and their loved ones worried and grieved far away from them, in silent rage at how easily they were sacrificed. Maybe they are turning their backs on us for the time being.

Maybe they are pondering strategies for our survival and whispering the answers into the ears of those who are listening.

Some, no doubt, are considering whether to re-board this plane careening toward a cataclysmic crash. Weighing unfinished business against unnecessary suffering. Fingering their gifts like prayer beads and wondering whether this iteration of humanity is worthy of receiving them. Deliberating whether to fill new lungs so soon after laboring to fill old ones. Pondering the pros and cons of returning to a world on the edge, to the pandemics to come, to parents and people who will be steeped in the trauma of unprecedented loss for years, decades, generations to come, to a planet in crisis.

Some will decide to throw their fate in with us once again, in spite of all they know and have known. Some will embody hope in ways we cannot fathom by making a leap of faith in us, in spite of what we have shown ourselves capable of. Some will choose to labor alongside us to redeem our future. Some will bet on the long game. Some will choose us.

Let us welcome them back with boundless gratitude, fierce love, and tender tears.

And fight like hell for the world we all deserve.

Surfacing

She can't remember when she decided to do it.

Why she chose that day to make the journey. They rarely surfaced these days.

No one really knows when the trips slowed from a daily ritual, thousands flooding out to the far reaches of the ocean, to an occasional trickle. Maybe they just fell out of the habit.

She felt a strong pull to remain below that morning. The connection to her fellow mermaids as they bent to their labor of love, uniting to heal all kin who came to the ocean, standing on its edge, souls raw, hearts full of time-traveling pain embedded deep in their cells, replenished fresh and daily, felt compelling, completing, a collective prayer, a concert in which she was instrument, musician, and audience. The joy of filling hearts with love, bodies with balm, and souls with visions of a world beyond the violence infusing every aspect of the one they live in.

Transmitting on the frequency of a ripple, a sparkle of sunlight, a glistening at dawn, were the hopes of millions of mermaids who transformed the ocean from a killing field, an open grave, a gas chamber, a boneyard—of a continent, of civilizations, of countless people—into something unimaginably beautiful, beyond human understanding, impossible, except for the inexorable truth of the balance of the universe: every horror has an opposite, although it is often one humans are powerless to see or create except in small glimpses, ephemeral moments, exceptional beings.

As she moved upward, she continued to wonder, absent-mindedly, why she had torn herself away.

Maybe she just wanted to see the full moon. It could easily be seen from her home beneath the waves through an elaborate system of mirrors crafted to bring the light of celestial bodies to the ocean floor, illuminating shades of aqua, silver, pearl, riotous color, and rich, soft, blue-Blackness. But maybe she needed to see it in first person, in its full, brilliant, raw ebullience.

Maybe she heard a call—although when she listened carefully within for the familiar pull, she felt nothing.

At first.

She began a slow undulation of her long, sleek, full, and powerful body, her tail expanding into a giant, glittering fan, turning her strong, beautiful face instinctively toward the moment where air and ocean meet, her locs flowing behind her, her heart pulling upward, guiding her through shafts of darkness becoming columns of light as the moon's visage came into view. She closed her gills and opened her lungs as she broke the surface, an act as instinctual as it was practiced, a transition between states of being, between now and then. It was painful, as always, and yet easier each time as her understanding of healing as a journey between, and not beyond, deepened.

She doesn't remember how long she stayed at the surface, frolicking in the waves, distilled moonbeams on her face, filling her heart with quicksilver, glistening on her blue-Black skin, elevating the vibration of her being to almost unbearable ecstasy.

Now she watched the moon set and the sun rise, reveling in the surreal purple transition between illuminated darkness and soft light. The call of her siblings to return was becoming stronger—the pull not one of obligation but of infinite joy in their collective song, in each other, and in the unique magic she made within the whole. The pull of profound love for the kinfolk who found their way to the water, some regally clothed in flowing white robes, some naked and mischievous, some shivering with trepidation and trust, some immersing themselves up to their necks at sunset, waiting for the centuries of shame, shackles, torture, grief, cages, and ankle monitors to melt away as dolphins play.

She was about to begin the journey downward when she saw the tiny ship, holding just one. The sailor's attention was fully focused on the dance between her sail and the wind, instinctively and often imperceptibly shifting her weight in response to the rise and fall of the air, the wash of the waves, the hum of the hull. She was fully in what she would clumsily call her "happy place," her face luminous, bearing an expression most people in her life had never seen and wouldn't recognize if they did, her mind temporarily free of endless to-dos and the constant pursuit of perfection. A deep and gleeful laugh bubbled up from the depths of the sailor's center, an expression of sheer joy.

She instantly felt the connection.

As the mermaid got closer, she saw with surprise that the sailor was pale, although the sun had called what melanin remained up to the surface of her skin, rendering it a shade of nut brown. But her eyes were the piercing blue-green of the mermaid's captors, and her facial features were theirs—the sailor bore almost no resemblance to kin.

And yet.

She knew the sailor was of them, almost unrecognizably transformed by what lay on the other side of the ship's landing. She felt it at the cellular level, the shared atoms, lineage, history—faintly at first, then more and more strongly. In fact, it was more powerful than she had felt in a while—leaving her wondering if the sailor was one of her direct descendants. There were so many she could never know yet dreamed of often.

It was then that the sailor noticed her with a sharp intake of breath, wonder, and awe. As was the case with most at the surface, she was unable to comprehend what she was seeing—a glorious manifestation of survival, of trauma transformed, resistance embodied, of impossibility made possible—a glowing, shimmering embodiment of love and liberation no human could imagine.

So, what the sailor saw instead was a dolphin—glorious in its own right but a far cry from the magical truth before her.

Yet, as she continued to gaze in wonder, the sailor felt an inexplicable lightness in her usually heavy heart, an uncontainable joy, an aliveness beyond measure, a sudden certainty that she was not alone, an intractable knowledge that somehow, survival of the unsurviveable was not only possible but undeniable.

For a moment, their eyes met as their atoms spoke to each other in soft greetings, murmurings of recognition, gentle inquiries, tentative touches, reconnecting what had been violently split apart across time and space—the sailor, open to the wonder of what she couldn't possibly know or understand, the mermaid bemused by the wonder of this unexpected seedling.

After a time, the repair begun, the connection solidified, their kinship written in the waves, they both slowly turned away—the sailor to follow the breath of wind, the mermaid to return to the depths below and to her task of transforming inhumanity into light.

She knew why she had come.

for adrienne and alexis for inspiring me, for all the women who encouraged me to write it, and for the full moon that called me to the window to put the words on the page.

PRACTICE
MAKES
PATTERNS

CREATES
CULTURE

WEAVES
NEW
WORLDS

Molly Costello

Keep Practicing the Future

Molly Costello

Tending My Mycelium Network

Acknowledgments

The process of birthing a book is never easy, and it was definitely harder for *Practicing New Worlds* than for any other I have brought into the world. I owe deep gratitude to adrienne maree brown and Charles Weigl of AK Press for the invitation to transform the ideas I initially shared on a panel at the 2019 American Studies Association conference into a book (I think we called it a pamphlet at the time, lol), and for their grace and patience as I found the right time to do it. Deep appreciation to the rest of the team at AK who brought this invitation to life and bent time and space to make it possible for me to submit the book I wanted and could feel proud of.

Special shoutout to beloved and skillful editor Jill Petty, who also served as midwife for *Invisible No More*—AK and the Emergent Strategy Series are fortunate beyond measure to have her on board to steward this body of work. *Practicing New Worlds* also benefited greatly from, and was significantly improved by, the editorial guidance of laurie prendergast, Onnesha Roychoudhuri, Victoria Law, and Lorna Vetters, all of whom would have told me to shorten this sentence. Thanks to Zach Blue and the entire production team for adapting and iterating schedules to create new possibilities for this book to emerge on time despite delays due to organizing and life commitments. I am always and forever grateful to Levi Craske for answering the bat signal to attend to details of fact checking and to laurie prendergast for copy editing.

I am incredibly honored and profoundly thankful to Amir Khadar for gracing the cover with their gorgeous and inspiring art—there were times when I kept writing solely out of a sense that the cover deserved to be filled and in the world—and to Molly Costello for agreeing to contribute her luscious pieces inspired by *Emergent Strategy* and to create original art for the poster celebrating the book's release, and to Wes Taylor and the Complex Movements crew for allowing me to reprint their glorious poetic emblems. Infinite thanks to ill weaver and Complex Movements for being willing to trust me with the process of collaborating to document their brilliance, and special appreciation to ill for being willing to walk me through and geek out over complexity science for hours on the deck and long road trips. During an episode of the *Emergent Strategy Podcast*, ill recalled Grace Lee Boggs saying that we need to be more like midwives that support the birth of movements that are already emerging. ill was a much-needed midwife to this book when it was emerging but firmly stuck in the birth canal. Last, but certainly not least, I am grateful to Lisa Bates, Walidah Imarisha, Shawn Taylor, and the Wakanda Dream Lab for contributing visionary fiction to illuminate our practice of new worlds. You also wouldn't be holding this book in your hands if Amanda Alexander and Scott Kurashige hadn't started the chain reaction by telling me about the 2019 ASA conference and asking me to speak at it, for which I am also profoundly thankful.

Of course, this book wouldn't exist if adrienne hadn't taken the risk of sharing the ideas in *Emergent Strategy* with the world. I am honored by her kind words and Introduction to *Practicing New Worlds* and grateful for the ways our paths have crossed over the past two decades in Detroit and beyond. As a coach, adrienne has accompanied me through some of the hardest periods of my life, supported me in stepping fully into myself as a writer as I worked on *Invisible No More*, and invited me into more joyful and easeful ways of being myself in the world. As a teacher and healer, she introduced me to and trained me in the somatic practices that have completely transformed my life. And as a beloved community member, she passed on her beautiful space when she moved away from Detroit—which has become one of the happiest homes I have ever had (#homejoy!). It seems fitting that *Practicing New Worlds* was largely written in the same physical space as *Emergent Strategy*, informed by countless conversations with the same people, in the same rooms. And to have the brilliant Black feminist genius and love evangelist Alexis, who I met at the same time and place as I first met adrienne—the Allied Media Conference—write the Foreword is clearly the universe, which Alexis is currently in the process of describing in the same mind-blowing, heart-opening, spiritually expanding Black feminist revolutionary way she communed with marine mammals in *Undrowned*, at work. Alexis's invitations to ancestral listening, Black feminist breathing, and creative practice in online classes offered through Mobile Homecoming, as well as the opportunity to commune at Blue Mountain Center and at our own self-created writing retreat have been instrumental to the emergence of *Practicing New Worlds*—and particularly to the visionary fiction within (as well as the courage to share it!).

I am blessed beyond measure by the incredible crew of doulas who cheered me on through this long labor, read multiple drafts, found diamonds in the rough of the earliest ones and encouraged me to dig deeper, participated in salons, answered late-night texts, ordered food for me, and continued to remind me that I could do it when I despaired that I couldn't. They consistently affirmed the value in this offering when I was consumed by doubt about its utility in this moment, and repeatedly expressed faith that I was the right person to offer it. They helped me get clarity about what it is and what it isn't. They encouraged me to practice emergent strategies by taking risks, being vulnerable, allowing myself to be seen, learning in public, experimenting with new ways of thinking and being, sharing creative work, and remembering that no one has all the answers—and there are no perfect ones. This book is infinitely better for the conversations and contributions of the people I interviewed. I am profoundly honored and grateful to each of them for taking the time to speak with me and share their insights, curiosities, critiques, rigor, and provocations. Deep thanks to Kat Aaron, Amanda Alexander, kai lumumba barrow, Autumn Meghan Brown, Erin Butler, Rachel Caïdor, Halima Cassells, Angélica Cházaro, Nandi Comer, Sage Crump, Trishala Deb, Ejeris Dixon, Woods Ervin, Alexis Pauline Gumbs, Shira Hassan, Kelly Hayes, Mia Herndon, shea howell, Mariame Kaba, Emi Kane, Mimi Kim, Daniel Kisslinger, Jenny Lee, N'Tanya Lee, Mia Mingus, Eva Nagao, Sheila Nezhad, Diana Nucera, Nikkita Oliver, Shannon Perez-Darby, Denise Perry, Kalayo Pestaño, Leah Lakshmi Piepzna-Samarasinha, Aishah Shahidah Simmons, LéTania Severe, Dean Spade, Maria Thomas, Adaku Utah, Lewis Raven Wallace, PG Watkins, and Damon Williams.

In addition to the beloved family, friends, and comrades listed above who participated in the creation of *Practicing New Worlds*, I am deeply indebted to those who held me through the process of writing it, including the entire Interrupting Criminalization team, the Community Resource Hub crew, and the In Our Names Network, Robyn Maynard, Joey Mogul, Matice Moore, Nate Mullen, Meilu Lee Mullen, Mars Marshall, Wes Ware, Sangodare Roxanne Wallace, Kyona Watts, Maurice Weeks, and Lauren Williams, as well as to Richard Brouillette and Remy Kharbanda. I am immeasurably grateful to the Abolitionist Cat for enduring and snuggling through yet another year of book writing and to my purple house family for accompanying me through it with food, laughter, game, movie, and dancefloor nights, barbecues, bonfires, fresh food and flowers, and a felt experience of community built on critical connections.

Last but not least, profound gratitude to the Allied Media Conference, Black Organizing for Leadership and Dignity, Blue Mountain Center, Mobile Homecoming, Hedgebrook, Hambidge, and all of the places that have made space for me to write and grow and invited me to stretch far beyond what I know to dream and practice the worlds I long for.

Notes

Introduction, Andrea J. Ritchie

1. Mariame Kaba and Andrea J. Ritchie, *No More Police: A Case for Abolition* (New York: The New Press, 2022); Andrea J. Ritchie, *Invisible No More: Police Violence Against Black Women and Women of Color* (Boston: Beacon Press, 2017); Joey L. Mogul, Andrea J. Ritchie, and Kay Whitlock, *Queer (In)Justice: The Criminalization of LGBT People in the United States* (Boston: Beacon Press, 2011).

2. Laura McTighe, with Women With a Vision, *Fire Dreams: Making Black Feminist Liberation in the South* (Durham: Duke University Press, forthcoming 2024).

3. Communities United for Police Reform, "The Community Safety Act," last accessed April 24, 2023, https://www.changethenypd.org/community-safety-act.

4. Fatal Force, "Police Shootings Database," *Washington Post*, last accessed April 16, 2023, https://www.washingtonpost.com/graphics/investigations/police-shootings-database.

5. To hear me explain what the doctrine of qualified immunity is and rant with fellow police "misconduct" attorney Joey Mogul about why ending qualified immunity in civil suits against police officers will do nothing to prevent police violence, you can visit the Interrupting Criminalization Instagram page (@interruptcrim): Andrea J. Ritchie (@invisiblenomorebook) and Joey Mogul (@jjmogul), Instagram Live video, February 7, 2023, https://www.instagram.com/p/CoYFYYiBFlc.

6. For example, see Mariame Kaba and Andrea J. Ritchie, "Why We Don't Say Reform the Police," *The Nation*, September 2, 2022, https://www.thenation.com/article/society/no-more-police-excerpt; Kaba and Ritchie, *No More Police*; Andrea J. Ritchie and Wes Ware, "Navigating DOJ Consent Decrees in the Context of Campaigns to Defund Police," Community Resource Hub, 2021, https://communityresourcehub.org/wp-content/uploads/2021/06/0602_DOJ_B.pdf.

7. Rachel Herzing, "Big Dreams and Bold Steps Toward a Police-Free Future," in *Who Do You Serve, Who Do You Protect?*, eds. Maya Schenwar, Joe Macaré, and Alana Yu-lan Price (Chicago: Haymarket Books, 2016). See also Kaba and Ritchie, *No More Police*, 131, for a discussion of "non-reformist reforms."

8. *So Is This Actually an Abolitionist Policy or Strategy?* collected by Interrupting Criminalization, Project Nia, and Critical Resistance, resource binder, June 30, 2022, https://criticalresistance.org/resources/actually-an-abolitionist-strategy-binder.

9. Grace Lee Boggs with Scott Kurashige, *The Next American Revolution: Sustainable Activism for the Twenty-First Century* (Oakland: University of California Press, 2012), 72.

10. Boggs and Kurashige, *The Next American Revolution*, xxi, 72.

11. Boggs and Kurashige, *The Next American Revolution*, 72.

12. Margaret J. Wheatley and Deborah Frieze, "Using Emergence to Take Social Innovations to Scale," The Berkana Institute, 2006, https://margaretwheatley.com/articles/emergence.html.

13. The James and Grace Lee Boggs Center was created to carry on the legacy of Grace Lee Boggs and Jimmy Boggs and to nurture the transformational leadership capacities of individuals and organizations committed to creating productive, sustainable, ecologically responsible, and just communities. For more information and to support their work, please visit https://www.boggscenter.org.

14. Sage Crump, A Cultural Strategy Toolkit, https://www.culturalstrategy.space. See also Boggs and Kurashige, *The Next American Revolution*, xvii.

15. Keeanga-Yamahtta Taylor, *How We Get Free: Black Feminism and the Combahee River Collective* (Chicago: Haymarket Books, 2017).

16. Boggs and Kurashige, *The Next American Revolution*, 49.

17. Charles Payne, *I've Got the Light of Freedom: The Organizing Tradition and the Mississippi Freedom Struggle* (Berkeley, CA: University of California Press, 1995), 253.

18. Boggs and Kurashige, *The Next American Revolution*, 50.

19. For more information on Dominionism, please see Frederick Clarkson, Political Research Associates, "101: Dominionism," Political Research Associates, November 4, 2022, https://politicalresearch.org/2022/11/04/101-dominionism; and Imara Jones #AntiTransHateMachine, *Translash Media*, https://translash.org/antitranshatemachine.

20. Elle Hardy, "The 'Modern Apostles' Who Want to Reshape America Ahead of the End Times," *The Outline*, March 19, 2020, https://the-outline.com/post/8856/seven-mountain-mandate-trump-paula-white.

21. Matthew N. Lyons, "Three-Way Fight Politics and the US Far Right," in *¡No Pasarán! Antifascist Dispatches from a World in Crisis*, ed. Shane Burley (Chico, CA: AK Press, 2022). See also Matthew N.

Lyons, *Insurgent Supremacists: The US Far Right's Challenge to State and Empire* (Montreal: Kersplebedeb, 2018).

22. Emmi Bevensee and Frank Miroslav, "It Takes a Network to Defeat a Network: (Anti)Fascism and the Future of Complex Warfare," in *¡No Pasarán! Antifascist Dispatches from a World in Crisis*, ed. Shane Burley (Chico, CA: AK Press, 2022).

23. For more on dual power strategies, please see Andrea J. Ritchie and Mariame Kaba, *No More Police*; Andrea J. Ritchie, "Abolition and the State: A Discussion Tool," Interrupting Criminalization (New York: Interrupting Criminalization, 2022), https://www.interrupting criminalization.com/abolition-and-the-state; Mijente, *Building Power Sin, Contra, y Desde el Estado*, video, April 12, 2022, https:// mijente.net/2022/04/building-power-sin-contra-y-desde-el-estado, and Paula X. Rojas, "Are the Cops in our Heads and Hearts?," *The Scholar and Feminist Online* 13, no. 2 (Spring 2016), https://sfonline .barnard.edu/paula-rojas-are-the-cops-in-our-heads-and-hearts, reprinted from *The Revolution Will Not Be Funded*, ed. INCITE! Women of Color Against Violence (Durham, NC: Duke University Press, 2015).

24. Lyons, "Three-Way Fight Politics and the US Far Right."

25. Lyons, "Three-Way Fight Politics and the US Far Right."

26. Suzanne Pharr, *Transformation: Toward a People's Democracy* (Blacksburg, VA: Virginia Tech Publishing, 2021), 13.

27. Emmi Bevensee and Frank Miroslav call this process "stigmergy," a mechanism of indirect coordination in which an action by one individual "stimulates the performance of a succeeding action by the same or a different agent." This phenomenon could describe, for instance, copycat mass shootings or attacks on spaces where LGBTQ people are gathered. Emmi Bevensee and Frank Miroslav, "It Takes a Network to Defeat a Network: (Anti)Fascism and the Future of Complex Warfare."

28. Pharr, *Transformation*, 19, 368.

29. Shane Burley, "Building Communities for a Fascist-Free Future," in *¡No Pasarán! Antifascist Dispatches from a World in Crisis*, ed. Shane Burley (Chico, CA: AK Press, 2022).

30. adrienne maree brown, *Emergent Strategy: Shaping Change, Changing Worlds* (Chico, CA: AK Press, 2017), 26; *The Emergent Strategy Podcast* can be found here https://podcasts.apple.com/us/podcast/the -emergent-strategy-podcast/id1553479340. For more information on the Emergent Strategy Ideation Institute (ESII), please visit https:// esii.org.

31. Charity Mahouna Hicks, "Wage Love," Emergence Media, video, December 15, 2014, https://emergencemedia.org/blogs/news/1629 0704-charity-mahouna-hicks-wage-love.

32. Ron Scott, *How to End Police Brutality: An Organizer's Manual* (Detroit: Detroit Coalition Against Police Brutality, 2015).

33. See "Remembering Ron Scott," Allied Media Projects, December 14, 2015, https://alliedmedia.org/news/remembering-ron-scott-watch-video-amc2010.

34. For more information on these and other campaigns around policing in Detroit, see Rae Baker, Pete Blackmer, Alex Lu, and Rebecca Smith, "Case Study Two—Knowing What Keeps Us Safe: A Report on the Green Light Black Futures Community Safety Survey," *Riverwise*, October 23, 2022, https://riverwisedetroit.org/article/case-study-2-building-black-futures-by-knowing-what-keeps-us-safe-a-report-on-the-green-lights-black-futures-community-safety-survey; Rukiya Colvin and Richard Feldman, "Some Call It Liberated Zones—Others: Peace Zones, Freedom Zones, Beloving Community and Healing—We Call It Home," *Riverwise*, September, 29, 2022, https://riverwisedetroit.org/article/some-call-it-liberated-zones-others-peace-zones-freedom-zones-beloving-community-and-healing-we-call-it-home; Emergent Strategy Ideation Institute and PG Watkins, "Honest Movement with PG Watkins," *Emergent Strategy Podcast*, podcast November 18, 2021, https://anchor.fm/emergentstrategy/episodes/Honest-Movement-with-PG-Watkins-e1afd10; "Campaigns," Detroit Justice Center, https://detroitjustice.org/campaigns.

35. Detroit Summer was a youth program founded by Jimmy and Grace Lee Boggs. For more information, please visit https://detroitsummer.wordpress.com.

36. For more information on the In Our Names Network, please visit https://www.inournamesnetwork.com.

37. Allied Media Projects "Critical Connections: Stories from Twenty Years of the Allied Media Conference," *Allied Media Projects*, podcast, https://podcasts.apple.com/us/podcast/critical-connections-stories-from-20-years-of-the/id1387213712.

38. See "A Chrysalis Year," Allied Media Projects, September 14, 2018, https://alliedmedia.org/news/chrysalis-year.

39. AirGo, Interrupting Criminalization and One Million Experiments, "Detroit Safety Team with Curtis Renee and John Sloan, III," *One Million Experiments*, podcast," April 21, 2022, https://soundcloud.com/one-million-experiments/episode-6-detroit-safety-team-with-curtis-renee-and-john-sloan-iii.

40. For more information on the Detroit Safety Team, please see https://www.redefinesafety.org.

41. AirGo, Interrupting Criminalization and One Million Experiments, "Detroit Safety Team" with Curtis Renee and John Sloan, III."

42. There are many places you can learn more about the history of

Detroit, including the Black Bottom Archives, "a community-driven media platform dedicated to centering and amplifying the voices, experiences, and perspectives of Black Detroiters through digital storytelling, journalism, art, and community organizing with a focus on preserving local Black history and archiving our present," http:// www.blackbottomarchives.com, and the Detroit Narrative Agency, which supports and develops media-based storytelling centering Black, Indigenous, and People of Color (BIPOC) to foster collective healing, power, and liberation, https://detroitnarrativeagency. org. See also Tiya Miles, *The Dawn of Detroit: A Chronicle of Slavery and Freedom in the City of the Straits* (New York: The New Press, 2019); Scott Kurashige, *The Fifty-Year Rebellion: How the US Political Crisis Began in Detroit* (Berkeley, CA: University of California Press, 2017); Heather Ann Thompson, *Whose Detroit: Politics, Labor and Race in a Modern American City* (Ithaca, NY: Cornell University Press, 2017); and Dan Georgakas and Marvin Surkin, *Detroit: I Do Mind Dying: A Study in Urban Revolution* (Chicago: Haymarket Books, 2012).

43. Check out Feedom Freedom Growers, https://feedomfreedom .wordpress.com, and Keep Growing Detroit, https://www.detroit agriculture.net.

44. Emergent Strategy Ideation Institute and PG Watkins "Honest Movement with PG Watkins."

45. For more information on Detroit Narrative Agency, please visit https://detroitnarrativeagency.org.

46. For more information on the People's Platform Detroit, please visit https://www.detroitpeoplesplatform.org.

47. Barbara Smith, "What I Believe," Robert L. Hess Memorial Lecture, The Ethyle R. Wolfe Institute for the Humanities, Brooklyn College of the City University of New York, March 16, 2023, https://www .youtube.com/watch?v=bAIs7VQ_n7M.

48. Beth E. Richie, *Arrested Justice: Black Women, Violence, and America's Prison Nation* (New York: NYU Press, 2012).

49. Kaba and Ritchie, *No More Police*, 281.

50. Hortense Spillers, "The Scholarly Journey of Hortense Spillers," *Brandeis Now*, February 1, 2019, https://www.brandeis.edu/now/2019/ february/hortense-spillers-qa.html.

51. Kaba and Ritchie, *No More Police*, 284.

52. Formerly INCITE! Women of Color Against Violence and then INCITE! Women and Trans People of Color Against Violence. For more on INCITE!'s history, see Angela Y. Davis, Gina Dent, Erica Meiners, and Beth Richie, *Abolition. Feminism. Now.* (Chicago: Haymarket Books, 2022) and visit www.incite-national.org.

53. Paula X. Rojas, "Are the Cops in Our Heads and Hearts?"

54. Sista II Sista, "Sistas Makin' Moves: Collective Leadership for Personal Transformation and Social Justice," in *Color of Violence: The INCITE! Anthology*, ed. INCITE! Women of Color Against Violence (Boston: South End Press, 2006).

55. Marina Sitrin, *Horizontalism: Voices of Popular Power in Argentina* (Oakland: AK Press, 2006), 2.

56. Sitrin, *Horizontalism*, 4.

57. Sitrin, *Horizontalism*, 10.

58. Sitrin, *Horizontalism*, 12.

59. For more information about YWEP, please visit https://www.youare priceless.org.

60. Shira Hassan, *Saving Our Own Lives: Liberatory Harm Reduction* (Chicago: Haymarket Books, 2022), 28.

61. brown, *Emergent Strategy*, 3.

62. brown, *Emergent Strategy*, 214 ("In my mind, this is a book about facilitation."). Mia Herndon, a former staff member of the Emergent Strategy Ideation Institute, describes emergent strategy as "an adaptive facilitation approach." See https://esii.org/local-engagement.

63. Emergent Strategy Ideation Institute, "Fractaling with adrienne, Mia, and Sage," *The Emergent Strategy Podcast*, podcast, March 24, 2022, https://podcasters.spotify.com/pod/show/emergentstrategy/ episodes/Season-2-Fractaling-with-adrienne--Mia-and-Sage -e1g6fil.

64. Emergent Strategy Ideation Institute and Sendolo Diaminah, "Devotion Strategy and Rigor with Sendolo Diaminah," *The Emergent Strategy Podcast,* podcast, October 21, 2021, https://podcasters .spotify.com/pod/show/emergentstrategy/episodes/Devotion--Strategy -and-Rigor-with-Sendolo-Diaminah-e19445k.

65. Leanne Betasamosake Simpson, *As We Have Always Done: Indigenous Freedom Through Radical Resistance* (Minneapolis: University of Minnesota Press, 2017).

66. Simpson, *As We Have Always Done*, 23.

67. Maurice Mitchell, "Building Resilient Organizations," *The Forge*, November 29, 2022, https://forgeorganizing.org/article/building -resilient-organizations.

68. INCITE!, *The Revolution Will Not Be Funded: Beyond the Non-Profit Industrial Complex* (Boston: South End Press, 2006; 2nd ed., Durham, NC: Duke University Press, 2017).

69. Mimi E. Kim, "Anti-Carceral Feminism: The Contradictions of Progress and the Possibilities of Counter-Hegemonic Struggle," *Affilia: Journal of Women and Social Work* 35, no. 3 (2020): 309–26, https://doi .org/10.1177/0886109919987827.

70. Andrea J. Ritchie, *#DefundPolice #FundthePeople #DefendBlackLives: The Struggle Continues* (New York: Interrupting Criminaliza-

tion, 2023), https://www.interruptingcriminalization.com/struggle
-continues.

71. Andrea J. Ritchie, #DefundPolice #FundthePeople #DefendBlackLives:
The Struggle Continues.

72. Rachel Herzing and Isaac Ontiveros, "Advice to New Abolitionists," video, March 18, 2021, https://www.youtube.com/watch?v=G8xo
FWCqQxs.

73. Boggs and Kurashige, The Next American Revolution, xxi.

74. Lorraine Hansberry, A Raisin in the Sun and The Sign in Sidney Brust-
ein's Window, ed. Robert Nemiroff (New York: Vintage Books, 1995),
115.

75. Kaba and Ritchie, No More Police; Ruth Wilson Gilmore, Abolition
Geography: Essays towards Liberation (Brooklyn, NY: Verso, 2022);
Davis, Dent, Meiners, and Richie, Abolition. Feminism. Now.; Alisa
Bierria, Jakeya Caruthers, and Brooke Lober, eds., Abolition Fem-
inisms, Vol. 1: Organizing, Survival, and Transformative Practice
(Chicago: Haymarket Books, 2022); Alisa Bierria, Jakeya Caruthers,
and Brooke Lober, eds., Abolition Feminisms, Vol. 2: Feminist Ruptures
Against the Carceral State (Chicago: Haymarket Books, 2022).

76. Smith, "What I Believe."

77. Simpson, As We Have Always Done, 19.

78. Carl Boggs, "Marxism, Prefigurative Communism, and the Problem
of Workers' Control," Radical America 11, no. 6 (November 1977): 100;
Carl Boggs, Jr., "Revolutionary Process, Political Strategy, and the
Dilemma of Power," Theory and Society 4, no. 3 (Autumn 1977): 359–93.

79. Prentis Hemphill taught me perfectionism is a profound commitment to never being satisfied; brown, Emergent Strategy, 22.

80. Daniel Kissinger, a Chicago organizer and co-producer of the
AirGo podcast, pointed out that limiting the readership for this book
to one-twelfth of the zodiac might not give it the broadest reach. I
conceded that it might be helpful for Virgos too (although adrienne
is a Virgo and she wrote Emergent Strategy) or maybe for all Earth
signs. Or maybe just anyone struggling with the question of how we
step out of what we've been doing to get to where we want to go.

Visionary Practice: Allied Media Projects Network Principles

1. More about AMP and the Network Principles can be found at
https://alliedmedia.org/network-principles.

Visionary Practice: Glimpses of Emergent Strategies

1. The Sailing for Social Justice workshop was facilitated by Tala Khanmalek and Audrey Kuo at the 2020 Allied Media Conference. The
workshop description can be found at https://amc2018.sched.com/
event/Es68/sailing-for-social-justice.

2. On June 24, 2022, in *Dobbs v. Jackson Women's Health Organization*, the US Supreme Court held that the Constitution of the United States does not protect a right to abortion, overturning *Roe v. Wade* (1973).

What Is Abolition?

1. Eric A. Stanley and Nat Smith, "Introduction," in *Captive Genders: Trans Embodiment and the Prison Industrial Complex*, eds. Eric A. Stanley and Nat Smith (Oakland: AK Press, 2015).

2. Mariame Kaba and Andrea J. Ritchie, *No More Police: A Case for Abolition* (New York: The New Press, 2022), 195–96.

3. Krista Tippett and Ruth Wilson Gilmore, "Ruth Wilson Gilmore: Where Life Is Precious, Life Is Precious," *On Being*, podcast, March 30, 2023, https://onbeing.org/programs/ruth-wilson-gilmore-where -life-is-precious-life-is-precious.

4. Tippett and Gilmore, *On Being*, "Ruth Wilson Gilmore."

5. Critical Resistance, "Our Communities, Our Solutions: An Organizer's Toolkit for Developing Campaigns to Abolish Policing," (New York: Critical Resistance, October 2020), https://criticalresistance. org/resources/our-communities-our-solutions-an-organizers-tool-kit-for-developing-campaigns-to-abolish-policing.

6. Interrupting Criminalization, "TJ Skill Up Institute: Skills/ Relationships/Structures Worksheet," 2021, https://www.interrupt-ingcriminalization.com/stool.

7. Sage Crump, "A Cultural Strategy Toolkit," https://www.cultural strategy.space. See also Grace Lee Boggs with Scott Kurashige, *The Next American Revolution: Sustainable Activism for the Twenty-First Century* (Oakland: University of California Press, 2012), xvii.

8. Susan Raffo, *Liberated to the Bone: Histories. Bodies. Futures.* (Chico, CA: AK Press, 2022), 162.

9. Mariame Kaba, *We Do This 'Til We Free Us: Abolitionist Organizing and Transforming Justice* (Chicago: Haymarket Books, 2021).

10. Tippett and Gilmore, "Ruth Wilson Gilmore"; Ruth Wilson Gilmore, "Abolition Geography and the Problem of Innocence," in *Abolition Geography: Essays towards Liberation* (Brooklyn, NY: Verso, 2022), 474–75.

11. Angela Y. Davis, *Are Prisons Obsolete?* (New York: Seven Stories Press, 2003).

12. Kelly Hayes and Mariame Kaba, "A Jailbreak of the Imagination: Seeing Prisons for What They Are and Demanding Transformation," in *We Do This 'Til We Free Us: Abolitionist Organizing and Transforming Justice*, ed. Tamara K. Nopper (Chicago: Haymarket Books, 2021).

13. adrienne maree brown and Walidah Imarisha, eds., *Octavia's Brood:*

Science Fiction Stories from Social Justice Movements (Oakland: AK Press, 2015).

14. adrienne maree brown, *Emergent Strategy: Shaping Change, Changing Worlds* (Chico, CA: AK Press, 2017), 56.

15. Andrea J. Ritchie, *Invisible No More: Police Violence Against Black Women and Women of Color* (Boston: Beacon Press, 2017).

16. brown, *Emergent Strategy*, 57.

17. Andrea J. Ritchie, "Building Alternatives Is Everybody's Job," Critical Resistance, video, December 17, 2017, https://www.youtube.com/watch?v=hWHW6bOGBgo.

18. Kaba and Ritchie, *No More Police*. See also Leigh Goodmark, *Imperfect Victims: Criminalized Survivors and the Promise of Abolition Feminism* (Berkeley, CA: University of California Press, 2023); Angela Y. Davis, Gina Dent, Erica R. Meiners, and Beth E. Richie, *Abolition. Feminism. Now.* (Chicago: Haymarket Books, 2022); Danielle Sered, *Until We Reckon: Violence, Mass Incarceration, and a Road to Repair* (New York: The New Press, 2019); Andrea J. Ritchie, *Invisible No More*; Beth E. Richie, *Arrested Justice: Black Women, Violence, and America's Prison Nation* (New York: NYU Press, 2012), and Survived and Punished, https://survivedandpunished.org.

19. National Domestic Violence Hotline, "Survivors of Domestic Violence Report Feeling Less Safe After Contacting Law Enforcement," last accessed April 26, 2023, https://www.thehotline.org/news/survivors-of-domestic-violence-report-feeling-less-safe-after-contacting-law-enforcement.

20. Mariame Kaba and Eva Nagao, *What About the Rapists?* (New York: Interrupting Criminalization, 2021), https://static1.squarespace.com/static/5ee39ec764dbd7179cf1243c/t/6109e65d5a8ce56464ff94eb/1628038750972/WATR+Zine.pdf.

21. Andrea J. Ritchie, *Shrouded in Silence: Police Sexual Violence—What We Know and What We Can Do About It* (New York: Interrupting Criminalization, 2021), https://www.interruptingcriminalization.com/breaking-the-silence.

22. Stephen Semler, "How Much Did the US Spend on Police, Prisons in FY2021?," *Speaking Security* newsletter, January 20, 2022, https://stephensemler.substack.com/p/how-much-did-the-us-spend-on-police.

23. Andrea J. Ritchie, "Police Responses to Domestic Violence: A Fact Sheet," (New York: Interrupting Criminalization, 2021), https://www.interruptingcriminalization.com/dvam.

Visionary Practice: To Build A Future Without Police And Prisons, We Have To Imagine It First

1. Ursula K. Le Guin, "Books Aren't Just Commodities," National Book Awards speech, *The Guardian*, November 20, 2014, https://www.theguardian.com/books/2014/nov/20/ursula-k-le-guin-national-book-awards-speech.

2. Wesley Lowery, "Why Minneapolis Was the Breaking Point," *The Atlantic*, June 10, 2020, https://www.theatlantic.com/politics/archive/2020/06/wesley-lowery-george-floyd-minneapolis-black-lives/612391.

3. Astead W. Herndon, "How a Pledge to Dismantle the Minneapolis Police Collapsed," *New York Times*, November 3, 2021, https://www.nytimes.com/2020/09/26/us/politics/minneapolis-defund-police.html.

4. adrienne maree brown and Walidah Imarisha, eds., *Octavia's Brood: Science Fiction Stories from Social Justice Movements* (Oakland: AK Press, 2015).

5. Walidah Imarisha, "Better Futures: Visioning in a Time of Crisis," Allied Media Projects, video, June 11, 2020, https://www.youtube.com/watch?v=S5vG7ZvoX_g.

6. Jeff Chang, "Culture Before Politics," *American Prospect*, December 6, 2010, https://prospect.org/culture/culture-politics.

7. The Wakanda Dream Lab and Policy Link, *Black Freedom Beyond Borders: Memories of Abolition Day* (New York: Policy Link, 2020), https://www.policylink.org/equity-in-action/webinars/black-freedom-beyond-borders_8-24-20; the *Black Freedom Beyond Borders* podcast is available at https://www.thebigwe.com/abolition day.

What Are Emergent Strategies?

1. Henry Mintzberg and James A. Waters, "Of Strategies, Deliberate and Emergent," *Strategic Management Journal* 6, no. 3 (July–September 1985): 257–72. http://strategy.sjsu.edu/www.stable/B290/reading/Mintzberg,%20H,%201985,%20Strategic%20Management%20Journal.%206%20pp%20257-272.pdf.

2. Mintzberg and Waters, "Of Strategies, Deliberate and Emergent."

3. Steven Johnson, *Emergence: The Connected Lives of Ants, Brains, Cities, and Software* (New York: Scribner, 2001).

4. Mintzberg and Waters, "Of Strategies, Deliberate and Emergent."

5. Leanne Betasamosake Simpson, *As We Have Always Done: Indigenous Freedom Through Radical Resistance* (Minneapolis: University of Minnesota Press, 2017), 3.

6. Simpson, *As We Have Always Done*, 8–9.

7. Simpson, *As We Have Always Done*, 23.

8. Simpson, *As We Have Always Done*, 24.

9. Learn more about Klee Benally's work at http://kleebenally.com/about. See also Morning Star Gali, "Broken Chains and Colonial Cages," in *Abolition for the People: The Movement for a Future Without Policing and Prisons*, ed. Colin Kaepernick (San Francisco: Kaepernick Publishing, 2021), and Nick Estes, *Our History Is the Future: Standing Rock vs. the Dakota Access Pipeline, and the Long Tradition of Indigenous Resistance* (Brooklyn, NY: Verso Books, 2019).

10. Robyn Maynard and Leanne Betasamosake Simpson, *Rehearsals for Living* (Chicago: Haymarket Books, 2022).

11. Margaret J. Wheatley, *Leadership and the New Science: Discovering Order in a Chaotic World* (Oakland: Berrett-Koehler Publishers, Inc., 2006).

12. Wheatley, *Leadership and the New Science*.

13. Margaret J. Wheatley and Deborah Frieze, "Using Emergence to Take Social Innovations to Scale," *The Berkana Institute*, 2006, reprinted at https://margaretwheatley.com/articles/emergence.html.

14. Wheatley and Frieze, "Using Emergence."

15. Wheatley and Frieze, "Using Emergence."

16. Wheatley and Frieze, "Using Emergence."

17. Wheatley and Frieze, "Using Emergence."

18. Wheatley and Frieze, "Using Emergence."

19. Wheatley and Frieze, "Using Emergence."

20. Andrea J. Ritchie, *#DefundPolice #FundthePeople #DefendBlackLives: The Struggle Continues* (New York: Interrupting Criminalization, 2023), https://www.interruptingcriminalization.com/struggle-continues. See also Ejeris Dixon, "Our Relationships Keep Us Alive: Let's Prioritize Them in 2018," *Truthout*, February 8, 2018, https://truthout.org/articles/our-relationships-keep-us-alive-let-s-prioritize-them-in-2018.

21. "Complexity science is the study of complex systems ranging from cells to cities to civilizations, the nervous system to the immune system to the human genome, to the internet to ecosystems, to social networks societies, and economies, and the ways that their operation is shaped by nonlinearity, randomness, collective dynamics, hierarchy, and emergence." Adapted from David Krakauer, ed., *Worlds Hidden in Plain Sight* (Santa Fe: SFI Press, 2019), https://www.santafe.edu/what-is-complex-systems-science. In other words, "Complexity science, also called complex systems science, studies how a large collection of relatively simple components—locally interacting with each other at small scales—can spontaneously self-organize to exhibit non-trivial global structures and behaviors at larger scales, often without external intervention, central authorities or leaders." #ComplexityExplained, "What Is Complexity Science," https://

complexityexplained.github.io. The Emergent Strategy Ideation Institute, founded by adrienne maree brown to create a practice space for organizers interested in emergent strategies, defines complex science as "the investigation of how relationships between parts give rise to the collective behaviors of a system and how systems interact to form relationships with environments." For more information, go to: https://esii.org/about.

22. Manlio De Domenico et al, *Complexity Explained*, May 2019 https://complexityexplained.github.io/ComplexityExplained.pdf.

23. Steven Johnson, *Emergence: The Connected Lives of Ants, Brains, Cities, and Software* (New York: Scribner, 2001).

24. Manlio De Domenico et al, *Complexity Explained*.

25. Johnson, *Emergence*, 74.

26. Manlio De Domenico et al, *Complexity Explained*.

27. Wheatley, *Leadership and the New Science*.

28. Manlio De Domenico et al, *Complexity Explained*.

29. Robin D.G. Kelley, "Back to the Future: Complex Movements Make Revolution," *Shift Space*, 2022, https://www.shiftspace.pub/back-to -the-future-complex-movements-make-revolution.

30. Design Justice Network, Complex Movements iconographic framework, https://designjustice.org/complex-movements.

31. For a gorgeous exploration of and tribute to Complex Movements's work, please read Kelley, "Back to the Future." You can also listen to their presentation "Eyeo 2017 Complex Movements: Invincible-ill Weaver, L05, Sage Crump & Wesley Taylor," Eyeo 2017, video, https://vimeo.com/233329636; Emergent Strategy Ideation Institute, and Complex Movements, "Shifting the Culture with Complex Movements," *The Emergent Strategy Podcast*, podcast, January 19, 2023, https://podcasters.spotify.com/pod/show/ emergentstrategy/episodes/Shifting-the-Culture-with-Complex -Movements-e1tmgeq/a-a96s4pk; and visit the Complex Movements page on emergence media: https://emergencemedia.org/ pages/complex-movements.

32. adrienne maree brown and ill weaver were partners at the time Complex Movements and the framework outlined in *Emergent Strategy* were evolving, and they remain family and collaborators.

33. *Complex Movements: Beware of the Dandelions*, Emergence Media, video, 2016, https://vimeo.com/196201236.

34. *Complex Movements: Beware of the Dandelions*, 2016 (on file with author).

35. John Arquilla and David Ronfeldt, *Networks and Netwars: The Future of Terror, Crime, and Militancy* (Santa Monica: Rand Corporation, 2001).

36. *Complex Movements: Beware of the Dandelions*.

37. Kelley, "Back to the Future.

38. *Complex Movements: Beware of the Dandelions.*

39. *Complex Movements: Beware of the Dandelions.*

40. Movement Generation defines translocal organizing as, "autonomous and place-based organizing that is tied together across communities with a unifying vision, shared values, aligned strategies and common frames. Through Translocal Organizing, we seek to build to scale not by creating larger and larger organizations with greater and greater concentrated power but by aggregating to scale by uniting across places." Movement Generation Justice and Ecology Project, "Resilience-Based Organizing and Translocal Organizing," last accessed April 24, 2023, https://movementgeneration.org/resilience-based-organizing.

41. adrienne maree brown, *Emergent Strategy: Shaping Change, Changing Worlds* (Chico, CA: AK Press, 2017), 20.

42. brown, *Emergent Strategy,* 24.

43. adrienne maree brown, *Holding Change: The Way of Emergent Strategy Facilitation and Mediation* (Chico, CA: AK Press, 2021), 12–13.

44. brown, *Holding Change,* 15–17; brown, *Emergent Strategy,* 42–50.

45. Mimi E. Kim, "Anti-Carceral Feminism: The Contradictions of Progress and the Possibilities of Counter-Hegemonic Struggle," *Affilia: Journal of Women and Social Work* 35, no. 3 (2020): 309–26.

46. Kim, "Anti-Carceral Feminism."

47. Ruha Benjamin, *Viral Justice: How We Grow the World We Want* (Princeton, NJ: Princeton University Press, 2022), 11.

48. Benjamin, *Viral Justice,* 13.

49. Benjamin, *Viral Justice,* 16.

50. Deepa Iyer, *Social Change Now: A Guide for Reflection and Connection* (Washington, DC: Thick Press, 2022).

Emergent Strategies and Abolition

1. Mariame Kaba and Andrea J. Ritchie, *No More Police: A Case for Abolition* (New York: The New Press, 2022).

2. Kelly Hayes, "We Need Collective Healing, Not Commodified 'Self-Care,'" *Movement Memos,* podcast, March 9, 2023, https://player.fm/series/movement-memos/we-need-collective-healing-not-commodified-self-care.

3. This evolution is extensively described in Angela Y. Davis, Gina Dent, Erica R. Meiners, and Beth E. Richie, *Abolition. Feminism. Now.* (New York: Haymarket Books, 2022); Beth E. Richie, *Arrested Justice: Black Women, Violence, and America's Prison Nation* (New York: New York University Press, 2012); Mimi Kim, "Dancing the Carceral Creep: The Anti-Domestic Violence Movement and the Paradoxical Pursuit of Criminalization, 1973–1986," (Berkeley, CA: ISSI Fellows

Working Papers, 2015), https://escholarship.org/uc/item/804227k6; and Emily Thuma, *All Our Trials: Prisons, Policing and the Feminist Fight to End Violence* (Champaign, IL: University of Illinois Press, 2019); as well as Kaba and Ritchie, *No More Police*, to name just a few resources on this topic.

4. Kaba and Ritchie, *No More Police*.
5. New York State Coalition Against Sexual Violence, "The Impact and Legacy of INCITE!" panel with Andrea J. Ritchie, Mimi Kim, Andrea Smith, Nan Stoops, facilitated by Spring Up, Ending Violence Without Violence: 2021 Conference, April 30, 2021, https://www.nyscasa.org/get-info/conferences.
6. Dr. Gabor Maté, MD, @gabaormatemd, Instagram post, July 8, 2021, https://www.instagram.com/p/CREmGMLsxgS. Of course, please read Gabor Maté, *The Myth of Normal: Trauma, Illness and Healing in a Toxic Culture* (New York: Penguin Random House, 2022). I haven't had a chance yet, but I will just as soon as I finish this book.
7. More information about Resonance Network can be found at https://resonance-network.org/who-we-are/about.
8. More about the We Govern project can be found at https://we-govern.org.
9. Find out more about One Million Experiments and the *One Million Experiments* podcast here https://millionexperiments.com.

Abolition Is Fractal

1. Emergent Strategy Ideation Institute and PG Watkins, "Honest Movement with PG Watkins," *The Emergent Strategy Podcast*, November 18, 2021, https://anchor.fm/emergentstrategy/episodes/Honest-Movement-with-PG-Watkins-e1afd10.
2. Mary Hooks, "The Mandate: A Call and Response from Black Lives Matter Atlanta," Southerners on New Ground, July 14, 2016, https://southernersonnewground.org/themandate.
3. Augusto Boal and Susana Epstein, "The Cop in the Head: Three Hypotheses," *The Drama Review* 34, no. 3 (1990): 35–42, https://doi.org/10.2307/1146067l; Paula X. Rojas, "Are the Cops in Our Heads and Hearts?" in *The Revolution Will Not be Funded: Beyond the Non-Profit Industrial Complex*, ed. INCITE! Women of Color Against Violence (Boston: South End Press, 2009), reprinted at *The Scholar and The Feminist Online* 13, no. 2 (Spring 2016), https://sfonline.barnard.edu/paula-rojas-are-the-cops-in-our-heads-and-hearts.
4. Robyn Maynard and Leanne Betasamosake Simpson, *Rehearsals for Living* (Chicago: Haymarket Books, 2022).
5. *American Revolutionary: The Evolution of Grace Lee Boggs*, directed by Grace Lee, (Brooklyn, NY: POV, 2013), https://www.pbs.org/pov/films/americanrevolutionary.

6. Abolitionist Toolbox Series, "Self-Accountability and Movement Building," workshop, September 12, 2020, https://accountable communities.com/events/self-accountability-movement-building. For more about the Accountable Communities Consortium, please see https://accountablecommunities.com.

7. Mia Mingus, "The Four Parts of Accountability and How to Give a Genuine Apology," *Leaving Evidence*, December 18, 2019, https:// leavingevidence.wordpress.com/2019/12/18/how-to-give-a-good -apology-part-1-the-four-parts-of-accountability.

8. adrienne maree brown, *Emergent Strategy: Shaping Change, Changing Worlds* (Chico, CA: AK Press, 2017), 52.

9. brown, *Emergent Strategy*, 55, 59.

10. Erin explained to me that the notion of fractals has deep roots in mathematical theories that evolved in numerous contexts on the African continent, with applications ranging from art to hair braiding to religion to the design of communities and cities. However, fractals were largely ignored in Western thought until the mid-1980s because Western mathematicians frankly couldn't understand them. For more information, check out Abdul Karim Bangura, "Review of Ron Eglash, *African Fractals: Modern Computing and Indigenous Design*" (New Brunswick, NJ: Rutgers University Press, 1999), *Nexus Network Journal,* vol. II (2000), https://link.springer.com/content/ pdf/10.1007/s00004-999-0019-3.pdf, and listen to "Ron Eglash: The Fractals at the Heart of African Designs," TED Talk, video, December 7, 2007, https://www.youtube.com/watch?v=7n36qV4Lk94.

11. Leanne Betasamosake Simpson, *As We Have Always Done: Indigenous Freedom Through Radical Resistance* (Minneapolis: University of Minnesota Press, 2017), 24.

12. From, "[there is a woman in this town]," in *Sinister Wisdom 102: The Complete Works of Pat Parker*, ed. Julie R. Enszer (Brookville, NY and Dover, FL: A Midsummer Night's Press and Sinister Wisdom, 2016), 160.

13. "Friends Take a Car Out of Action," Creative Interventions Storytelling and Organizing Project (STOP), audio recording and written transcript, https://www.creative-interventions.org/friends-take-a-car -out-of-action.

14. Creative Interventions, *The Creative Interventions Toolkit: A Practical Guide to Stop Interpersonal Violence* (Chico, CA: AK Press, 2022). Also available en Español/in Spanish and as an interactive web version, and the *Creative Interventions Workbook: Practical Tools to Stop Interpersonal Violence* (2021) can be found at https://www .creative-interventions.org/toolkit.

15. brown, *Emergent Strategy*, 22.

16. Mia Mingus, "Pods and Pod Mapping Worksheet," Transform

Harm, June 13, 2016, https://transformharm.org/ca_resource/pods
-and-pod-mapping-worksheet. More information about the Fireweed
Collective webinar series *Mad Maps: Paths to Personal and Collective Transformation*, can be found at https://vimeo.com/showcase/
fireweedcollective. See also The Icarus Project, *Madness and Oppression: Paths to Personal Transformation and Collective Liberation* (New
York: Icarus Project, 2015), https://fireweedcollective.org/publication/
madness-oppression-paths-to-personal-transformation-and-collective
-liberation, and The Icarus Project, "35 Practice: Mad Maps with The
Icarus Project's Rhiana Anthony," *Healing Justice*, podcast, April 30,
2019, https://irresistible.org/podcast/35penglish.

17. Mia Mingus, "Pods: The Building Blocks of Transformative Justice
and Collective Care," SOILTJP, March 16, 2023, https://www.soiltjp.
org/our-work/pods; Mingus is drawing and building on the work of
the Bay Area Transformative Justice Collective, originally published
in 2016 as Mia Mingus for the BATJC, "Pods and Pod Mapping
Worksheet," BATJC, June 2016, at https://batjc.wordpress.com/
resources/pods-and-pod-mapping-worksheet.

18. Mia Mingus for the Bay Area Transformative Justice Collective,
"Pods and Pod Mapping Worksheet."

19. Oakland Power Projects, "Mission," last accessed April 24, 2023,
https://oaklandpowerprojects.org/mission.

20. Critical Resistance, "The Oakland Power Projects," undated, http://
criticalresistance.org/wp-content/uploads/2015/03/TheOakPower
Proj_rept_target1_v3WEB.pdf.

21. Rachel Herzing for Build the Block, *Developing Alternatives to
Policing in the Arab and Muslim Community* (Oakland: Critical
Resistance, 2020), https://criticalresistance.org/resources/build
-the-block-report-developing-alternatives-to-policing-in-the-arab
-muslim-community.

22. Herzing, *Developing Alternatives to Policing in the Arab and Muslim
Community*.

23. For more about the Anti Police-Terror Project, MH First program, please see https://www.antipoliceterrorproject.org/mental
-health-first and https://millionexperiments.com/projects/mental
-health-first. See also Mimi E. Kim, Megyung Chung, Shira Hassan, and Andrea J. Ritchie, *Defund Police, Invest in Community Care:
A Guide to Alternative Mental Health Responses* (NYC: Interrupting
Criminalization, 2021), https://www.interruptingcriminalization.com
/non-police-crisis-response-guide. Relationships Evolving Possibilities (REP) is a network of dedicated abolitionists showing up to
support others in moments of crisis or urgency, with care and respect
for the full dignity and autonomy of the people in crisis. More information about REP can be found at https://repformn.org/about. On

the nationwide shift toward non-police crisis response after 2020, see
AirGo and Interrupting Criminalization, "REP with Signe Victoria
Harriday," *One Million Experiments,* podcast, March 24, 2022, https://
soundcloud.com/one-million-experiments/episode-5-rep-with-signe
-victoria-harriday, and Susan Raffo, *Liberated to the Bone: Histories.
Bodies. Futures.* (Chico, CA: AK Press, 2022), 116–125.

24. Cat Brooks and James Burch, *Oakland Is Reimagining Public Safety,*
Version 2.0 (Oakland: Anti Police-Terror Project/The Defund Police
Coalition, 2021), https://search.issuelab.org/resource/oakland-is
-reimagining-public-safety-version-2-0.html; Anti Police-Terror
Project, "Refund. Restore. Reimagine. Oakland Is Ready to
Reimagine Public Safety," https://www.antipoliceterrorproject.org/
oakland-is-ready-to-reimagine-public-safety; Interrupting Criminalization, *Navigating Public Safety Task Forces: A Guide from the
Ground,* (New York: Interrupting Criminalization, 2021), https://
www.interruptingcriminalization.com/task-forces; Anti Police-Terror Project, "Defund Police Coalition Priority Recommendations,"
APTP, https://www.antipoliceterrorproject.org/defund-coalition
-priority-recommendations.

25. See Interrupting Criminalization, "Skills, Relationships, Structures Worksheet, TJ Skill Up," 2021, https://www.interrupting
criminalization.com/stool.

26. Mimi E. Kim, "Anti-Carceral Feminism: The Contradictions of
Progress and the Possibilities of Counter-Hegemonic Struggle,"
Affilia: Journal of Women and Social Work 35, no. 3 (2020): 309–26.

27. Maurice Mitchell, "Building Resilient Organizations," *The Forge,*
November 29, 2022, https://forgeorganizing.org/article/building
-resilient-organizations.

28. More information about API Chaya can be found at: https://www
.apichaya.org.

29. Shane Burley, "Kops and Klan Go Hand in Hand: An Interview with
Kelly Hayes," in *¡No Pasarán! Antifascist Dispatches from a World in
Crisis,* ed. Shane Burley (Chico, CA: AK Press, 2022), 384.

30. Shane Burley, "Building Communities for a Fascist-Free Future," in
¡!No Pasarán! Antifascist Dispatches from a World in Crisis, ed. Shane
Burley, ed. (Chico, CA: AK Press, 2022).

31. Burley, "Building Communities for a Fascist-Free Future."

32. Dean Spade, *Mutual Aid: Building Solidarity During This Crisis (And
the Next)* (New York: Verso Books, 2020).

33. brown, *Emergent Strategy,* 113.

34. Spade, *Mutual Aid,* 17.

35. Mutual Aid Disaster Relief, "Mutual Aid 101: #WeGotOurBlock,"
toolkit, April 2020, https://mutualaiddisasterrelief.org/wp-content/
uploads/2020/04/NO-LOGOS-Mutual-Aid-101_-Toolkit.pdf.

36. "The Coronavirus Solidarity Poster and Postcard Project," Interrupting Criminalization, last accessed April 24, 2023, https://www.interruptingcriminalization.com/postcards.

37. Amy Goodman, "Solidarity Not Charity: Mutual Aid and How to Organize in the Age of Coronavirus," *Democracy Now*, radio program, March 20, 2020, https://www.democracynow.org/2020/3/20/coronavirus_community_response_mutual_aid.

38. Shira Hassan, *Saving Our Own Lives: Liberatory Harm Reduction* (Chicago: Haymarket Books, 2022), 83–93; Spade, *Mutual Aid*, 10–11.

39. For more information on Black Mama's Bail Out and National Bail Out, please visit https://www.nationalbailout.org.

40. Spade, *Mutual Aid*, 40–41.

41. Destinee Adams, "What It's Like Being an Abortion Doula in a State with Restrictive Laws," *NPR*, radio program, October 19, 2022, https://www.npr.org/2022/10/19/1123778633/abortion-doula-north-carolina; Harmeet Kaur, "It's a Stressful Time to Be an Abortion Doula. But Many Say They Aren't Quitting," *CNN*, July 15, 2022, https://www.cnn.com/2022/07/15/health/abortion-doulas-roe-v-wade-wellness-cec/index.html.

42. Emergent Strategy Ideation Institute and Adaku Utah, "Minding Your Relations with Adaku Utah," *The Emergent Strategy Podcast*, podcast, September 22, 2022, https://anchor.fm/emergentstrategy/episodes/Minding-Your-Relations-with-Adaku-Utah-e1ohv89. See also AirGo and Interrupting Criminalization, "Chicago Abortion Fund with Alicia Hurtado," *One Million Experiments*, podcast, June 30, 2022, https://millionexperiments.com/podcast/season-1/podcast-episode-7.

43. Emergent Strategy Ideation Institute and Utah, "Minding Your Relations."

44. Emergent Strategy Ideation Institute and Utah, "Minding Your Relations."

45. Emergent Strategy Ideation Institute and Utah, "Minding Your Relations."

46. The *Detroit Future Youth Curriculum Mixtape* is a compilation of workshops and media developed by each of the twelve DFY partner organizations. Detroit Future Youth Network, *Detroit Future Youth Curriculum Mixtape*, Emergence Media, August 2012, https://emergencemedia.org/products/detroit-future-youth-curriculum-mixtape.

47. For more information on the In Our Names Network, please visit https://www.inournamesnetwork.com.

48. For more information on the Building Coordinated Crisis Response Learning Space hosted by Interrupting Criminalization, please visit https://www.interruptingcriminalization.com/practice-space.

49. For more information on the Beyond Do No Harm Network, please visit https://www.interruptingcriminalization.com/bdnh.

50. See, for example, Andrea J. Ritchie, Mariame Kaba, and Woods Ervin, *The Demand Is #DefundthePolice #FundthePeople #DefendBlackLives: Concrete Steps Toward Divestment from Policing and Investment in Community Safety* (New York: Interrupting Criminalization, June 2020), https://filtermag.org/wp-content/uploads/2020/06/Defund-Toolkit.pdf; Andrea J. Ritchie, *The Demand Is Still #DefundthePolice #FundthePeople #DefendBlackLives: Lessons From 2020* (New York: Interrupting Criminalization, 2022), https://www.interruptingcriminalization.com/defundpolice-update; Andrea J. Ritchie, *#DefundPolice #FundthePeople #DefendBlackLives: The Struggle Continues* (New York: Interrupting Criminalization, 2023), https://www.interruptingcriminalization.com/struggle-continues.

51. Ritchie, *#DefundPolice #FundthePeople #DefendBlackLives*; Ritchie, *The Demand Is Still #DefundthePolice*.

52. Ritchie, *#DefundPolice #FundthePeople #DefendBlackLives*; Ritchie, *The Demand Is Still #DefundthePolice*.

53. See, for example, Community Resource Hub and Action Center on Race and the Economy, *A Revenue Generation Playbook: How to Fully Fund Our Communities* (2021), https://communityresourcehub.org/wp-content/uploads/2021/05/0602_RGPlaybook_B.pdf.

54. Maria Thomas, "Abolition and the State," Volume 2 of Abolition and the State zine series, Interrupting Criminalization, 2023.

55. On an episode of *Complexity*, a podcast on complexity science hosted by the Santa Fe Institute, the host and guests note that while the goal of creating a decentralized, networked society is "the fundamental idea of the twentieth century," it is important to be mindful that networks "can easily be captured and weaponized by powerful players." The Santa Fe Institute, "Glen Weyl and Cris Moore on Plurality, Governance, and Decentralized Society," *Complexity*, podcast, December 9, 2022, https://complexity.simplecast.com/episodes/97/transcript.

Visionary Practice: Relationships Evolving Possibilities

1. Interrupting Criminalization and Project Nia, REP, One Million Experiments, vol. 6, zine, March 2022, https://files.cargocollective.com/c1000528/REP.pdf.

2. Susan Raffo, *Liberated to the Bone: Histories. Bodies. Futures.* (Chico, CA: AK Press, 2022), 123.

3. Raffo, *Liberated to the Bone*, 123.

4. One Million Experiments, "Relationships Evolving Possibilities," https://millionexperiments.com/projects/relationships-evolving

-possibilities; Relationships Evolving Possibilities, https://repformn
.org; *AirGo* and Interrupting Criminalization, "REP with Signe
Victoria Harriday," *One Million Experiments,* podcast, March 24,
2022, https://soundcloud.com/one-million-experiments/episode-5
-rep-with-signe-victoria-harriday.
5. *AirGo* and Interrupting Criminalization, "REP with Signe Victoria
Harriday."
6. *AirGo* and Interrupting Criminalization, "REP with Signe Victoria
Harriday;" Raffo, *Liberated to the Bone,* 124.
7. Raffo, *Liberated to the Bone,* 124.
8. *AirGo* and Interrupting Criminalization, "REP with Signe Victoria
Harriday."
9. Raffo, *Liberated to the Bone,* 125.
10. Raffo, *Liberated to the Bone,* 125.

Visionary Practice: Young Women's Empowerment Project
1. More information about the Young Women's Empowerment Project
(YWEP), including an audio documentary about their work and
their incredible research reports, *Girls Do What They Have To Do
To Survive* (2009) and *Bad Encounter Line* (2012), can be found at
https://youarepriceless.org.
2. Shira Hassan, *Saving Our Own Lives: Liberatory Harm Reduction*
(Chicago: Haymarket Books, 2022), 28–29.
3. Young Women's Empowerment Project, "Street Youth Rise Up,"
last accessed April 23, 2023, https://youarepriceless.org/our-work/
our-campaign; emi koyama, "Announcing System Failure Alert!"
Eminism, December 18, 2012, http://eminism.org/blog/entry/367.

Abolition Is Decentralized and Rooted in Interdependence
1. adrienne maree brown, *Emergent Strategy: Shaping Change, Changing
Worlds* (Chico, CA: AK Press, 2017), 83.
2. #ComplexityExplained, "What Is Complexity Science," https://
complexityexplained.github.io.
3. Meghan Auker Becker, "Cornell University Students Sit-in for
Divestment from Apartheid South Africa, 1985," Global Non-
violent Action Database, July 7, 2010, last accessed April 24, 2023,
https://nvdatabase.swarthmore.edu/content/cornell-university
-students-sit-divestment-apartheid-south-africa-1985.
4. Sarah A. Soule, "The Student Divestment Movement in the United
States and Tactical Diffusion: The Shantytown Protest," *Social Forces*
75, no. 3 (1997): 855–82, https://doi.org/10.2307/2580522.
5. Deepa Iyer, *Social Change Now: A Guide for Reflection and Connection*
(Washington, DC: Thick Press, 2022).

Notes

6. William Yang Taipei, "How Hong Kong Protests Are Inspiring Movements Worldwide," *Deutsche Welle*, October 21, 2019, https://www .dw.com/en/how-hong-kong-protests-are-inspiring-movements -worldwide/a-50935907.

7. For more information on Southern Movement Assemblies, please visit https://www.southtosouth.org.

8. Project South, *People's Movement Assembly Organizing Handbook* (Atlanta: Southern Movement Assemblies, 2016), https://global -uploads.webflow.com/604d498fe7b051681b80cba5/604f2fbc9 05975577fd19657_5fe166c501bdb57dac79d434_PMA-Handbook.pdf; see also Jackson People's Assembly, https://jxnpeoplesassembly.org; the US Social Forum, https://www.ussocialforum.net; the World Social Forum, https://globalisering.no/wp-content/uploads/2018/12/ World-Social-Forum-Charter-of-Principles.pdf; the Black Nashville Assembly, https://www.blacknashvilleassembly.org; and Black Visions, "The Path Forward," https://www.blackvisionsmn.org/ path-forward. For more information on Marissa Alexander, please see "Marissa Alexander TED Talk," video, Survived and Punished, June 1, 2019, https://survivedandpunished.org/2019/06/01/marissa -alexander-ted-talk.

9. Emily Schmall, "How India's Farmers, Organized and Well-Funded, Faced Down Modi," *New York Times*, November 22, 2021, https://www .nytimes.com/2021/11/20/world/asia/india-modi-farmer-protests .html.

10. For more information on the Indian farmers' protests, see Emily Schmall, "How India's Farmers, Organized and Well-funded, Faced Down Modi;" "Medha Patkar on Farmers Protest, Interview with Medha Patkar, New Delhi 2020," *Media India Group*, December 3, 2020, video, https://www.youtube.com/watch?v=wJn1Lp3hEks; "Farmer's Protest Against Vulgar Inequity in This Country: Medha Patkar," *NDTV*, video, November 28, 2020, https://www.youtube.com /watch?v=m4e06Etz4nQ; and Nitish Pahwa, "India Just Had the Biggest Protest in World History," *Slate*, December 9, 2020, https:// slate.com/news-and-politics/2020/12/india-farmer-protests-modi .html.

11. For more information on decentralized movements in Central and South America, please see Paula X. Rojas, "Are the Cops in Our Heads and Hearts?" in *The Revolution Will Not be Funded: Beyond the Non-Profit Industrial Complex*, ed. INCITE! Women of Color Against Violence (Boston: South End Press, 2009), reprinted at *The Scholar and The Feminist Online* 13, no. 2 (Spring 2016), https://sfon-line.barnard.edu/paula-rojas-are-the-cops-in-our-heads-and-hearts; Marta Harnecker, *A World To Build: New Paths Toward Twenty-First Century Socialism* (New York: Monthly Review Press, 2015); Marina

Sitrin, *Horizontalism: Voices of Popular Power in Argentina* (Oakland: AK Press, 2006); and "What Is the MST?" Friends of the MST, last accessed April 24, 2023, https://www.mstbrazil.org/content/what -mst.

12. For more information on the movements referenced here, see Kelly Hayes, "Latin American Feminism Has Much to Teach US Left on How to Fight for Abortion," *Movement Memos*, podcast, April 7, 2023, https://truthout.org/audio/latin-american-feminism-has-much -to-teach-us-left-on-how-to-fight-for-abortion/https://truthout .org/audio/latin-american-feminism-has-much-to-teach-us-left -on-how-to-fight-for-abortion; and "Reflections on the Chilean Uprising," *The Forge*, October 2022, https://forgeorganizing.org/ issues/reflections-chilean-uprising.

13. Krista Tippett and Ruth Wilson Gilmore, "Ruth Wilson Gilmore: Where Life Is Precious, Life Is Precious," *On Being*, podcast, March 30, 2023, https://onbeing.org/programs/ruth-wilson-gilmore-where -life-is-precious-life-is-precious.

14. Leah Lakshmi Piepzna-Samarasinha, *The Future Is Disabled: Prophesies, Love Notes, and Mourning Songs* (Vancouver: Arsenal Pulp Press, 2022), 76.

15. Sins Invalid, *Skin, Tooth, and Bone: The Basis of Movement Is Our People*, 2nd ed. (San Francisco: Dancers Group, 2019), https://www. sinsinvalid.org/disability-justice-primer.

16. Andrea J. Ritchie and BLM Chicago, "Epicenter: Chicago: Reclaiming a City from Neoliberalism," (Somerville, MA: Political Research Associates, 2019), https://politicalresearch.org/2019/06/05/epicenter-chicago-reclaiming-a-city-from-neoliberalism.

17. Piepzna-Samarasinha, *The Future Is Disabled*, 95.

18. Piepzna-Samarasinha, *The Future Is Disabled*, 104.

19. Piepzna-Samarasinha, *The Future Is Disabled*, 78, 102.

20. Piepzna-Samarasinha, *The Future Is Disabled*, 100.

21. Piepzna-Samarasinha, *The Future Is Disabled*, 100.

22. Piepzna-Samarasinha, *The Future Is Disabled*. 102–103.

23. Piepzna-Samarasinha, *The Future Is Disabled*, 103–104.

Abolition Is Adaptive and Intentional

1. adrienne maree brown, *Emergent Strategy: Shaping Change, Changing Worlds* (Chico, CA: AK Press, 2017), 69.

2. brown, *Emergent Strategy*, 71.

3. Steven Johnson, *Emergence: The Connected Lives of Ants, Brains, Cities, and Software* (New York: Scribner, 2001), 20.

4. Manlio De Domenico, et al., *Complexity Explained*, May 2019, https://complexityexplained.github.io/ComplexityExplained.pdf.

5. brown, *Emergent Strategy*, 94.

6. brown, *Emergent Strategy*, 67.
7. On June 24, 2022, in *Dobbs v. Jackson Women's Health Organization*, the US Supreme Court held that the Constitution of the United States does not protect a right to abortion, overturning *Roe v. Wade* (1973).
8. Kelly Hayes, "Abolition Is About Escaping the Death Trap of 'Normalcy,'" *Movement Memos*, podcast, November 17, 2022, https://truthout.org/audio/abolition-is-about-escaping-the-death-trap-of-normalcy.

Abolition Is Nonlinear and Iterative

1. MPD150, *Enough Is Enough: A 150-Year Performance Review of the Minneapolis Police Department* (2016, updated summer 2020), https://www.mpd150.com/report. MPD150 is a community-based initiative challenging the narrative that police exist to protect and serve. MPD150 sunset in 2020; more information about MPD150 can be found here https://www.mpd150.com.
2. Manlio De Domenico, et al., *Complexity Explained*, May 2019, https://complexityexplained.github.io/ComplexityExplained.pdf.
3. De Domenico, et al., *Complexity Explained*.
4. De Domenico, et al., *Complexity Explained*.
5. Interrupting Criminalization and Project Nia, *1MExperiments Discussion Guide: Organizing on a 500-Year Clock* (New York: One Million Experiments, 2023), https://static1.squarespace.com/static/5ee39ec764dbd7179cf1243c/t/63fff5006cd7d40863a0ad7d/1677718784263/1ME+Discussion+Guide+2.pdf.
6. Laura Newberry, "When the World Feels Like It's Caving In, Can Hope for the Future Dig Us Out?" *Los Angeles Times*, November 8, 2022, https://www.latimes.com/california/newsletter/2022-11-08/mental-health-hope-future-group-therapy.
7. Barbara Sostaita, "Free Radicals: Abolition's Roots in Healing Are a Key to Its Future," *Bitch Media*, July 1, 2020, bitchmedia.org/article/abolition-healing-connected-essential.
8. brown, *Emergent Strategy*, 106.

Visionary Practice: Harm Free Zones

1. Decolonize This Place, @decolonizethis, Twitter post, March 1, 2023, 8:31 a.m., https://twitter.com/decolonize_this/status/1630923635887165442.
2. Ejeris Dixon, "Building Community Safety," in Ejeris Dixon and Leah Lakshmi Piepzna-Samarasinha, eds., *Beyond Survival: Strategies and Stories from the Transformative Justice Movement* (Chico, CA: AK Press, 2020); Ejeris Dixon, "What Alex Taught Me," *The Scholar and Feminist Online*, 15, no. 3 (2019), https://sfonline.barnard.edu/what-alex-taught-me; Sista II Sista, "Sistas Makin' Moves," in

Color of Violence: The INCITE! Anthology, ed. INCITE! Women of Color Against Violence (Boston: South End Press, 2006).

3. DecolonizeThisPlace, @decolonize_this, Twitter post, March 1, 2023, 8:31 a.m., https://twitter.com/decolonize_this/status/1630923635887165 442.

4. The Creative Interventions Story Telling and Organizing Project (STOP), "Community Responds to Domestic Violence," audio recording, Creative Interventions, https://www.creative-interventions .org/community-responds-to-domestic-violence.

5. The Creative Interventions Story Telling and Organizing Project (STOP), "Community Responds to Domestic Violence."

6. For more information on UBUNTU, please visit https://iambecaus eweare.wordpress.com.

7. New York City Harm Free Zone Working Group, "Document of Principles and Agreement," *Daring to Dream: Crafting a Harm Free Zone*, SpiritHouse, March 17, 2020, https://www.spirithouse-nc.org/ journal/2020/3/17/daring-to-dream.

8. New York City Harm Free Zone Working Group, "Document of Principles and Agreement." For more information about the NYC Harm Free Zone Project, see Critical Resistance, "NYC Harm Free Zone Project," December 11, 2007, https://criticalresistance.org/projects/ harm-free-zone-project and NYC Harm Free Zone Collective, "Harm Free Zones: Rethinking Restorative Justice," *WIN Magazine*, Summer 2007, https://www.warresisters.org/win/win-summer-2007/ harm-free-zones.

Visionary Practice: Freedom Square

1. Damon Williams and Daniel Kisslinger, "Freedom Square," *AirGo*, podcast, recorded July 27, 2016, https://soundcloud.com/airgoradio/ ep-53-freedom-square.

Abolition Is Cooperative and Focused on Collective Sustainability

1. Steven Johnson, *Emergence: The Connected Lives of Ants, Brains, Cities, and Software* (New York: Scribner, 2001), 224.

2. Johnson, *Emergence*, 31, 73.

3. Johnson, *Emergence*, 31.

4. Johnson, *Emergence*, 76–77.

5. Johnson, *Emergence*, 74.

6. Johnson, *Emergence*, 73.

7. Alexis Pauline Gumbs, *Undrowned: Black Feminist Lessons from Marine Mammals* (Chico, CA: AK Press, 2020), 55.

8. Gumbs, *Undrowned*, 58.

9. Gumbs, *Undrowned*, 51, 56.

10. Deepa Iyer, "Intro to Solidarity Economies," *Solidarity Is This*, podcast, July 20, 2022, https://solidarityis.org/our-work/solidarity-is-this-podcast/pastepisodesofsit/2022sit/sito722. See also Solidarity Economy Principles Project, "What Do We Mean by a Solidarity Economy?" last accessed April 24, 2023, https://solidarityeconomyprinciples.org/what-do-we-mean-by-solidarity-economy.

11. Solidarity Economy Principles Project, "What Do We Mean by a Solidarity Economy?"

12. For more information on Queer the Land, please visit http://www.queertheland.org.

13. US Federation of Worker Cooperatives, "What Is a Worker Cooperative," last accessed April 24, 2023, https://www.usworker.coop/what-is-a-worker-cooperative.

14. Maria Thomas, "Abolition and the State," vol. 2 of the Abolition and the State zine series, Interrupting Criminalization, 2023.

15. Vijay Prashad and Subin Dennis, "An Often Overlooked Region of India Is a Beacon to the World for Taking on the Coronavirus," *People's Dispatch*, March 24, 2020, https://peoplesdispatch.org/2020/03/24/an-often-overlooked-region-of-india-is-a-beacon-to-the-world-for-taking-on-the-coronavirus. For more information on the women's cooperative movement in Kerala, please see https://thekudumbashreestory.info/index.php/what%E2%80%99s-kudumbashree.

16. Deepa Iyer, "Intro to Solidarity Economies."

Abolition Builds Resilience and Fosters Transformation

1. Association for Child and Adolescent Mental Health, "Resilience—A Complexity Science Approach: Professor Anne-Laura Van Harmelen 'In Conversation,'"*ACAMH*, podcast, https://www.resilience.org/the-science-of-resilience.

2. adrienne maree brown, *Emergent Strategy: Shaping Change, Changing Worlds* (Chico, CA: AK Press, 2017), 126.

3. brown, *Emergent Strategy*, 133.

4. Association for Child and Adolescent Mental Health, "Resilience."

5. Mimi E. Kim, "Anti-Carceral Feminism: The Contradictions of Progress and the Possibilities of Counter-Hegemonic Struggle," *Affilia: Journal of Women and Social Work* 35, no. 3 (2020).

6. Kim, "Anti-Carceral Feminism," 323.

7. Kim, "Anti-Carceral Feminism."

8. Kim, "Anti-Carceral Feminism."

9. "Steps to End Prisons and Policing: A Mixtape on Transformative Justice" by The Transformative Justice Collaborative is a collection of nine video workshops and webinars; it is available at https://just-practice.org/steps-to-end-prisons-policing-a-mix-tape-on-transformative-justice. See also Mariame Kaba and Shira Hassan,

Fumbling Towards Repair: A Workbook for Community Accountability Practitioners (Chicago: Project NIA, 2019).

10. You can find most of these at transformharm.org, abolitionisttools.com and interruptingcriminalization.com.

11. The Wakanda Dream Lab and Policy Link, *Black Freedom Beyond Borders: Memories of Abolition Day* (New York: Policy Link, 2020), https://www.policylink.org/equity-in-action/webinars/black-freedom-beyond-borders_8-24-20; readings are also available at https://www.thebigwe.com/abolitionday.

Visionary Practice: Albina Zone

1. "Verseland Slam Poetry Finalist Sekai Edwards Performs 'Displaced,'" *The Oregonian*, video, May 6, 2015, https://www.youtube.com/watch?v=vX6yKMUoumU.

Abolition Creates More Possibilities (That We Can't Currently Imagine)

1. adrienne maree brown, *Emergent Strategy: Shaping Change, Changing Worlds* (Chico, CA: AK Press, 2017), 77–78.

2. brown, *Emergent Strategy*, 77–78.

3. brown, *Emergent Strategy*, 77–78.

4. Emergent Strategy Ideation Institute, Walidah Imarisha, and Calvin Williams "Dreaming While Black with Walidah Imarisha and Calvin Williams," *The Emergent Strategy Podcast*, podcast, April 29, 2021, https://podcasters.spotify.com/pod/show/emergentstrategy/episodes/Dreaming-While-Black-with-Walidah-Imarisha-and-Calvin-Williams-evu005.

5. Emergent Strategy Ideation Institute, Imarisha, and Williams, "Dreaming While Black."

6. Emergent Strategy Ideation Institute, Imarisha, and Williams, "Dreaming While Black."

7. Emergent Strategy Ideation Institute, Imarisha, and Williams, "Dreaming While Black."

8. The Wakanda Dream Lab and Policy Link, *Black Freedom Beyond Borders: Memories of Abolition Day* (New York: Policy Link, 2020), https://www.policylink.org/equity-in-action/webinars/black-freedom-beyond-borders_8-24-20; the *Black Freedom Beyond Borders* podcast is available at https://www.thebigwe.com/abolitionday.

9. See Mariame Kaba, "Justice: A Short Story," in *We Do This 'Til We Free Us* (Chicago: Haymarket Books, 2021); Barbara Ransby, "Letter from the Year 2071," *In These Times*, July 15, 2021, https://inthesetimes.com/article/letter-from-ancestors-revolutionary-future.

10. See Alexander Reid Ross, "Surreal Antifascism, 1921–45," in *¡No*

Pasarán! Antifascist Dispatches from a World on Fire, ed. Shane Burley (Chico, CA: AK Press, 2022), 448.

11. For more information on Gallery of the Streets, please visit https://www.kailbarrow.com/portfolio and https://www.galleryofthestreets.org. Interestingly, kai and I were invited to do an event focused on Black women's experiences of police violence in 2015 at the height of #SayHerName. I remember struggling to mesh my policy-based talk with her expansive and immersive experiential offering—and that, unsurprisingly, people who attended the event were clearly far more deeply moved and shifted by the art than the policy.

12. Vibranium is a fictional substance that is extremely valuable and somehow makes Wakanda possible. As someone who is not deep into any of the sci-fi or comic book universes, I don't pretend to understand any more than that.

13. See the chapter "Tricks and Tensions" in Mariame Kaba and Andrea J. Ritchie, *No More Police: A Case for Abolition* (New York: The New Press, 2022) and Andrea J. Ritchie, *Abolition and the State: A Discussion Tool* (New York: Interrupting Criminalization, 2022), https://www.interruptingcriminalization.com/abolition-and-the-state.

14. brown, *Emergent Strategy*, 21.

15. brown, *Emergent Strategy*, 53.

16. adrienne maree brown, *Pleasure Activism: The Politics of Feeling Good* (Chico, CA: AK Press, 2019).

17. Here, Rachel is paraphrasing Cornel West's famous saying that "justice is what love looks like in public."

18. Leah Lakshmi Piepzna-Samarasinha, *The Future Is Disabled: Prophesies, Love Notes and Mourning Songs* (Vancouver: Arsenal Pulp Press, 2022), 308.

19. Piepzna-Samarasinha, *The Future Is Disabled*, 312.

20. Piepzna-Samarasinha, *The Future Is Disabled*, 314.

21. Barbara Smith, "What I Believe," Robert L. Hess Memorial Lecture, The Ethyle R. Wolfe Institute for the Humanities, Brooklyn College of the City University of New York, March 16, 2023, https://www.youtube.com/watch?v=bAIs7VQ_n7M.

22. Steven Johnson, *Emergence: The Connected Lives of Ants, Brains, Cities, and Software* (New York: Scribner, 2001), 75.

23. Ruth Wilson Gilmore, *Golden Gulag: Prisons, Surplus, Crisis, and Opposition in Globalizing California* (Berkeley, CA: University of California Press, 2007), 242.

A Note on Wave-Particle Duality

1. Robyn Maynard, Andrea J. Ritchie, and Leanne Betasamosake Simpson, "The Role of the State in Abolitionist Futures," *Haymarket Books Live*, podcast, October 26, 2022; https://podcasts.apple

.com/us/podcast/the-role-of-the-state-in-abolitionist-futures/ idı555589534?i=1000587819796, October 26, 2022; William C. Anderson, Dean Spade, and Harsha Walia, "No Borders! No Prisons! No Cops! No State?," Barnard Center for Research on Women, online conversation, November 15, 2022, https:// bcrw.barnard.edu/event/no-borders-no-prisons-no-cops-no -war-no-state/; Center for Place, Culture and Politics at the Graduate Center, CUNY, "The State: Abolitionist? Fascist? Communist? Bourgeois?" CPCP 2023 Annual Conference, May 4–5, 2023, https://pcp.gc.cuny.edu/2023/04/cpcp-2023-annual-conference -the-state-abolitionist-fascist-communist-bourgeois. See also "Tricks and Tensions," in Mariame Kaba and Andrea J. Ritchie, *No More Police: A Case for Abolition* (New York: The New Press, 2022); and Andrea J. Ritchie, *Abolition and the State: A Discussion Tool* (New York: Interrupting Criminalization, 2022), https://www.interrupting criminalization.com/abolition-and-the-state.

2. Robin D.G. Kelley, "Freedom Dreams and the Socialist Project," Socialism 2022 conference, https://www.youtube.com/watch ?v=6vIIrtBvtKM.

Practice (A Conclusion)

1. To learn more about the Black brilliance of BOLD, please visit https://boldorganizing.org.

2. Emergent Strategy Ideation Institute and Adaku Utah, "Minding Your Relations with Adaku Utah," *The Emergent Strategy Podcast*, podcast, September 22, 2022, https://anchor.fm/emergentstrategy/ episodes/Minding-Your-Relations-with-Adaku-Utah-e1ohv89.

3. Emergent Strategy Ideation Institute Adaku Utah, "Minding Your Relations."

4. Talia Levin, "How to Fight a Holy War," *The Sword and the Sandwich*, podcast, February 21, 2023, https://theswordandthesandwich .substack.com/p/how-to-fight-a-holy-war.

5. Jane McAlevey, *No Shortcuts: Organizing for Power in the New Gilded Age* (London: Oxford University Press, 2016).

6. Kelly Hayes and Mariame Kaba, *Let This Radicalize You: Organizing and the Revolution of Reciprocal Care* (Chicago: Haymarket Books, 2023).

7. Kelly Hayes, "Prepping for the Apocalypse Means Building Community," *Movement Memos*, podcast, October 22, 2022, https:// truthout.org/audio/prepping-for-the-apocalypse-means-building -community; Chris Begley, *The Next Apocalypse: The Art and Science of Survival* (New York: Basic Books, 2021).

8. Hayes, "Prepping for the Apocalypse."

9. Hayes, "Prepping for the Apocalypse."

10. Robyn Maynard and Leanne Betasamosake Simpson, *Rehearsals for Living* (New York: Haymarket Books, 2022), 44.

11. Hayes, "Prepping for the Apocalypse."

12. Kung Li Sun, *Begin the World Over* (Chico, CA: AK Press, 2022).

13. Emergent Strategy Ideation Institute, "Minding Your Relations."

14. Emergent Strategy Ideation Institute and Sendolo Diaminah, "Devotion Strategy and Rigor with Sendolo Diaminah," *The Emergent Strategy Podcast*, podcast, October 21, 2021, https://podcasts .apple.com/us/podcast/devotion-strategy-and-rigor-with-sendolo -diaminah/id1553479340.

15. For more information about Stop Cop City, please visit: https:// stopcop.city; https://defendtheatlantaforest.org; and Micah Herskind, "The Fight to Stop Cop City has Decades-Old Roots," *Prism Reports*, March 2, 2023, https://prismreports.org/2023/03/02/fight -stop-cop-city.

16. Micah Herskind, "Mapping the Prison Industrial Complex: A Tool for Abolitionist Organizers," (New York: Interrupting Criminalization, 2022), https://files.cargocollective.com/c1012822/Mapping PICHandout.pdf.

17. Stop Cop City Solidarity, "Solidarity with the Frontlines," https:// www.stopcopcitysolidarity.org.

18. Timothy Pratt, "'Assassinated in Cold Blood': Activist Killed Protesting Georgia's 'Cop City'" *The Guardian*, January 21, 2023; https://www .theguardian.com/us-news/2023/jan/21/protester-killed-georgia-cop -city-police-shooting.

19. Atlanta Community Press Collective, @atlanta_press, Twitter post, March 11, 2023, 12:50 p.m., https://twitter.com/atlanta_press/sta- tus/1634612794703204354.

20. Micah Herskind, "This Is the Atlanta Way—A Primer on Cop City," *Scalawag*, May 2, 2023, https://scalawagmagazine.org/2023/05/ cop-city-atlanta-history-timeline; "Opposition Grows to Atlanta 'Cop City' as More Forest Defenders Charged with Domestic Terrorism," *Democracy Now*, video, March 9, 2023, http://www.democracy now.org/2023/3/9/cop_city_arrests_protests; Herskind, "The Fight to Stop Cop City has Decades-Old Roots," CrimethInc., "Balance Sheet: Two Years against Against Cop City–Evaluating Strategies, Refining Tactics," *CrimethInc.*, February 28, 2023, https:// crimethinc.com/2023/02/28/balance-sheet-two-years-against -cop-city-evaluating-strategies-refining-tactics; Hannah Riley and Micah Herskind, "Atlanta's 'Cop City' Is Putting Policing Before the Climate," *Teen Vogue*, January 30, 2023, https://www.teen vogue.com/story/stop-cop-city-tortugita-oped; Kelly Hayes, "The Death of a Forest Defender at 'Stop Cop City,'" *Movement Memos*, podcast, January 26, 2023, https://truthout.org/audio/the-death

-of-a-forest-defender-at-stop-cop-city/; and Micah Herskind, "Cop City and the Prison Industrial Complex in Atlanta," *Mainline*, February 7, 2022, https://www.mainlinezine.com/cop-city-and-the-prison-industrial-complex-in-atlanta.

21. CrimethInc., "Balance Sheet."
22. CrimethInc., "Balance Sheet."

Conversations

Unless otherwise noted, quotes are from individual and collective conversations that took place between 2019 and 2023.

Adaku Utah
Aishah Shahidah Simmons
Alexis Pauline Gumbs
Amanda Alexander
Angélica Cházaro
Autumn Meghan Brown
Damon Williams
Daniel Kisslinger
Dean Spade
Denise Perry
Diana Nucera
Ejeris Dixon
Emi Kane
Erin Butler
Eva Nagao
Halima Cassells
Jenny Lee
kai lumumba barrow
Kalayo Pestaño
Kat Aaron
Kelly Hayes
Leah Lakshmi Piepzna-Samarasinha
LéTania Severe
Lewis Raven Wallace
Maria Thomas
Mariame Kaba
Mia Herndon

Mia Mingus
Mimi Kim
N'Tanya Lee
Nandi Comer
Nikkita Oliver
PG Watkins
Rachel Caïdor
Sage Crump
Shannon Perez-Darby
shea howell
Sheila Nehzad
Shira Hassan
Trishala Deb
Woods Ervin

Index

Aaron, Kat, 101–2, 142, 153–54
abolition: abolitionist
   principles, 45–46; Black
   feminism and, 22–23,
   36–38, 41, 46, 48, 49–50,
   89–90, 160–63, 226–35,
   241; collective care and,
   23, 34–36, 90–93; decentralized movements and,
   129–39; disability justice
   and, 137–39; emergent
   strategy and, xviii–xx,
   89–93; pleasure and joy
   and, 233–35; translocal
   organizing and, 69, 83,
   118–22, 158–63, 285n40; use
   of term, 45–49; visionary
   organizing and, 49–54,
   225–26, 227–33
Accountable Communities
   Consortium, 97, 287n6
adaptation: adaptation principle, 41–43, 60–61, 64–66;
   intention and, 141–47
Ahmed, Fahd, iv
AirGo (podcast), 120, 171–78,
   276n39, 288n23, 290n42,
   291n4, 296n1
"Albina Zone" (Bates), 190,
   207–23
Alexander, Amanda, 136, 270
Alexander, Marissa, 134, 293n8

Allied Media Projects (AMP):
   Allied Media Conference
   (AMC), xviii, 15–20, 40,
   41–43, 83, 230–32, 239;
   AMP Network Princi-
   ples, 39–40; AMP Seeds
   program, 18; *Critical Connections* (podcast), 16–17;
   overview of, 18, 39–40,
   276n37–38, 279n1
American Revolutionary (2013),
   97
"A Moment of Truth" (2020),
   90–91
Another Politics is Possible (APP) study group,
   23–24, 102
anti-apartheid movements,
   131–32, 243
anti-globalization movements,
   8, 132, 133–34
Anti Police-Terror Project
   (Mental Health First),
   107, 288n23, 289n24
anti-violence organizing, 53,
   90–92, 230
API Chaya, 108–9, 289n28
Arab Resource and Orga-
   nizing Center (AROC),
   106–7
As We Have Always Done
   (Simpson), 30, 65–66, 99

305